From the Ledge

A Conversation with Comfort

RAY COMFORT

Overcoming Depression
& Suicidal Thoughts

First printing: October 2018

New Leaf Press, P.O. Box 726, Green Forest, AR 72638
New Leaf Press is a division of the New Leaf Publishing Group, Inc.

ISBN: 978-0-89221-761-8

Please consider requesting that a copy of this volume be purchased by your local library system.

Printed in the United States of America

Please visit our website for other great titles:
www.newleafpress.com

For information regarding author interviews,
please contact the publicity department at (870) 438-5288.

New Leaf Press
A Division of New Leaf Publishing Group
www.newleafpress.com

Depression is a very complex issue, and while it may have a genuine biological basis, many experts believe the vast majority of cases diagnosed as organic depression really aren't.

This content shouldn't be construed as medical advice; please consult your doctor before making any decisions regarding medication.

Contents

Chapter 1

The Golden Gate Bridge

From his bird's eye view, he peered into the foggy bay, as if his solution might be out there just beyond his sight.

Why was he hesitating to take his life? All he had to do was lean forward from the railing and simply freefall into the treacherous depths below, yet he felt as compelled to stay as he did to jump. It wouldn't be painless, but it would be quick, and a lot less painful than this life, he figured.

He felt so hopeless, with no more reason to live. And yet he wanted to.

Oh, how he wanted to.

• • •

I'm not a big fan of crowds. That's why I chose very early on a Tuesday morning, when there are fewer tourists, to walk across the iconic Golden Gate Bridge. I wanted to get a good sunrise picture for an upcoming publication and the bridge offered an ideal place from which to take the photo. The forecast hadn't mentioned fog, but typical for San Francisco, fog came from nowhere that particular morning. Pea soup. I was deciding whether to turn back or wait for it to clear when I noticed the shadowy figure in the fog about 20 feet from me.

Someone had climbed over the steel railing and was perched precariously on a narrow ledge — and just as precariously on the edge of this life. The ledge was actually about a 30-inch-wide beam, spanning 220 feet of the icy, gray waters of the San Francisco Bay.

As I carefully approached, I saw it was a young man, in his early to mid twenties, with short blondish hair. I was fully aware that a sudden move or the wrong words from me could end in tragedy, so I said a quick prayer for wisdom.

I began by gently asking for his name, telling him mine, and that I'm a Christian and would like to talk with him.

He seemed startled by my approach, but he remained fixed in his spot. "Is that some sort of stage name, for people who need a ray of hope and a little comfort?" he replied wryly.

I assured him that it was my real name and that all I was asking was for him to listen. I'm aware that experts often say to get a suicidal person to talk, but I was afraid talking about his problems may prompt him to jump, and I didn't know how much time he would give me. So, funny as it may sound, I *did* want to give him a ray of hope and some comfort, as quickly as I could. "Even as difficult and painful as your circumstances are right now, you still have tremendous worth. I believe that I can give you some good reasons not to take your life," I said.

"I've already made up my mind. I'm going to jump. You can't tell me anything new that I haven't heard before," he informed me. "And when I jump, what are you going to do? You're going to walk away a failure. Your little speech didn't work. Your little 'God solutions' are irrelevant to the big problems that I have. I've got friends who died and God didn't help them."

"What's your name?" I gently prompted again.

"I'm not giving it to you."

"If you've already made up your mind to jump, you have nothing to lose by listening. Will you give me your word that you won't jump until you hear me out?"

"Why should I give you my word?"

"Okay. You don't know me and you don't know what I'm going to say," I admitted. "Will you let me tell you what happened to my friend's brother?"

"I couldn't care less what happened to your friend's brother. But go ahead," he sighed. "Tell me about your stupid friend's stupid brother."

I wasn't sure how to read his attitude, whether he was still on the verge of jumping or willing to listen, but every minute he continued to talk with me was giving *me* a ray of hope. I continued, "My friend's name is Stuart Scott, and this actually happened in Utah in 2012. A group of masked men with knives took Stan, his younger brother, knocked him out, cut open his chest, and took out his heart. And no one did a thing to stop them."

"Seriously, that's one of the sickest things I've ever heard. There is so much evil in this life!" he exclaimed, his agitation level rising. "That's the kind of thing that gets me so depressed. Everywhere I look I see nothing but horrible things happening. And so how is this supposed to make me change my mind about killing myself?"

"As it stands, you think it was horrible," I quickly told him. "You only think so because you're missing some vital information. What they did wasn't bad. It was good."

"Go ahead, Mr. Wise Guy. Change my mind," he mocked.

"They were surgeons."

"What do you mean?"

"They were heart surgeons who put on their masks, took their scalpels, knocked the man out with anesthesia, cut open his chest, took out his diseased heart that was killing him, and gave him a heart transplant. Those brilliant men saved his life!"

"Oh," he said, meekly.

"*Oh* is right. Just 30 seconds ago you thought that what they did was evil, but now with the missing information you've had a radical change of mind. Just three little words changed your mind from something being despicably evil to being wonderfully good. That little bit of information gave you another perspective, so that you could see the truth."

"Okay . . . point made. What's that got to do with me standing on the edge of this bridge? It doesn't change my mind about jumping. I'm still going to do it."

"No, the point hasn't yet been made," I said. "The point is, you've made up your mind to take your life, but I'd like to share some information that will give you another perspective. Your life matters, but you think life isn't worth living because you are seeing your situation from your limited point of view. All I'm asking is that you listen to a few words that I believe are going to change everything for you. Will you please hear me out? Just let me run through the reasons that I believe will show you that what you are doing is the wrong thing to do. I don't mean morally wrong. I mean 'wrong' in the sense of it not being in your best interest."

"Okay. I get it. If the information is as radical as you say it is, and it does change my perspective, I give you my word that I won't jump. But I don't think it's going to happen."

"Let's give it a try," I said with a sense of relief. "But I need to know that you won't take offense at anything I say. This is because I'm going to talk about God and other things that may make you feel guilty."

"You make me laugh. I'm on the ledge of the Golden Gate Bridge, about to jump. I have never felt this bad in all my life, and you think you're going to make me feel worse?" He shook his head in disbelief, then added in utter defeat, "I already feel guilty. I feel about as alone as anyone can get. There is no point and no purpose in existing any longer. And you know what? I don't even believe in God; I believe in science and reason. So you have an impossible task. But go ahead. Do your thing."

"Thank you," I replied, greatly encouraged. I knew that *nothing* was impossible. . . .

Chapter 2

A Wicked Do-Nothing God

I had been standing on the bridge's walkway, while the young man stood on the ledge, about three feet below, on the other side of the railing. Each time he answered me, it was without looking me in the eye. I wanted to make more of a connection with him, so I asked his permission to sit near him. If I couldn't talk him down off the ledge, just yet, I hoped to at least get him to sit down; that way he'd be less likely to plunge off the bridge while we talked. He agreed. As I sat on the damp sidewalk and looked through a gap in the rail, he was turned slightly so that I could now see most of his face.

"Since you don't believe in God, let's start there," I began. "It's tragic that there's been a recent revival in atheism, so that millions of young people, like you, have been taught to believe there's no evidence for the existence of God. Rather, they see what they think is evidence that God doesn't exist. Just look around at all the starving children, deadly earthquakes, and cancer that kills millions each year."

"Add to that all the evil that goes on in the world, and how can anyone think there is a loving God who takes care of His creation?" he eagerly chimed in. "No; it's more like if there is a God, He's wicked to stand by and do nothing while evil is happening. What sort of father could allow his children to suffer horribly while he stands by and watches? Religion has done nothing to help humanity." He was on a roll now and was becoming more animated. "In fact, its existence has brought evil with it. We would be better off without religion. Think of the thousands of children who have been molested by pedophile priests, and all the simple-minded idiots who give money to rich, slick TV preachers. Religion is responsible for more wars than anything else in history. There is no way you can justify the existence of a loving God in the face of all this!"

"What you're saying is true. These are legitimate arguments," I conceded. It was encouraging to hear him express his views, and these were thoughts that I've heard shared by countless people. "There *is* evil in the world. It's overflowing with evil. But that doesn't deal with the premise of atheism. Atheism claims that there is no God, but you're just saying that if there is a God, He's evil.

"Let's say a man maintains that he built a skyscraper from the foundation to the hundredth floor. He has the credentials and the experience, and other buildings he can point to, to substantiate the fact that he built the skyscraper. Your argument is that the man is a thief and a liar, and *therefore* the building had no builder. That's an illogical leap. Whether the builder is morally good or bad is irrelevant. Every building has to have a builder. It can't build itself.

"You may be offended at God's seeming inaction when it comes to evil, or at man's evil use of religion," I argued, "but it doesn't negate the fact that we have this intellectual problem of the whole of nature in front of us. Where did it come from? It is scientifically impossible for it to have made itself."

"I thought you were going to offer some evidence of God's existence," he scoffed as he turned toward me. "I want something scientific, something I can hold onto. I don't want this blind faith — believing in some invisible Being in the sky when there is no evidence. Give me evidence and I will listen."

The plentiful gray-and-white seagulls were cawing as they circled directly above us. They were probably just after an early morning feed, but I couldn't help seeing them as circling vultures, smelling death below. It was as though they were goading him with, "Jump. Jump. . . ."

"Okay, I will give you scientific evidence," I began. "Do you believe that a book could make itself? Do you think that it could form its own pages filled with coherent information? There was nothing, then ink fell from nowhere onto paper that came from nowhere, and not only formed itself into sensible sentences, but also into sequential page numbers on each page. More colorful ink formed itself into full-color photos of roses, sunsets, and hummingbirds. Then the book designed its own cover. Could a book make itself from nothing?"

"Of course not. That's ridiculous."

"That's right. It is utterly impossible. Are you familiar with DNA?"

"Of course," he said.

"Scientists often refer to DNA as the book of life. It is not only filled with coherent information, but scientists describe it as having letters forming paragraphs and chapters. And this isn't ordinary information; it's *programming* information. Your DNA is so complex that it defies human imagination. From the moment you were conceived, your DNA gave instructions on how to make your eyes, your ears, your skin, your hair, your blood type, your personality . . . everything about you was written in your DNA from the moment you were conceived."

"Your point?"

"What would you think of the mentality of someone who really believed that a physical book could make itself?" I asked. "To be politically incorrect, he would be crazy. Nobody in his right mind would believe that a book could make itself. So here's my point. What would you think of the intellectual capacity of someone who really believed that DNA made itself? In other words, an atheist. To believe even for a moment that the unspeakably complex programming in DNA made itself makes the person who believes that a book created itself seem sane. Atheism is thoughtless. It is unscientific and senseless. Any rational human being who professes to be an atheist and says that DNA made itself has to be hiding something. They can't be serious."

As I paused to take a breath I wondered whether this was having any impact, but I couldn't see his expression clearly. "So there is your scientific proof for the existence of an intelligent Mind that brought everything into existence. It is outside the realm of possibility for nature to have made itself."

He was quiet for several moments before responding. "Okay, so I guess I'm not an atheist," he answered slowly. "Big deal. It doesn't change anything," he added, a little more defiantly. "It just leaves you with the problem of who this Creator is, why He doesn't say something about Himself, and why He allows evil."

"Good point. That *is* a problem."

Chapter 3

The Problem of Evil

I hadn't planned to be out this long (I suppose neither of us did), and a cool breeze cut through my jacket and brought a chill. My hands were freezing. I wanted to put them in my pockets as we talked, but I didn't want to look even slightly casual. It was miserable, wet, and cold. But the conversation was warming up. "Okay, so now we're back to the character of our Creator. Why would a loving God allow evil?

"Everywhere we look in our world we see evil. It often comes to us as breaking news. A police officer has been shot to death. A white officer has been arrested because he killed an unarmed black youth. A young girl has been viciously raped and left for dead, and the attacker has never been brought to justice. These sorts of things happen every day and are part of human existence. There is evil everywhere."

I continued to reason with him, "But here's the question that needs to be asked: How do we know that evil is evil? What is our point of reference? Is the murder of a cop wrong? If so, why is it wrong? Is rape wrong? How about theft? If so, who says it's wrong? Society? Does rape then become right if society legalizes it? Is murder moral if it is sanctioned by society? If a government under someone like Hitler allows the killing of what they call 'undesirables,' is that morally okay? If society in future generations legalizes pedophilia, does pedophilia become morally acceptable? If not, why not? Societal morality is a slippery slope.

"It is morality that separates man from the beasts," I explained. "Humans have an innate knowledge of right and wrong, and that's why we set up court systems. We have a conscience — a built-in knowledge of what is good and what is evil. Where did that come from? Some of it is obviously shaped by society, but that doesn't explain why every society navigates in some way by the human conscience.

"The existence of evil needs a reference point."

"But that still doesn't deal with your problem of God being evil because of His inaction," the young man argued. "If He was good, He wouldn't let people starve to death, let little kids get cancer, or let young girls be raped and murdered. So you've convinced me that there is a Creator, but I'm convinced that the Creator is evil and I don't want to have anything to do with Him. He even stood by and did nothing while His 'chosen people' were slaughtered by the Nazis. So much for your loving God," he sneered.

"Actually, the problem is bigger than God's inaction with the Holocaust. If you look at the record of the Bible, He also let His people suffer in Egypt and in Babylon. And not only that, if you look at the Christian message, He let His Son be crucified. You may have heard that when Jesus was on the Cross He cried out, 'My God, My God, why have You forsaken Me?' Isn't that evidence that God is unloving? But don't be too quick to come to any conclusions. Remember how a little information can give you a completely new perspective and change your mind in seconds."

"Let me ask you a question," he interjected, as another cold breeze blew and sent a chill down my spine. "Do you own a house? Have a well-paying job? A family who loves you?"

"Yes," I nodded. "I do have a wife and kids who love me, I have a good job, and we've had our own home for about 20 years. It's not a mansion, but it keeps the rain out. Why do you ask?"

"Because I have none of those things. When I was 14 my dad ran off with another woman, abandoning his family and ripping my mom's heart out. I haven't seen him since. After my parents divorced, my mom shacked up with some guy who started out nice, but turned out to be a no-good drunk. He spent all her money, and we lost our house because we couldn't keep up with the payments. I hate my father for doing that to us."

"But that's no reason to want to kill yourself."

"Right. It isn't. My problem started when I got some girl pregnant a couple years ago. We were both at a party one night, half-drunk. I didn't care about her, and so when I found out, I pressured her to have an abortion," he confided. "It was no big deal at the time — just pay out a few hundred bucks and the problem goes away. Someone told me that she ended up cutting her wrists. She didn't die, but she's apparently in some psych ward somewhere. When I heard that, I began to have an overwhelming feeling of guilt. My conscience was eating at me."

He paused, as if weighing whether to continue. Then he went on: "I started using drugs, just recreational at first, to numb the pain. But pretty soon I got addicted, and a few weeks later I got canned at my job for missing too much work. So I started stealing from anyone I could, and then dealing, to keep my habit going. I got caught for possession and had to do three months in jail, followed by 12 weeks of counseling. What a waste of time! Nobody cares."

"What about your family? I'm sure you have people who care about you."

"Sure, until I started lying and stealing from them. My friends say they can't trust me and won't have anything to do with me, and my mom is heartbroken over what I've done with my life. My girlfriend just broke up with me, saying she can't put up with my anger any longer, that I keep taking everything out on her. I don't know why I do that, but I just get so upset at the littlest things. She kicked me out, so now I have nowhere to live. I keep hurting all the people I care about, and I can't take it anymore." He slumped his shoulders and looked deflated, weary of life and its problems.

"I'm sorry you're going through all that. I'm sure that's very painful. But, it's not you they are rejecting," I tried to assure him. "It's the drugs. Do you know what addiction does to you? It steals your dignity. It puts chains around your neck, on your ankles and wrists, and makes you a slave. Then it takes a whip and gives you pain if you don't let it master you. You don't care about eating, or your health, or even hygiene. People become objects to be used and lied to."

"Yeah," he groaned in agreement, "and I've given my mother so much grief she doesn't even want to see me. So I'm alone. Really alone. Seriously, you're the first person I've talked to in depth in a long time . . . and I don't even know you. And with all that happened, I still can't forget about what I did. I keep asking myself if I killed my own kid. I can't handle that thought. Did I do that?"

"What are you trying to do?" I asked nervously. "Do you want me to say something and have you jump? If you don't mind, I'd rather not talk about that now. I want to ask you something. How long have you been getting bouts of depression?"

"Who said I'm depressed? Are you just assuming that, because I'm sitting on this ledge?"

His response struck me as slightly humorous, given the circumstances. "Kind of," I said. "You wouldn't want to end your life if you were bursting with joy each morning because you love life. That comes into it. But there is another reason I asked. It's because you said you hate your father. Do you have chronic depression?"

"I suppose," he shrugged.

"When did it start?"

He didn't take long to answer. "When I was about 14."

"Around the time your dad left?" I probed.

"Pretty much. But after what he did to my mom, I hated him and was happy to see him go."

"I think your depression is tied directly to your hatred toward your father," I suggested. "Hatred always has baggage. It eats away at the human soul. The Bible says. . . ."

Apparently I had struck a nerve and his demeanor suddenly changed. He turned directly toward me with a scowl on his face. "You know what? You're starting to make me mad with your 'The Bible says.' Who do you think you are?" he spat. "You remind me of my father and it's making me feel physically sick. He used to say exactly that, 'The Bible says . . .' all the time. He would make me go to church and sit through meaningless drivel. You know what that does to a ten-year-old? I hated it. He was such a hypocrite. He said one thing and did another . . . 'believe in God,' and then he runs off with a woman at his work. You know what else he did? He bought gifts for her with my mom's money. I really hate him, and your 'The

You Are Not Alone

"Am I a God near at hand," says the Lᴢᴢᴢ, *"and not a God afar off? Can anyone hide himself in secret places, so I shall not see him?"* says the Lᴢᴢᴢ; *"Do I not fill heaven and earth?"* (Jeremiah 23:23–24)

"The Lᴢᴢᴢ is near to those who have a broken heart, and saves such as have a contrite spirit." (Psalm 34:18)

"The Lᴢᴢᴢ is near to all who call upon Him, to all who call upon Him in truth." (Psalm 145:18)

"Do not be afraid; do not be discouraged, for the Lᴢᴢᴢ your God will be with you wherever you go." (Joshua 1:9; NIV)

"For He Himself has said, 'I will never leave you nor forsake you.' So we may boldly say: 'The Lᴢᴢᴢ is my helper; I will not fear. What can man do to me?'" (Hebrews 13:5–6)

"Lo, I am with you always, even to the end of the age." (Matthew 28:20)

"Fear not, for I am with you; be not dismayed, for I am your God. I will strengthen you, yes, I will help you, I will uphold you with My righteous right hand." (Isaiah 41:10)

"Yea, though I walk through the valley of the shadow of death, I will fear no evil; for You are with me; Your rod and Your staff, they comfort me." (Psalm 23:4)

"Nevertheless I am continually with You; You hold me by my right hand." (Psalm 73:23)

Bible says' is making me want to jump to end it all." Both his voice and his hands were trembling with anger.

"*Please* don't jump," I pleaded. "I'm sorry. I'll be careful with my words. I don't want to stir anything up. If I cause any more problems like that, just tell me."

Chapter 4

Stay in the Chair

"Again, I'm sorry. I didn't know about your dad," I said. "I'm trying to do the right thing."

His reaction wasn't the only thing making me more cautious. The fog was beginning to thin a little, and with the daylight, I was concerned that he might decide to go ahead and jump if someone spotted us. We were making some headway, but I didn't think he was ready to rejoin the land of the living just yet.

"Well, whatever you do, don't try to make me feel guilty about hurting loved ones by my suicide. I know that tactic. Oh, I've thought about that," he said as he leaned back a little, like he was starting to relax. Earlier, I could see the tension in his jaw as though he were grinding his teeth. That suddenly stopped. "I have thought about how my mom will react when she hears the news. Well, don't worry, nobody's going to have to find my dead body hanging in the closet. No one will have to clean my brains off a wall. I've thought it out: what's going to kill me is the impact of the water. It'll be quick and clean. Sure, they'll have a nice funeral; there will be a few tears shed and some people may feel guilty. But they'll get over it.

"I also know that you want to get the suicidal person to talk — I've seen all that on TV. That it's healthy for me to let out my feelings and be distracted from what I'm planning to do. So I'll accommodate you; I'll talk. I'm going to tell you what's going on in my brain. It'll be a great case-study for the experts."

Finally, he was beginning to really open up about his thoughts, and for that I was grateful. I was happy to offer a listening ear.

"You know what's going on in my brain? Fear. Pure terror," he said emphatically, sitting up straight again and looking me in the eye. "It's so powerful it almost takes my breath away. Seriously. I can feel my heart beating in my chest. It's like there are two people living inside my head. No, I'm not schizophrenic and I don't need to see a shrink. One of the voices is cold and calculating. It's pure logic, like Mr. Spock. It tells me that if I want to get out of this mess, if I want to rid myself of this pain and the feeling of hopelessness, this is the logical thing to do. Just jump. It says, 'It will be out of your hands. Gravity will take over and in a second or two you'll hit the water and it will all be over. Simple.'

"But there's another part of me that's like a terrified child. That voice is quietly pleading with me, saying, '*What are you doing?* You can't do this! You value your life. What if right after you jump you suddenly realize you've made the worst mistake of your life? It will be too late.'"

"Keep talking. I'm listening." *And praying,* I thought. I'd often heard that those who consider suicide don't really want to *die*, they just want to end their pain. It was a relief, in a sense, to see that was the case with this young man. His circumstances could be changed and the pains of life dealt with. As long as he was breathing, there was hope.

He continued, "I'm going to be honest with you. Mr. Spock is stronger than the child. I'm afraid he's going to win this battle. Deep down, I want you to talk me out of this — but then what's going to happen after you're gone and his voice comes back even stronger? It will be back to square one. Hopelessness. Helplessness. I can't stand it anymore. Day after day. Even while I'm talking, Spock is pulling me closer to the edge and whispering to me to jump. Please help me!" he pleaded. "Please say something that will help me."

"I can help you. Not because I've been trained in psychology, but because I know exactly how you feel," I openly confessed. We had more in common than he suspected. "I know the feeling of hopelessness. I know the feeling of a fear that is so strong, it takes your breath away. So I ask you to do two things. Number one, and it's the most important one at this moment, don't listen to Mr. Spock. He's not your friend, he's your enemy. Can you do that?"

"I'll try."

"Second, I want you to trust me. By that I mean, simply believe that my motives are pure in wanting to help you. I don't get paid for this. I am almost as scared as you are, because in a sense your life is in my hands. If I say the wrong thing, or you take something the wrong way, or think that I don't care about you, you could just give up and let go. If you truly trust me, that won't happen. Can I trust you to do that?"

He took a deep breath and exhaled slowly. "I can't promise anything, but I'll do my best to work with you. I don't want to die. But neither do I want to live. So you've got a pretty big task."

"Don't I know it!" Now it was my turn for a deep breath. "But I'm going to give it everything I've got, because, you may not believe it, but I love you and really do care about you, even though I don't know you. Just the fact that you are talking to me is a tremendous encouragement. I have hope, and I hope that I can pass that hope on to you.

"I know that you didn't want to tell me your name. You probably think that I'll call your family. I won't do that. Would you please do me the courtesy of giving it to me? There's an important reason for this," I explained. "I'm going to say things that may seem offensive to you, and to be quite honest, if I can use your name, it will make it easier for me. Please?"

"John," he said quietly, with a half-nod.

"Okay, John," I smiled. "I appreciate that. I'm going to do to you what a dentist does to his patients. He wants to save their teeth, so he's going to go over them one by one looking for decay. If he sees some, he is going to probe it. There is a reason for this. He wants to convince you that your teeth need to be repaired or you're going to lose them. So the temporary pain he causes is for your long-term benefit.

"I'm here because I care about your life. I think you are worth saving. I *know* you are," I stressed. "You are much more than the animal that evolutionists say you are. You're not just a cosmic accident; you're a moral human being made in the image of God. I believe that you have great worth in the sight of your Creator. But like the dentist, the only way I can convince you of that is to cause you some short-term pain. Here is where trust comes in. I want you to trust me for a moment while I probe. Just sit still and let this happen. The end result is worth it."

John mustered as much enthusiasm as you would expect in a dental exam. "Go ahead, Mr. Dentist. I'll stay in the chair."

"I'd like you to do more than stay in the chair. I'd like you to open your mouth wide and let me probe. By that I mean, open your heart to me for a few moments, and be really honest. Can you do. that?"

"I've already shared more with you than I have with anyone else in years. So, yeah, no problem."

"Do you think you're a good person?"

The Greatest Mistake

"Anywhere from one-third to 80% of all suicide attempts are impulsive acts, according to The New England Journal of Medicine . 24% of those who made near-lethal suicide attempts decided to kill themselves less than five minutes before the attempt, and 70% made the decision within an hour of the attempt." — Corey Adwar[1]

"I just vaulted over, and I realized, at that moment, this is the stupidest thing I could have done. I instantly realized that everything in my life that I'd thought was unfixable was totally fixable — except for having just jumped." — Ken Baldwin[2]

"Instant regret, powerful, overwhelming. As I fell, all I wanted to do was reach back to the rail, but it was gone. I thought, 'What have I

1. "The Role Of Impulsiveness Is One Of The Saddest Things About Suicide," Business Insider, Aug. 13, 2014; https://www.businessinsider.com/many-suicides-are-based-on-an-impulsive-decision-2014-8.
2. ABC7 News, "Second Chances: 'I survived jumping off the Golden Gate Bridge.'" By Natasha Zouves, Thursday, May 18, 2017; http://abc7news.com/society/second-chances-i-survived-jumping-off-the-golden-gate-bridge/2010562/.

"Of course. I've made mistakes, just like everyone else. But, I'm basically good." In a sharp contrast to his previous demeanor, John was suddenly sounding more self-confident.

"How many lies have you told in your whole life? I'm not talking about telling your grandma that her hair is nice, when you think it looks like an abandoned bird's nest. I'm talking about bold-faced lies."

"In my whole life?" He shrugged. "Hundreds."

"What do you call somebody who has told hundreds of lies?"

"A liar."

just done? I don't want to die. God, please save me.' I recognized that I made the greatest mistake in my life." — Kevin Hines[3]

Of 515 people who were thwarted from leaping off the Golden Gate, just 6 percent went on to kill themselves. "Ninety percent of them got past it. They were having an acute temporary crisis, they passed through it and, coming out the other side, they got on with their lives." — Dr. Richard Seiden[4]

"I attempted suicide by laying on a set of railroad tracks, and I was run over by 33 freight train cars. I lost both of my legs, but I was still conscious and alive. Thank God! . . . God had given me a second chance to go to heaven and spend eternity with Him. I realized my life wasn't mine to take, and I asked Him to forgive me. . . . I am here now with more strength, joy, peace, and purpose than I ever imagined." — Kristen Anderson[5]

---

3. Ibid.
4. "Where Are They Now? A Follow-up Study of Suicide Attempters from the Golden Gate Bridge," Richard H. Seiden, Ph.D., M.P.H. University of California at Berkeley; http://seattlefriends.org/files/seiden_study.pdf.
5. http://www.reachingyouministries.com/Kristen.html.

"You mentioned earlier that you stole things to feed your drug habit. What do you call somebody who steals?" I asked.

"A thief."

"So, what are you?"

"A lying thief," John replied. "But I still think I'm good at heart."

"Have you ever used God's name in vain?"

"All the time."

"Jesus said, 'Whoever looks at a woman to lust for her has already committed adultery with her in his heart.' Have you ever looked at a woman with lust?"

Like almost every male, his reply was emphatic. "Of course!"

"Okay, John, this is where I need you to hold still. Don't flake on me. Please don't get mad, feel hurt, or listen to Mr. Spock. I'm going to tell you the truth about your teeth. Remember, I'm only doing this because I'm seeking your well-being," I said gently. "I'm not judging you; but you have just told me that you are a lying, thieving, blasphemous adulterer at heart. And that's only four of the Ten Commandments, God's moral Law. There are another six we haven't even looked at. So here is the big question: If God judges you by the Ten Commandments on the Day of Judgment, will you be innocent or guilty?"

"I will be guilty as charged," he readily admitted. "If I get judged by that standard."

"Would you go to heaven or hell?"

"If I was judged by the Ten Commandments, I would end up in hell, for sure."

"Does that concern you?"

John shook his head. "No, because I don't believe in hell."

"That doesn't make any difference. If a judge condemned a guilty man to the electric chair, and the criminal said that he didn't believe in the electric chair, it wouldn't change a thing. They would take him away and execute him, despite his beliefs.

"The Bi . . . the Scriptures say more about hell than they do about heaven. They warn that God will have His day of justice. He is going to punish the evil that so concerned you earlier. Not only murderers and rapists, but also liars and thieves," I added. "You wanted God to do something, and He's going to do it thoroughly,

Call on God for Help

"I lift up my eyes to the mountains — where does my help come from? My help comes from the LORD, the Maker of heaven and earth." (Psalm 121:1–2; NIV)

"He shall call upon Me, and I will answer him; I will be with him in trouble; I will deliver him and honor him. With long life I will satisfy him, and show him My salvation." (Psalm 91:15–16)

"I sought the LORD, and He heard me, and delivered me from all my fears." (Psalm 34:4)

"In the day when I cried out, You answered me, and made me bold with strength in my soul." (Psalm 138:3)

"From the end of the earth I will cry to You, when my heart is overwhelmed; lead me to the rock that is higher than I." (Psalm 61:2)

"When my soul fainted within me, I remembered the LORD; and my prayer went up to You, into Your holy temple." (Jonah 2:7)

"My soul, wait silently for God alone, for my expectation is from Him. He only is my rock and my salvation; He is my defense; I shall not be moved." (Psalm 62:5–6)

"He heals the brokenhearted and binds up their wounds." (Psalm 147:3)

"Let us therefore come boldly to the throne of grace, that we may obtain mercy and find grace to help in time of need." (Hebrews 4:16)

but He is holding off, waiting for you to repent and trust the Savior. He doesn't want you to end up in hell. So now you see that His inaction against evil actually has a legitimate purpose. It's for your good."

I paused to see how he was taking this. I definitely didn't want him to jump up out of the chair — or off of the bridge. "Please tell me if I'm talking too much, or if you are quietly getting mad at me. I will stop immediately if that's the case. How am I doing, John?"

"Carry on. I can handle the probing."

I continued, "Do you remember how you said that religion has caused more wars than anything else in history? Here are the historical facts. During the 20th century, more people were slaughtered in warfare than in all the preceding 19 centuries combined. Around 70 million people died in the first two world wars, neither of which were religious. They were political. Most of the wars fought in the 20th century were similar to the Vietnam and Korean Wars — they were political in nature and had nothing to do with religion. So to say that religion has caused more wars in history than anything else is just not true.

"That being said, religion — meaning the manmade religious system — can't help anybody. It is merely man trying to earn everlasting life by doing religious deeds — fasting, praying, facing Mecca, sitting on hard pews, living a good life, etc. None of these things will bribe God, the Judge of the universe, to compromise eternal justice. The only thing that can save us from hell is the mercy of the Judge.

"Can you understand how seeing your own sins changes things?" I pressed John, whose head was now hanging down. "No longer are you an innocent, sinless human being standing in judgment over Almighty God. Now you can see yourself as an evil and justly condemned criminal pointing a holier-than-thou finger at a morally perfect Judge.

"What are you going to do? If you jump from the bridge and die in your sins, your fate is sealed eternally. 'Damned' means just that. There is no way out of hell. You may feel your life is hopeless now, but that can be changed. However, you won't have a hope in hell, if you end up there. One second in hell will make you realize how much you should have valued everything you had on earth. Think about what you used to love and live for," I implored. "A cool drink to satisfy a raging thirst on a hot day. Or your favorite homemade foods, like your mom used to make, when you're really hungry. Or think of a song that brings back such great memories it makes you smile. In hell there will only be thirst with not a drop to quench it, agonizing pain with no relief, and tormenting fear with no end. It's a place of terrifying punishment, so horrible it defies the imagination, and I desperately don't want you to go there."

My new friend was awfully quiet, and I hoped that he sensed my genuine concern for him, despite these harsh words. "If this sort of talk is beginning to scare you, thank God that it is. Fear is not your enemy, John; in this case, it's your friend. Fear will keep your hand away from a flame and your feet from the edge of a thousand-foot cliff. And if your brain is doing what it should, fear should make you pull back from the very thought of taking your precious life. It was God's incredible gift to you, and you didn't even bother to thank Him. Instead, you ignored Him, and treated Him with contempt. You even spit in His face by using His name as a cuss word. Again, is this getting too heavy for you?"

"No," he answered somberly.

"Right now there is a battle going on in your mind. We have a very real spiritual enemy, who seeks to steal, kill, and destroy us. Satan, the enemy of your soul, wants you to jump. He'd like nothing more than for you to seal your doom in hell. Who are you going to listen to? The devil, who hates you, or God, who is the lover of your soul?"

I paused to see John's reaction and I silently prayed he was thinking seriously about these things. I continued, "Do you remember how we talked about God's supposed inaction when it came to Jesus on the Cross? Here's some information that will change your perspective. Jesus of Nazareth wasn't merely the Son of God. That title actually meant that He was Almighty God in human form. Now, I'm a little nervous because I want to use that phrase your father used to use. So bear with me. This is what the Bible says: 'God was manifested in the flesh.' 'In the beginning was the Word, and the Word was with God, and the Word was God. . . . And the Word became flesh and dwelt among us.' The Bible says, 'God was in Christ reconciling the world to Himself.' God created for Himself a human body and filled that body as a hand fills a glove. Jesus was the express image of the invisible God. He was born as a human being, lived a morally perfect life, and suffered and died on the Cross to take the punishment for the sin of the world. We broke God's Law, the Ten Commandments, and Jesus paid our fine.

"If you're in court and are found guilty, if someone pays your fine, the judge can let you go and still be just. When Jesus was on the Cross He cried out, 'It is finished!' In other words, the debt had been paid for our sin. Now God can let us go; He can dismiss our case. He can commute our death sentence and let us live forever, because the fine was paid by another."

"So why did Jesus cry out, 'My God, My God, why have You forsaken Me' — what you mentioned earlier?" John asked.

"Psalm 22, written 800 years earlier, explains that when the sin of the world was laid upon Jesus, God, being holy, turned His back on sin. That's why Jesus cried out in torment. Such was His love for you and me.

"Then after Jesus had suffered for our sins, He rose from the dead and defeated our greatest enemy — death itself. The Scriptures say that it was not possible that death could hold Him. Through His Resurrection, life overcame death. And now all who repent and trust in Jesus Christ alone as their Savior will receive forgiveness of sins and be granted the gift of everlasting life. Do you think I'm speaking the truth?"

With a slight shrug John answered honestly, "I don't know."

Chapter 5

The Bad Side of Pride

Iwas growing more encouraged that I'd been able to speak with John this long, and that he was patient during the painful probing. As the morning sunlight was breaking through the clouds, I hoped a light was dawning in the darkness of his heart. I also hoped that the lifting fog hadn't alerted the authorities to John and I. I was quietly trusting that there was some sort of divine intervention allowing us to continue.

"What part doesn't make sense?" I gently prompted him.

"Oh . . . it makes sense," he said hesitantly, still sounding a bit unsure. "You've done a good job. I've never heard it put like that before. My problem is that I have so many questions — about heaven, my dad, the abortion, and a whole stack of other things."

"Could I ask you to set those questions aside for the moment?" I asked. "They're important, but there is something even more important."

"No problem," John replied.

"We're all made in God's image and have similar basic desires in life. Our common goal in life is to be happy. No human being in his right mind sets out to be unhappy. We have that desire because we have been made like that. Suicide only becomes an option when the fear of life overcomes our intuitive will to live.

"Let me ask you a question, John. It's a personal question and one I want you to think about for a moment before you answer. Are you afraid of dying?"

"There's nothing to think about. I'm not afraid of dying; I never have been," he said without hesitation. "I told you, I don't believe in hell, so what's there to fear? I'm afraid of the *way* I might die. I don't want some long, drawn-out, painful, cancerous death. I think people should have the right to choose how and when they're going to die. That's why I'm here today. If I could have found a better way to die than jumping, I would have chosen it. The jump scares me, but death itself? No," he shook his head. "I welcome it."

"John, there's something else we all have in common. The Bible, God's instruction book for humanity, tells us that all mankind 'through fear of death have been living all their lives as slaves to constant dread' [Hebrews 2:15; TLB]. It says every human being is a slave to the fear of death. We live in a constant dread of it. I have asked hundreds of people if they are afraid of dying, and I found out something interesting about the answer. People who are humble of heart will admit that they are afraid of dying. They will admit that they think about it all the time and it haunts them. Just like the Bible says.

"But people who are proud won't admit that they have a haunting fear of death," I added, "because it makes them seem vulnerable and weak. So when you tell me that you don't fear death, I hope you don't mind me saying this, John, but I don't believe you. I believe what the Scriptures say about you, because they have proven themselves to be true. The Bible is no ordinary book. It is clearly supernatural in origin, despite what skeptics say about it.

"I have read the Bible every day without fail since April 24, 1972. I have studied it and searched for the supposed mistakes and scientific inaccuracies. They don't exist. They are only in the minds of those who hate the Bible, because it speaks from beginning to end of a God who will hold them accountable."

I paused to give him a chance to respond, but he continued to quietly listen. I knew I was talking a lot, but wanted to share my personal story in case he could relate. "Let me tell you why I am a Christian. At the age of around 20 I became aware of my own fear of death. I wasn't conscious that that was what it was. It was more a sense of heaviness that sat deep within me at the thought that everything I loved — my wife, my mom and dad, everything — was going to be ripped from my hands by this thing called death. This great blackness was swallowing up all of humanity. Nobody spoke about it, but everybody knew it was coming. It didn't matter how rich you were or how politically powerful or famous, death was coming for you. And there's nothing any of us could do about it. All my happiness seemed so futile because it would some day be popped like a bubble by the sharp pin of reality.

"When I read about the millions who suffer from chronic depression, I can identify with them, because that's the feeling that I had before I came to Christ. It was a feeling of helplessness and hopelessness. There is an elephant in the room waiting to stomp on all of us, and only those who are humble of heart are willing to admit that it scares them.

"Do you think that might be the case with you?"

"Maybe," John half-agreed. Then he sighed. "I take that back. I'm not being honest with you. I *am* afraid of dying," he added quietly. "Terrified. I have been since I was little and it dawned on me that I was going to end up like my grandparents. Dead. I didn't want to admit it to you because I was embarrassed. I guess that's pride."

"It sure is. We are afraid of what people think of us. I appreciate you admitting it. Most of humanity doesn't see anything wrong with pride. But when people have marriage difficulties, you'll often find that pride is what is destroying the relationship. Rather than apologize and say, 'Honey, I was wrong,' pride lifts its ugly head and says, 'I would rather die than apologize.' Pride would rather destroy what was once a good marriage and leave children scarred for life without a father or mother, than back down in humility.

"That sort of pride is a poison, and it is the same pride that holds people back from finding everlasting life. The Book of Psalms says, 'The wicked, through the pride of his countenance, will not seek after God.'

"Pride says, 'I would rather go to hell than apologize to God.' But one second in that terrible place will show that such arrogance is spoken out of ignorance," I continued. "Listen to what Jesus said about that place: 'If your hand or foot causes you to sin, cut it off and cast it from you. It is better for you to enter into life lame or maimed, rather than having two hands or two feet, to be cast into the everlasting fire. And if your eye causes you to sin, pluck it out and cast it from you. It is better for you to enter into life with one eye, rather than having two eyes, to be cast into hell fire' [Matthew 18:8–9].

"In other words, as much as you value your precious eye, if it causes you to sin, put your finger into your eye socket and gouge it out. And then don't put it down where you can pick it up again. Cast it from you! The imagery is fearful. Think about how you value your eyes. Would you sell one of them for a million dollars?"

"No way," John replied.

"Would you sell both for a hundred million?"

He shook his head.

"Of course you wouldn't. Your eyes give you a window into this beautiful world. If you sold both of your eyes you would be in darkness for the rest of your life. Your eyes are without price. But here Jesus is saying that sin is so serious in God's sight that it would be far better for your eyes to be ripped out than for them to cause you to sin.

"In fact, sin is so serious in the eyes of a Holy God that He proclaimed the death sentence upon all those who transgress His Law, and damnation in a terrible place called hell. What you don't realize, John, is that not only has God seen your lying and stealing, but He has heard every word that has come out of your mouth and seen every thought that has gone through your mind.

"Nothing is hidden from the eyes of Him to whom we must give an account. It was that knowledge that caused me to tremble on the night of my conversion," I confessed. "I didn't realize that God saw my thought-life. He saw my sexual fantasies and what the Bible calls evil imaginations. And every time I sinned, I was storing up His wrath.

"Hey, this is some pretty weighty stuff. Are you still with me, John?"

"Still with you," he mumbled. "And thinking."

Chapter 6

Scary Picture

With the serious topics we were talking about, we both were absorbed in the conversation and oblivious to the growing bustle of traffic passing by. I could feel the bridge shaking as the bigger trucks rumbled past. By now I was convinced that God had led me to the bridge that morning and that He had provided the opportunity to reach out to John.

"I have painted the biblical portrait of God, and it's a scary picture," I acknowledged. "It is filled with wrath and judgment. Nevertheless, it is based on God's revelation of Himself.

"If I told you anything about Him that wasn't in line with Scripture, I would be doing you the ultimate disservice. It would mean that you would have a wrong understanding of your state before God, wouldn't see your need for a Savior, and would end up in hell. And as I said, John, I am desperate for that not to happen to you.

"But there is something you need to know about this holy and just Creator. He is also loving, compassionate, and rich in mercy. Jesus told three parables to illustrate this. One was about a shepherd who discovered that one of his sheep was missing. So he left 99 sheep and went in search of the 1 that was lost. When he found it, he lovingly put it on his shoulders and brought it back to safety. That's a picture of the lost sinner."

"Yes, that rings a bell. I remember learning about that story back in Sunday school," John added. "Maybe all that time wasn't a waste. . . ."

"Good to know you recall some of what you heard," I noted. "That's one reason why Jesus told stories — they're memorable. The second parable that Jesus gave was about a woman who lost a coin and searched everywhere for it. When she found it she called her friends and rejoiced that she had found that which was lost. Again, this is a picture of our worth in the sight of God. We are lost, but we are worth finding as far as God is concerned. He rejoices when one sinner comes to repentance."

John's head quietly nodded, either in recognition or agreement, or both. But something else was wonderfully evident. He had turned toward me so that we could look at each other as we spoke, and we were beginning to see eye to eye.

"And finally, Jesus culminated with the story of the lost son. A young man was burning with lust. His hormones kicked in, and like a wild stallion he didn't want to be corralled in his father's household. So he asked his father for his inheritance and then went to a foreign land, away from the eyes of his father, so that he could enjoy the high life. The young man spent all of his money on wild parties and prostitutes. After his money ran out, all of his friends left him, and when a famine came to the land, the only job he could find was feeding pigs in a pigsty.

"As he sat, looking at the pig food, he had a revelation," I continued. "He realized that he was so hungry that he wanted to pick up the filthy corn cobs and eat them. That's when he came to his senses and said, 'Even my father's servants have it better than this. I will go back to my father and say, "I have sinned against heaven and in your sight. Please take me on as a hired servant."' And so he got up out of that filthy pigsty and went back to his father.

"His father, who had been looking for him, saw him at a distance and had compassion on him. He ran to him, fell upon his neck and kissed him. He called for a robe for him and ring for his finger, and he rejoiced, saying, 'My son was once dead and is alive again!' [Luke 15:15–22]

"The picture of the father watching for his lost son is a picture of God waiting for you to return to Him."

John was looking down, and he put his hand to his chin to rub it thoughtfully. I was pleased to see him slowly nodding again at these stories.

"The greatest revelation you will ever have, John, is to realize that your desires have been for filthy pig food. You have wallowed

You Are Loved

"Yes, I have loved you with an everlasting love; therefore with lovingkindness I have drawn you." (Jeremiah 31:3)

"What is man, that You should exalt him, that You should set Your heart on him?" (Job 7:17)

"But God demonstrates His own love toward us, in that while we were still sinners, Christ died for us." (Romans 5:8)

"For God so loved the world that He gave His only begotten Son, that whoever believes in Him should not perish but have everlasting life." (John 3:16)

"In this the love of God was manifested toward us, that God has sent His only begotten Son into the world, that we might live through Him." (1 John 4:9)

"But God, who is rich in mercy, because of His great love with which He loved us, even when we were dead in trespasses, made us alive together with Christ (by grace you have been saved)." (Ephesians 2:4–5)

"Oh give thanks to the LORD, for He is good; for his steadfast love endures forever!" (Psalm 118:1; ESV)

"I am persuaded that neither death nor life, nor angels nor principalities nor powers, nor things present nor things to come, nor height nor depth, nor any other created thing, shall be able to separate us from the love of God which is in Christ Jesus our Lord." (Romans 8:38–39)

"Behold what manner of love the Father has bestowed on us, that we should be called children of God!" (1 John 3:1) in the filth of sin and loved every minute of it. That's the evilness of our nature: we love the darkness and hate the light. The Bible says that we drink in iniquity like water.

"And where has your sin left you? It has destroyed relationships, cut you off from those you care about, and given you a sense of futility and despair. And it has culminated in thoughts of suicide — to a point of doing yourself the ultimate harm. The pleasure it promised has been outweighed by the pain that it brought. The question is, will you come to your senses?" I gently implored.

"Let me tell you something very personal. Before I was a Christian, I lived for lust. Like every other red-blooded young man, I took great pleasure in looking at girls sexually. But the night of my conversion, when I learned Jesus said that if we looked with lust we committed adultery in our heart, it was like an arrow hit my chest. I knew I was guilty a million times over," I honestly admitted. Yet I was confident this was something John could identify with. "I knew that I had angered God by my sins, but I wasn't sorry. I still wanted to hold onto them. After all, what was left in life if I couldn't look with pleasure at beautiful women? Knowing that I had sinned just made me feel guilty and fearful with no desire to change.

"I want you to listen closely to a story I'm going to tell you. A young boy was once told by his father that a certain vase was priceless. The child was forbidden to touch it or even go near the glass case in which it was displayed. During a trip to the store some time later, the boy noticed an identical-looking vase that cost only five dollars. From then on, not only did the son doubt his father's credibility, but he also lost all reverence for that 'priceless' vase. In fact, one day while his father was out, the boy decided to take a closer look at it. He opened the glass door and carefully handled the family heirloom. It was much lighter than the one in the supermarket, but there was no doubt about it — they were identical!"

I continued, "As he wondered why his father would lie to him about its value, he heard a car pull into the driveway. In his haste to return the vase to the cabinet, he struck it on the glass case and shattered it into a thousand pieces! The child began to tremble with fear. Suddenly he remembered that he had five dollars in his piggy bank and consoled himself with the fact that he could easily replace it. When the father entered the house, the child flippantly called out, 'Dad, I broke that vase thing in the cabinet. It's okay, though. I can get another one at the store with the five dollars I've got in my piggy bank.'

"His father turned pale. He approached his son, placed his hands on the boy's shoulders, looked him in the eyes, and said, 'Son, that was no cheap imitation vase. That was an antique worth $25,000!' "

John seemed to wince at that. I carried on with my illustration: "The seriousness of what the boy had done suddenly hit him. His mouth went dry. Tears welled in his eyes. He broke down sobbing and fell into his father's arms, saying, 'I'm sorry . . . I'm so sorry!'

"His father wiped his tears and said, 'Son, there's no way you are going to be able to pay for that vase. It's going to take everything I've got, but I'll pay for a new one myself.' Conflicting emotions gripped the child — horror on one hand that his father would go to such expense, and yet gratitude that he would do such a thing for him despite his deliberate disobedience. Unutterable relief and unspeakable appreciation consoled his grief.

"So, John, let's see how perceptive you are. What produced the boy's sorrow?"

"It came when he saw the seriousness of what he had done," John replied, "revealed in the cost the father would have to pay to make things right."

"That's right," I affirmed. "At the moment, you are aware of the fact that you have broken God's Law into a thousand pieces. But no doubt you're not too concerned, because, like most people, you think that if you face God your good will outweigh your bad — you can make things right yourself. But you can't!

"What did it cost God to justify us — to make things right? The Scriptures tell us that we were not redeemed with silver and gold but with the precious blood of Christ. Our forgiveness was purchased with the unspeakably cruel suffering of Jesus of Nazareth. If you want to catch a glimpse of the cost of our redemption, look to the battered and bruised body of the Son of God as He hung on the Cross to take the punishment for the sin of the world. See the blood stream from His wounds. Hear His cry of anguish, 'My God, My God, why have You forsaken Me?' as His soul was made an offering for sin. That was the cost," I said, my voice quaking. I never failed to be gripped with emotion as I considered what Christ had done for me.

"If I gave my life for you, if I stepped in front of a bullet and took it in the chest so that you could live," I added, "it should break your heart. How much more should your heart be broken for your own sins, as you look at what Jesus did for sinners two thousand years ago? The Bible tells us, 'God demonstrates His own love toward us, in that while we were still sinners, Christ died for us' [Romans 5:8]. He did that for us. That's how much value we have to God.

"John, here's something else for you to think about. You are wanting to commit suicide. You want to end life as you know it. Why then not end it all in a different way? When someone is born again, they become a completely new person. The Bible says that old things pass away and all things become new.

"So if you're wanting to end it all, John, here is a way out that will cost you nothing but your pride. Instead of throwing yourself off the Golden Gate Bridge and ending up in hell, throw yourself into the arms of a faithful Creator, and end up in heaven."

A car honking as it buzzed past startled us both momentarily, and John looked up. With the water below now growing visible through large holes in the fog, that was definitely safer than looking down. It was then that I saw something that moved me. He closed his eyes tightly and furrowed his brow. With his lips pursed, he let out a long sigh. He probably did it unconsciously, but it revealed his stirred emotions. It was as though he was trembling in his heart. It seemed he was beginning to believe what he was being told, and the implications were breathtaking.

"What do you want — pain and suffering for eternity?" I continued. "By throwing yourself off the bridge you will lose everything, including every pleasure. By throwing yourself into the arms of Almighty God, you will get to keep your precious life, even though you don't value it at the moment. If you do come to Christ today, you will look back in horror at this moment with the thought that you might have chosen hell over heaven, merely by letting gravity take over."

John leaned back and closed his eyes again as he listened, his resistance softening. This time there was no furrowed brow or tight lips. Something was happening.

"None of us are worthy of the gift of everlasting life, but in God's eyes we are worth the life of His Son," I emphasized. "What are you going to do in response to such sobering thoughts? Keep your pride, and jump? Or are you willing to humble yourself and apologize to God for your rebellion against His will after He so graciously gave you life?

"John, think about life. Get your mind off the bad things for a moment, and think of the good things . . . the good things that God gave you. You have eyes. You can see color — the blueness of the sky and the magnificence of a sunrise. You can hear the songs of birds, and the sound of music. Think of all the food you can enjoy. Think of love and laughter. I'm not saying that you should just ignore your pain and be positive. I'm saying more than that — that life is an incredible gift from God to you. It's not something to be trifled with, but looked on with awe. Get up out of the pigsty and run to your Creator. Do that and He will meet you halfway. He will have compassion on you and embrace you as His son."

Chapter 7

No Excuse

By now I was sure that there had been divine intervention. As I glanced over my shoulder I could see that drivers were looking in our direction as they sped past. I was eager for us both to get down off the bridge, and wanted to share one more analogy with my friend. I no longer had any interest in taking a sunrise picture; there was something of far more value that I was concerned about.

"John, there's one more thought I'd like to leave with you. May I?"

"Sure," he replied, suddenly sounding a little anxious. "You're not going to leave me, are you? I'm beginning to. . . ."

"Of course not! I just want to tell you a true story about a little village in Italy that sits in a deep valley, surrounded by snow-capped mountains. The village, Viganella, is hidden from the sunshine for three freezing months of every year, and those three sunless months are not only cold, they tend to be gloomy and depressing.

"However, the local residents had a bright idea," I explained. "They installed a giant mirror on the mountainside, and it reflected the warmth of sunlight directly into the heart of that dark little town.

"John, I know your life right now seems to be dark, gloomy, and depressing. Life is filled with pain, suffering, and death. But the Bible says that to those who sat in the shadow of death, a light has dawned. Heaven shone its glorious light down to earth in the person of Jesus Christ, the one who said, 'I am the light of the world.'

"Even in the midst of this world's darkness, God has given us light — the light of the glorious gospel. Those who draw near to God can bask in the warmth of His love. If you turn from your sins and trust in Christ, Jesus promises that you will never walk in darkness again. Does that make sense?"

John was silent for a few moments, then asked, "You know what?"

"What?"

"Everything is starting to make sense," he said slowly. "I don't mean about my dad and the other issues that seemed so important. I mean everything makes sense that you've said about God, my sin, and what Jesus did on the Cross. I have no excuse for the things I've done. I feel physically sick at what I have become. I even accused Almighty God of being evil! For the first time in my life I understand what happened on that Cross. That was the payment for my sin!

"Could you pray for me? Right now!" John pleaded. "I want to pray but I can't. I can't face God. I have never in my life had such an overwhelming desire to kill myself as I do right now. Mr. Spock is screaming in my head for me to jump — seriously! Please pray!" he exclaimed, his voice shaking.

I bowed my head and earnestly prayed, "Father, in the name of Jesus, I stand against every work of darkness. I break every principality and power in John's life, through faith in the name of Jesus. Please help him. I pray that at this very moment, light will flood his soul and that by Your mercy and Your amazing grace, he will pass from death to life. In Jesus' name I pray. Amen."

"Dear God, I . . . I killed my own child," John began praying, sounding much calmer now. With a refreshing honesty, he opened his heart to his Creator. "I have hated my father. I have used other people for my own selfish needs. I have incessantly lied and stolen, and been filled with sexual fantasies. Help me to get up out of this pigsty. You gave me life, yet I used Your name as a cuss word. I have sinned against You. Please forgive me. Thank You for what You did on the Cross. I put my trust in Jesus Christ as my Savior. From this day forward I will live for Him. In His name I pray. Amen."

His eyes, which moments before darted with fear, were now peaceful and resolute. "Would you be kind enough to take my hand and help me up? I want to get away from this place. I have things to do. . . ."

Chapter 8

Out of the Mouths of Lions

The following day as I waited near the counter in my favorite burger restaurant, I was delighted to see a familiar face approaching. "John, I'm so pleased you could make it," I said with a broad smile as I gave him a hug. "Like I mentioned yesterday, I have a few important things I want to share with you." Among other things, I wanted to make sure he was okay, but he was far better than that. For the first time I saw a smile on his face, and his eyes were clear and bright and full of life.

"How could I not come? I love burgers — especially In-N-Out. Yesterday I was miserable and wanted to kill myself and today I'm a Christian being treated to In-N-Out. Gone from hell to heaven in 24 hours." He paused to ponder the dual meaning of that thought, and added, "Literally. I can't believe what's happened. Seriously, what you told me was the truth, and I'm excited to hear more."

"Did you want onions? There's such a crowd, I took the liberty of placing your order just before you got here."

"Yes, thanks," John said. "You know what I did yesterday? I went home . . . to my mom! I called her first, and when I told her what had happened, that I'd become a Christian, she burst into tears. Well, we both did. I told her I was so sorry for all the pain that I had caused her. When I got off the bus near her apartment, she was standing at the gate looking for me. When she saw me, she ran toward me and hugged me. It was just like that story Jesus told of the father running to his son. Incredible!"

I couldn't stop smiling as John spoke. He hardly took a breath between sentences. "Hold that thought," I said. "Here's your meal.

Let's get out of this noise and eat outside. I noticed a table under a tree."

He just smiled slightly, took the food, and carried on speaking with the same wide-eyed intensity.

"And you won't believe this. After dinner, I dug out my old Bible and was reading it. The *Bible!*" John flashed a big grin as he paused, then shook his head as if he couldn't believe it either. "I spent hours reading it and hardly slept a wink last night! I read Psalm 139 and it was so amazing I kept reading it over and over — well, I don't mean I read just *that Psalm* for hours," John chuckled, then continued. "It says that God knows me. From my birth. I've never said one word without Him being aware of it. He created me in my mother's womb, it says. You know what? The fact that God sees me doesn't freak me out anymore. I don't feel any guilt. Realizing that He sees me makes me feel good, knowing I'm not alone. Am I talking too much?"

"Not at all!" I laughed. "This is making my day. But, you're going to have to hold that thought again. Let's give God thanks for the food."

John was seated, and without saying a word clasped his hands together and once again furrowed his brow. I was about to open my mouth when he beat me to it.

"Dear God, we are so grateful for this day, for the sunrise, for my mom, and for saving me from such a terrible death." His voice cracked slightly. "And thank you for my new friend, for the sound of birds, for music and color. For Jesus and the Cross. . . . Oh, and for this food. Amen."

"Amen."

The smell of the fries was suddenly overpowering. I picked one up and placed it on my grateful taste buds.

John didn't miss a beat. He continued, "I had read parts of the Bible a few times when I was in church as a kid but last night it was like it was a different book. I couldn't put it down. I felt like a kid in a candy store."

"Because *you're* different. God gave you a new heart and put His Spirit within you, so you'll find you now have different desires. The way the Bible puts it is that you've been born again and are now a new creature in Christ," I said.

"You ain't kidding. Brand new. It's like a totally new world has opened to me. I can't stop thinking about Jesus, and what He did on the Cross — *for me*. And you know what? I've been saying 'Praise the Lord' and meaning it. You know, not in mockery."

I smiled again. "That's wonderful."

"I have so many questions for you. But, I also have one very real fear."

"What's that?"

"I'm afraid that I will lose what I've found. It's a little weird to say this, but I can't describe the feeling of joy. And I have a peace that I never had before."

"You've no worries there," I assured him. "You have God's promise that He will never leave you. Ever. Not even death can separate you from Him."

"Wow, really? That's incredible." John let out a sigh of relief. "Okay, first question — the big one I've been thinking about. What am I going to do if I get depressed? If Mr. Spock starts again, telling me to end it all? How should I deal with thoughts of suicide?"

"Well, let's look at the suicide aspect first. Are you familiar with the story of the Philippian jailer?" I asked.

"I've heard that they have harsh jail sentences for drug users. One of my old friends got two years for less than half an ounce of weed."

"No. Philippian, not the Philipp*ines*. It's a story in the Bible about a jailer who wanted to commit suicide because he thought he messed up at his job."

"Seriously? Just because he messed up?"

"Yes. His employer had a rule that if you blew it, you were put to death. And he thought that he had blown it."

John's eyes sparkled with interest. "Okay. You have me hooked. Give me the details."

"It's in the Book of Acts. Two Christians were beaten and then thrown in prison for upsetting the locals."

"What did they do?"

"They cast a demon out of a girl. She had been following them for a long time, yelling out stuff, and one of the Christians, a man named Paul, lost his patience and cast out the demon."

"Do you really believe in that sort of thing? A literal demon?"

The words caught the ear of the young woman sitting behind John. She was sporting devilish tattoos and had brass rings through her nose and in her bottom lip. She turned around slightly and gave a strange look first at John and then at me. I managed a courtesy smile, and answered his question. I could tell that she was straining to hear my answer above the noise of the patio.

"Of course. The Bible has a lot to say on the subject. Anyway, Paul and his friend were beaten and their feet were locked in stocks, and they lay in a cold, dark dungeon, bleeding from their wounds. You know what they did? They sang praises to God."

John looked genuinely mystified. "That's a little weird. Why would they do that?"

"Even in what some may think was a hopelessly depressing situation, they trusted Him. Whatever happens to a Christian happens only by God's permissive will. It may not be His perfect will, but He has permitted it because He can work it out for the Christian's good. More ketchup?"

"Sure, thanks." I sat speechless as I watched him pick up all three of the remaining paper cups of ketchup and smother not more than a dozen fries, and saw them disappear under a sea of red sauce. He continued, "But how on earth could getting beaten up and sitting bloodied and in pain in a cold dungeon work out for their good? Can't see that happening."

I smiled and said, "Would you like to hear what did happen?"

"Of course."

"They're sitting in prison singing hymns . . . let me read it to you. Hang on — I have a Bible on my phone."

As I reached for my phone, John licked ketchup from his thumb. "Here's another thing that's weird. You know what I like to do? I fry an egg and slip it in between the patties. An Aussie made me one once. Now I do it all the time," he commented as he bit into his burger.

"I love eggs . . . ah, here it is. Acts 16:25. Tell you what, take my phone and you read it. Out loud. This burger's got me salivating."

"Okay. Verse 25?"

"Yes. Verses 25 through 31."

John began reading aloud: "'But at midnight Paul and Silas were praying and singing hymns to God, and the prisoners were listening to them. Suddenly there was a great earthquake, so that the foundations of the prison were shaken; and immediately all the doors were opened and everyone's chains were loosed. And the keeper of the prison, awaking from sleep and seeing the prison doors open, supposing the prisoners had fled, drew his sword and was about to kill himself.' So this is the guy who was going to commit suicide. Why would he do that?"

"He was a *Roman* jailer," I explained, between bites. "Under Roman law, if a guard lost his prisoners he was to be put to death for failing his responsibility. Or worse, he would suffer the punishment that was due to his prisoners. It was an effective way to make sure everyone was diligent when guarding prisoners. If his were gone, come sunrise, he would suffer some grizzly death as an example to other jailers who might decide to free condemned prisoners. So he decided to speed up the process."

"That makes sense." John nodded, then he resumed his reading: "'But Paul called with a loud voice, saying, "Do yourself no harm, for we are all here." Then he called for a light, ran in, and fell down trembling before Paul and Silas. And he brought them out and said, "Sirs, what must I do to be saved?" So they said, "Believe on the Lord Jesus Christ, and you will be saved, you and your household."' Wow. How cool!"

I set my burger down for the moment. "So when the Philippian jailer was going to kill himself, Paul stopped him. He called out, 'Do yourself no harm, for we are all here!'"

"Kind of like what you did for me," John inserted.

"Right. But think about this. Why did Paul call out? He had a good reason for remaining silent and letting the jailer kill himself. The doors were open and that would have been one less obstacle on the way out. But suicide is never a good choice; it is a *harmful* choice. This was a human being, made in the image of God, and Paul couldn't let the man take his own life."

"So, what does that mean?" John asked as he took a bite and awaited the answer.

"What does what mean?"

Caught with a mouthful, John responded with a muffled, "Made in the image of a God." After he quickly swallowed he added, "You mentioned that yesterday, too."

"It means that God created us in His likeness, with some of His attributes. We are aware of our existence. Consciousness. We can appreciate music and beauty, love and laughter. We have a sense of morality and with it an intuitive passion for justice. Animals don't set up court systems and prosecute other animals that violate some law they have put in place. But humans do. We are unique in creation."

"Wow — I seem to be saying *wow* a lot lately — I've never thought about the difference. I've been told that we are all animals. The whole evolution thing."

"And if you read further," I added, "you will see that the jailer and his whole family came to Christ, and he ended up tending to Paul and Silas's wounds. Then the Romans let them go!"

"So it *did* work out for their good. Amazing."

"Yes. And *there's* the reason no one should ever even think about committing suicide."

A fry on its way to John's mouth paused midair as he asked quizzically, "How do you mean?" Then it found its target.

"Think of what happened. The jailer thought he had good reason to kill himself. The doors were open, so he naturally assumed the prisoners were gone. Life was over. He would never see his beloved family again and would be put to death. It was a hopeless situation, so he may as well do it himself and get it over with.

"But he was wrong — he was not alone. The prisoners were still there! When God is in the equation, what may seem to be a hopeless, depressing, and impossible situation isn't. This is because with God, nothing is impossible." I smiled as I thought of John's comment when we first met: that convincing him life was worth living was "an impossible task." *Truly, nothing is impossible with God.*

There Is Hope

"For I know the thoughts that I think toward you, says the LORD, thoughts of peace and not of evil, to give you a future and a hope." (Jeremiah 29:11)

"Why are you cast down, O my soul? And why are you disquieted within me? Hope in God, for I shall yet praise Him for the help of His countenance." (Psalm 42:5)

". . . lay hold of the hope set before us. This hope we have as an anchor of the soul, both sure and steadfast. . . ." (Hebrews 6:18–19)

"Let us hold fast the confession of our hope without wavering, for He who promised is faithful." (Hebrews 10:23)

"Be of good courage, and He shall strengthen your heart, all you who hope in the LORD." (Psalm 31:24)

"Now may the God of hope fill you with all joy and peace in believing, that you may abound in hope by the power of the Holy Spirit." (Romans 15:13)

"Now hope does not disappoint, because the love of God has been poured out in our hearts by the Holy Spirit who was given to us." (Romans 5:5)

"This I recall to my mind, therefore I have hope. Through the LORD's mercies we are not consumed, because His compassions fail not. They are new every morning; great is Your faithfulness. 'The LORD is my portion,' says my soul, 'Therefore I hope in Him!'" (Lamentations 3:21–24)

"Uphold me according to Your word, that I may live; and do not let me be ashamed of my hope." (Psa. 119:116)

"So you're saying that no matter what situation I find myself in, even if there seems to be no way of escape, God can do the impossible," John summarized. "And so if I kill myself, I stop Him from delivering me. I stop the solution."

"Exactly. I'm impressed. Do you know the story of Moses at the Red Sea?"

"You mean the two-by-two . . . the animals and the ark thing?" John happily continued to work over his burger and fries as I talked.

"No, that was Noah." I couldn't help grinning at this common case of mistaken identity. "Moses was leading the nation of Israel through the wilderness, and they were being chased by an angry enemy — the Egyptian army. They were between a rock and a hard place, trapped at the edge of a sea with no way of escape. But instead of thinking about suicide to get out of an impossible situation, Moses told the people, 'Stand still and see the salvation of God.' Salvation just means deliverance. In other words, even though the situation looked impossible, he trusted God to help. And God did a miracle by opening the sea and providing a way of escape.

"It was a similar situation with a man named Joseph, who found himself in prison wrongly charged with attempted rape. Instead of considering killing himself, he patiently trusted God. And he was delivered. Daniel was tossed into a den of hungry lions, simply for praying to God, and was left overnight. He trusted God and was delivered from their mouths," I concluded, as I hungrily stuffed a few fries in mine.

"Okay. So that's the answer to my question about thoughts of suicide," John summed up. "If they come back, I need to look to God and trust Him."

"Yes, that's the first principle of Christianity. It's foundational," I stressed. "Whatever life throws at you, show that you believe that He will work things out for your good by singing hymns to God, even though you are in pain and chains hold you to your dilemma. Perhaps God will send a miracle your way. You will never know what will happen until you totally trust Him. And singing His praise no matter how bad things may seem is evidence of your trust. Suicide should therefore never be an option. Listen to this wonderful promise in Romans 8:28, and put it in your memory bank so that you

You Can Trust God

"But I trust in the LORD. I will rejoice and be glad in your steadfast love, because you have seen my affliction; you have known the distress of my soul." (Psalm 31:6–7; ESV)

"To you, O LORD, I lift up my soul. O my God, I trust in you." (Psalm 25:1,2)

"Trust in the LORD with all your heart, and lean not on your own understanding; in all your ways acknowledge Him, and He shall direct your paths." (Proverbs 3:5–6)

"Who walks in darkness and has no light? Let him trust in the name of the LORD and rely upon his God." (Isaiah 50:10)

"You will keep him in perfect peace, whose mind is stayed on You, because he trusts in You." (Isaiah 26:3)

"Blessed is the man who trusts in the LORD, and whose hope is the LORD." (Jeremiah 17:7)

"Whenever I am afraid, I will trust in You." (Psalm 56:3)

"The LORD is my strength and my shield; my heart trusted in Him, and I am helped." (Psalm 28:7)

"In God I have put my trust; I will not be afraid. What can man do to me?" (Psalm 56:11)

"Keep my soul, and deliver me; let me not be ashamed, for I put my trust in You." (Psalm 25:20)

"I will say of the LORD, 'He is my refuge and my fortress; my God, in Him I will trust.'" (Psalm 91:2) never forget it: 'And we know that all things work together for good to those who love God, to those who are the called according to His purpose.' Got it?"

"Got it. *All* things," John repeated. Fries all gone, he popped the last bite of burger in his mouth and crumpled up the wrapper.

"Man, I enjoyed that! You know what I like? The taste of salt that explodes in your mouth when that first hot fry hits the tongue. It's incredible." He shook his head in amazement and added, "This is really strange."

"What's strange?"

"I never used to think like this. Seriously! Fries were just fries. Stick them in the mouth, chew, swallow. Now I have a whole new appreciation for everything. Did you see the sunrise today? Amazing."

"Yes. It certainly was," I agreed. "Back to Romans 8:28. This doesn't just mean that God will give you light at the end of the tunnel. The promise is that He will work out the situation *for your own good.* He will use your dilemma for your benefit. You may see that in this life, or it may be in eternity. In the Book of Hebrews, particularly in chapter 11, you will read about what are often called the heroes of faith, men and women who were put in terrible situations, and yet they trusted God to work things out for good. It would be helpful for you to read that chapter."

"Okay, I will."

Chapter 9

The Slap in the Face

"Gentlemen, are you enjoying your meal?" The waiter, dressed in white with a bright red apron and white hat, was a tall, lanky youth.

I looked at his nametag and replied, "It's great. Thanks, Matthias," as I handed him a card. "Did you get one of these? It's six free movies. They are award-winning, seen by millions. The site is on the back of the card: FullyFreeFilms.com."[1] [1 You can find these "Movie Gift Cards" on LivingWaters.com.]

Matthias smiled from ear to ear, and turned the card over. "Is this for me? No way! Thank you, sir."

As Matthias walked away, John grabbed one of the cards from the small pile that was on the table. "So what are these?"

"They're Christian films," I said, adding that people love being given a card where they can watch six free movies.

"Can I have one? Or a few? I can share them with some friends . . . if they'll speak to me again."

"Certainly. If you remember, you had asked about what to do when you start to feel depressed."

"Yeah. I would appreciate hearing your thoughts on that," John said.

I polished off my hamburger, ate the last delectable fry, and debated whether to lick my fingers. Then I dove into the next topic of our conversation. "The Bible does have something to say about that, too. Some preachers wrongly promise a bed of roses, when the Christian life can sometimes be a whole stack of thorns. Painful thorns. Did you know that quite a number of biblical figures struggled with depression? Take Jonah for instance."

"Are you telling me that Jonah felt down in the mouth?"

"Very funny," I chuckled.

"Did that really happen?"

"Did what really happen?"

"Did Jonah really get swallowed by a whale?" John asked. "Or is it some sort of Bible lesson about life's circumstances being over-whelming?"

"Well, the Bible does say that a massive fish swallowed Jonah. This is the way I handle strange Bible stories like this," I offered. "I keep in mind that the Scriptures say that God has chosen foolish things to confound the wise, and this certainly is a foolish-sounding story. It is humbling to believe it. It's a stumbling-block for proud people. But Jesus said it literally happened, so I don't doubt it for a second. The premise is that God can do anything. He's not bound by natural laws — that's what 'supernatural' means. Anyway, God used Jonah as a prophet to deliver the people of Nineveh from judg-ment, and that caused Jonah to go into a big sulk. He actually did get down in the mouth, and hand-in-hand with his pouting came depression — so much so that he sat down and wanted to die. He was actually being childish."

John interjected, "Are you saying that this is what happens with all depression? That people just need to grow up and face life?"

"Definitely not. But it was in this case," I explained, as I took a quick sip. "Jonah was upset that God didn't judge the city, but rather He showed them mercy. If Jonah had a loving heart he would have rejoiced. Instead, his shallow attitude made him jealous and his anger brought on depression. Love fortifies us against such sinful attitudes. A loving person will be glad when good things happen to others. So, John, learn a prophet-able lesson: Don't be shallow in character by letting anger and jealousy into your heart. Anger gives place to the devil, but love keeps the doors shut tight.

"There's a great definition of love from the famous chapter so often quoted at weddings. Well, it used to be, anyway," I added. "One of the modern translations says this (I committed it to memory years ago): 'Love is patient and kind. Love is not jealous or boastful or proud or rude. It does not demand its own way. It is not irritable, and it keeps no record of being wronged. It does not rejoice about injustice, but rejoices whenever the truth wins out. Love never gives up, never loses faith, is always hopeful, and endures through every circumstance.' That's from 1 Corinthians 15." I paused to think. "Hang on; that's the resurrection chapter. It's from chapter 13. So much for my memory," I grinned.

"The Bible shows us Jonah's warts. How would you like that?" I asked.

"Like what?"

"How would you like to be featured in the world's most famous book, with all of your personal whining and weaknesses displayed? But that's what we have in the Scriptures. We see the good, the bad, and the ugly (that was a great film, by the way). The Bible says that these things were written for our instruction, so that 'we through the patience and comfort of the Scriptures might have hope.' We watch them walk onto landmines, in the hope that we won't follow in their steps."

"And I thought the Bible was just a dry, old history book," John marveled. "Since I became a Christian, it's as though . . . I don't know how to explain this . . . it's as though every word is alive. I didn't realize it's so applicable to my life."

I had to smile at that. "Okay, John. Give me a summary of what we have learned from Jonah about what not to do. How can we save ourselves some pain?"

"Well, his angry attitude was childish and unloving. If he was loving, he would have been happy about the good fortune of others."

"That's right," I noted. "Love protects us from sin and its bedfellows, one of which is depression. Have you heard of Job?"

"All I have ever heard is the saying about having the patience of Job. My dad used to mumble that when things didn't go right." This time when John mentioned his father, there was no tone of anger in his voice like there had been the day before.

"Yeah. If anyone was justified in being depressed, it was Job. The Bible says he was a rich man who had everything in life, including being blameless in the eyes of God. He wasn't without sin, but he was better than most. Yet life hit him like a ton of bricks. In one day, he lost all of his wealth and all of his kids were killed in a tragedy. Then he lost his health. Job's suffering was so great that he cursed the day he was born. On top of that, his friends told him that God was punishing him for his sins — which wasn't the case.

"God allowed the storms to pile up on Job for some unknown reason," I continued. "Other than, of course, to teach us how we should react when storms come our way. We are called, like Job, to be patient in tribulation. When we look at the whole picture of his life, though, we see that God not only restored all that he had originally lost, He even gave Job twice as much and blessed him more than before. So it worked out for his good. And that's the consolation that should help us to be patient in tribulation. It really is just a matter of Romans 8:28. Do you remember that verse?"

"Yes. All things work together for good."

"Right. But what's the last part?" I prompted.

"Something about being called."

" 'All things work together for good to those who love God, to those who are the called according to His purpose.' The promise is to those who love God. In other words, if you are walking away from the purpose and will of God, it's probably not going to work for your good. I say 'probably' because some Christians may make a wrong business or relationship decision that turns out to be a disaster. They come back to God with a massive mess and, in His kindness, He may work it out for their good. But it sure would have been easier to wait on the Lord for His wisdom before making some life-changing decision. So always commit what you do into God's hands, and if things don't go the way you expect, you can rest in the promise of Romans 8:28. That will help to lift the weight of depression from your shoulders."

John said, nodding, "I'll try to remember that."

"Job wasn't the only one who cursed the day of his birth. So did the prophet Jeremiah, who endured such grief for years that he's known as 'the weeping prophet.' Both Job and Jeremiah wished they'd never been born. Others were more direct and actually prayed to die. In addition to Jonah, the prophet Elijah and Moses both asked God to kill them. It's interesting to note that these men didn't take their own lives by suicide; instead, all three appealed to God to take their lives from them. What do you make of that?"

"Hmm." John thought a moment before replying. "Okay. Tell me if I'm getting the message right. Instead of killing themselves, they knew that their life belonged to God, and as the giver of life, He was the only one with the right to take it. How's that?"

I felt like a father who had just watched his toddler take his first steps. "Bang on," I said. "Nailed it. I think it's very important to realize that these were real people who suffered from real depression, and they were honest with God in pouring out their hearts. When they felt despair, they looked to Him for help. And we should do the same."

"They are so famous it's easy to lose sight of the fact that they were just like us," John observed.

"Yes. The Scriptures show them experiencing the same trials and difficulties that we do, and in many cases we are even given the solutions. For instance, Moses wanted to die because he couldn't bear the heavy burdens he was carrying alone, so God gave him helpers to lighten his load. The same principle is true for you. If you share your concerns with a friend or family member, it will help lighten your burdens and keep your problems from feeling overwhelming."

I continued, "The prophet Elijah, after he had an especially trying time, was exhausted and despondent, and God told him to have some food and water, along with rest. How many times do we neglect the simple care of our bodies? Failing to eat right and get a good night's sleep can wear on our emotional and physical health, and lead to depression. So follow your Creator's advice to keep depression in check."

"Wow! This is all really good stuff!" John exclaimed. "I had no idea all this was in there."

It was so good to see his enthusiasm. Being a small part in a chain of divinely orchestrated events in his life was a huge highlight for me. This life so often doesn't turn out well. Every day people kill themselves, and no one gets to give them another perspective. But it had turned out wonderfully well with John. I loved his hunger for the things of God, and I could hardly wait to share more with him.

I said, "Yeah, the Bible is like that. It's an instruction book for life . . . and for death. Somebody thought of a great acronym using the word 'Bible': Basic Instructions Before Leaving Earth."

The Bible on Suicide

"Know that the LORD, *He is God; it is He who has made us, and not we ourselves." (Psalm 100:3)*

"You have granted me life and favor, and Your care has preserved my spirit." (Job 10:12)

"Thus says the LORD *who made you and formed you from the womb, who will help you. . . ." (Isaiah 44:2)*

"Look, every life belongs to Me." (Ezekiel 18:4; CSB)

"Thus says the LORD, *who created you . . . 'I have called you by your name; you are Mine.' " (Isaiah 43:1)*

"And in Your book were all written the days that were ordained for me, when as yet there was not one of them." (Psalm 139:16; NASB)

"Do not be overly wicked, nor be foolish: why should you die before your time?" (Ecclesiastes 7:17)

"Whoever sheds man's blood, by man his blood shall be shed; for in the image of God He made man." (Genesis 9:6)

"You shall not murder." (Exodus 20:13)

"Do you not know that your body is the temple of the Holy Spirit who is in you, whom you have from God, and you are not your own? For you were bought at a price; therefore glorify God in your body and in your spirit, which are God's." (1 Corinthians 6:19–20)

"I shall not die, but live, and declare the works of the LORD.*" (Psalm 118:17)*

John grinned. "I like that!"

"So do I. There's more. Even King David battled deep depression. Do you know his story?"

"Yes. About Goliath."

"That was a different battle. He had one with a bigger giant, and lost."

"I didn't know that."

"Well, I think you will identify with it," I began. "David was walking on the rooftop of his palace when he spotted one of his neighbors — a beautiful woman named Bathsheba — bathing herself. This giant was lust."

"Okay. I get it."

"Instead of fighting this Goliath, David surrendered to it. He committed adultery with her, and then when she became pregnant with his child, he didn't abort her baby; he aborted her husband. The king had him killed. Then he married Bathsheba, and all was well. Neat and tidy. Except that God saw his sin."

"I guess we didn't cover that one in Sunday school. So what happened?"

I could only read John's lips, and concluded that he had said something about Sunday school. Just to our left, a mother seemed oblivious to the fact that her toddler sounded like the engines of a 777 at full thrust. The child's bag of fries had fallen to the ground, and she was too busy feeding another one of her offspring to be concerned with his problem. After what seemed like an eternity, she took a handful of fries from her own supply and slapped them on a napkin in front of him. Immediate silence. Golden silence. I was pleased, and carried on.

"Well, David's sin weighed heavily on him and led him into a deep depression — not unlike your situation."

"That's true," John acknowledged. "It was my sin that got me into a quicksand of hopelessness. The more I struggled, the deeper I went. Wow . . . thank God He saved me."

I continued, "As David's conscience was eating away at him, he poured out his great sorrow in several psalms. Listen to his words, here in Psalm 38." I looked it up on my phone and began reading portions:

" 'I am troubled, I am bowed down greatly;
I go mourning all the day long. . . .
I am feeble and severely broken;
I groan because of the turmoil of my heart. . . .
For I am ready to fall,
And my sorrow is continually before me.
For I will declare my iniquity;
I will be in anguish over my sin. . . .
Make haste to help me,
O Lord, my salvation!'

"When David eventually confessed his sin and cried out to God for mercy, he got it . . . because God is rich in mercy. God forgave him and washed away all of his sins. The words of David's prayer are recorded in Psalm 51 — it's such a beautiful example of confession and repentance, be sure to read it sometime."

"Psalm 51. Okay, I will," John replied, looking deep in thought. He paused and then added, "Let me ask you: God forgave him? Even for murder?"

"Yes . . . even for murder."

"Seriously? So are you saying that when God forgave my sins He also forgave the fact that I terminated the life of my own child?"

"Yes," I assured him. "The moment you trust in Christ, you are completely forgiven every single sin."

John clenched his fist and held his bent forefinger to his bottom lip, as tears welled in his eyes. I waited a few seconds for him to get his composure.

"So, John," I asked, "what would you say is the point of David's story? What can we learn about how to avoid sliding into depression?"

"Well, people can become depressed when they're struggling with guilt over unconfessed sin — like I was. So the solution is to cry out to God for mercy — like David did — and they'll find forgiveness."

"That's right. God gave you a conscience for your protection, so make sure you listen to it. Confess any sin as soon as you are aware of it. The Bible says that he who covers his sins will not prosper, but whoever confesses and forsakes them will have mercy."

Your Guilt Can Be Removed

"Have mercy upon me, O God, according to Your lovingkindness; according to the multitude of Your tender mercies, blot out my transgressions. Wash me thoroughly from my iniquity, and cleanse me from my sin. . . . Wash me, and I shall be whiter than snow."
(Psalm 51:1–7)

"If we confess our sins, He is faithful and just to forgive us our sins and to cleanse us from all unrighteousness." (1 John 1:9)

"For I will be merciful to their unrighteousness, and their sins and their lawless deeds I will remember no more." (Hebrews 8:12)

"I, even I, am He who blots out your transgressions for My own sake; and I will not remember your sins." (Isaiah 43:25)

"As far as the east is from the west, so far has He removed our transgressions from us." (Psalm 103:12)

"You will cast all our sins into the depths of the sea." (Micah 7:19)

"There is therefore now no condemnation to those who are in Christ Jesus, who do not walk according to the flesh, but according to the Spirit." (Romans 8:1)

"But if we walk in the light as He is in the light, we have fellowship with one another, and the blood of Jesus Christ His Son cleanses us from all sin." (1 John 1:7)

"Excuse me, sir. Are these Christian movies?" It was Matthias. He was still holding the card.

"Yes, they are," I replied.

"Great! I can't wait to watch them. I'm a Christian."

John seemed mesmerized with the conversation. "I became a Christian yesterday!" he chimed.

"No way!" Matthias reached out and shook John's hand. "Congratulations. That's wonderful. Did you see the Bible verses under your cups?"

John tipped his cup, dribbling water on the table. "Proverbs 3:5. Wow! That's so cool."

Matthias automatically took out his rag and wiped off the table. "Nice to meet you. I'd better get back to work. Thanks again for the movies."

I smiled, turned to John and said, "Nice guy. Okay, back to what we were talking about. The New Testament offers a few more ways to avoid depression. In addition to being beaten and thrown in jail, the Apostle Paul endured tremendous hardships — far more than most of us ever will — yet he considered them to be 'light afflictions' compared to the glories that awaited him in heaven. By keeping the eternal view in mind, he was able to not lose heart."

I continued, "Paul also described how he and the disciples had conflicts and fears, were troubled on every side, and had no rest. Little wonder then that he wrote, 'We were burdened beyond measure, so that we despaired even of life.' But he went on to say this occurred so that 'we should not trust in ourselves but in God who raises the dead.'

"Our option as Christians is to trust in God. So here's another verse for you to commit to memory. It's actually the one that's on your cup. Say it after me: 'Trust in the LORD with all your heart. . . .'"

"Trust in the LORD with all your heart . . ." John repeated.

"And lean not on your own understanding."

"And lean not on your own understanding. Got it."

"That's from the Book of Proverbs, which is the cream of the wisdom of Solomon. By the way, did you know there was a point where even the wisest man who ever lived found everything distressing and said he hated life? As Solomon discovered, the only lasting meaning in life is found in trusting God."

"Wow, I didn't know. And he was quite a wise guy, huh?"

"The original." I grinned. "And that brings us to Jesus — our ultimate example. God in the flesh. But because Jesus was also a man, He can sympathize with our pain and weaknesses. The Bible says He was 'a Man of sorrows and acquainted with grief,' and there were times when He was so troubled that He groaned in His spirit. The night before He knew He would be crucified, He said that His soul was 'exceedingly sorrowful, even to death.' Does that sound familiar?"

"Yes, it does," John agreed. "That's about how I felt. That's surprising."

"Here's an important verse — let me read it to you, from the Book of John. When Jesus was praying in the garden that night He said, 'Now My soul is troubled, and what shall I say? "Father, save Me from this hour"? But for this purpose I came to this hour.' Do you know what He was talking about?"

"Of course. Jesus came to earth for the purpose of giving His life as a payment for our sins. *My* sins," John added, smiling.

"That's right. Jesus never considered taking His life, even for a moment. Throwing Himself off a high building, like Satan had tempted Him to — or off a bridge — would have prevented Him from fulfilling the purpose for His life. And the same is true for you. God created you for a purpose and gave you life for a reason. There is meaning to your existence here on earth, and you need to look to God to know what that is.

"What I'm saying is that God could use you to say to this generation, like Paul did, that they are not alone and that they should do themselves no harm," I suggested. "Speaking of God using you, tell me, how would you have handled you?"

He looked puzzled. "What do you mean?"

"How would you have handled coming across someone sitting on the edge of eternity on a ledge of the Golden Gate Bridge?"

John wrinkled his brow. "I don't know."

"Well, what was the turning point in our conversation?"

Your Life Has Purpose

"Everyone who is called by My name, whom I have created for My glory; I have formed him, yes, I have made him. . . . This people I have formed for Myself; they shall declare My praise." (Isaiah 43:7–21)

"But you are a chosen generation, a royal priesthood, a holy nation, His own special people, that you may proclaim the praises of Him who called you out of darkness into His marvelous light." (1 Peter 2:9)

"Jesus Christ, who gave Himself for us, that He might redeem us from every lawless deed and purify for Himself His own special people, zealous for good works." (Titus 2:13–14)

"For we are His workmanship, created in Christ Jesus for good works, which God prepared beforehand that we should walk in them." (Ephesians 2:10)

"And this is eternal life, that they may know You, the only true God, and Jesus Christ whom You have sent." (John 17:3)

"that you may walk worthy of the Lord, fully pleasing Him, being fruitful in every good work and increasing in the knowledge of God." (Colossians 1:10)

"'You shall love the LORD your God with all your heart, with all your soul, and with all your mind.' This is the first and great commandment." (Matthew 22:37–38)

"Go into all the world and preach the gospel to every creature." (Mark 16:15)

"The turning point. . . ." He picked up his cup of water, took a sip, and said, "When you first approached me, I was really annoyed. You being there complicated things. I didn't want to have anything to do with you. But there was something in your tone. I think it was a gentleness . . . and a love. I could feel a genuine concern. The turning point didn't come until I began to understand the Cross, but that story of the man having his heart cut out of his chest, by the surgeons, was like a hard slap in my face. It suddenly made me doubt what I was planning to do."

"So that's all you need. Love and gentleness along with the gospel."

"I can do that. There are others I know who are struggling with depression, and I want to share with them what I've learned. This is the answer to every human problem."

"Well, let's say that if the world obeyed the gospel, if they did what you have done — turned from sin and trusted the Savior — life would certainly be better for the human race." There is a wonderful walk-on-water enthusiasm with a new Christian. I didn't want to dampen John's belief that God can fix this broken world. The only hindrance is humanity. So I chose my words carefully. "Think about it. Experts tell us they don't know the cause of chronic depression that leads to suicide, let alone the cure. The best they can do is try to treat the symptoms: mental illness, guilt, self-hatred, a sense of futility, and the agony of hopelessness.

"After many years of seeing chronic depression and suicide grow into an epidemic, I'm convinced, seriously (as you like to say), that the only answer to this terrible dilemma is the gospel of Jesus Christ. It promises a sound mind, complete release from the burden of guilt, purpose for existence, a reason to live, freedom from the fear of death, and the living hope of eternal life. Hopelessness leaves the moment we are born again.

"So despite the fact that we all have our emotional ups and downs, of all people on earth who shouldn't be depressed to thoughts of suicide, it's us Christians. We know God loves us; He proved that with the Cross. He has forgiven all of our sins and granted us everlasting life! Think of that for a moment. Then He promises to work all things out for our good. *All* things.

"However, I'm not saying we won't ever feel down as Christians, or even experience depression at times," I added. "Life is filled with trials, and the evil that we talked about, but in Christ we always have hope."

John leaned forward slightly and put his palms on the now clean table. "Well, then, let me ask you another question," he said. "I've had friends who became Christians, and for a while things went well with them. They got off of drugs and alcohol, but then suddenly they went back to their old lives! Seriously, what's with that?"

"They were more than likely something called 'false converts' — the Bible speaks a lot about that. Many people think they become a Christian by praying a prayer or joining a church, instead of what the Bible commands: repent and trust in Christ. Those friends who 'fell away' did so probably because they came to Christ to have their problems fixed, rather than have their sins forgiven. So they weren't truly born again."

Leaning back on his chair again, he said, "Anyway, the reason I brought it up is that I'm afraid *I'll* fall away!"

It was a legitimate concern for a new Christian. I replied, "As I mentioned, nothing can separate you from God's love. Not even death. The Bible says that He who has begun a good work in you will complete it, and that He is able to keep you from falling and present you faultless before the presence of His glory with exceeding joy. So you can trust that He's not going to let you go.

"It's that same trust that will give you victory over depression. Your faith will give you a joy that will sing hymns in the dungeon. And when the enemy whispers for you to kill yourself, the Scriptures say to submit yourself to God and resist the devil, and he will flee from you. Look to God's Word as your guide, and suicide will no longer be an option."

After a study on the subject of suicide, *The American Journal of Psychiatry* reported:

"Religiously unaffiliated subjects had significantly more lifetime suicide attempts . . . subjects with no religious affiliation perceived fewer reasons for living, particularly fewer moral objections to suicide."

Offering Hope

In her book, Hope Prevails: Insights from a Doctor's Personal Journey through Depression, *Christian psychologist Dr. Michelle Bengtson said that every week she saw patients with mental health disorders and depression. She would diagnose the condition and make treatment recommendations. However, with all her expertise, she fell into the dark and deep valley of depression herself.*

She said, "My greatest shock came when I tried the same treatment suggestions I typically offered my patients — and they didn't work. I tried medication, I participated in therapy, I ate right and exercised dutifully . . . for me those things weren't enough. Only when I started to understand what depression does to us spiritually, as well as what it cannot do, and then started cooperating with God did I finally begin to experience the chains of depression falling off."

She concluded, "In the midst of my battle, hope was elusive. I wasn't sure I would survive. Actually, I wasn't sure I wanted to survive. But hope — the belief in a purpose, the belief in something better — can make all the difference. Without hope, what reason do we have to get up in the morning? With hope, we want to move forward, press on, get to the other side, and then share with others what we have learned to offer them hope during their times of trial."

"In my thirty years as a practicing psychotherapist, I've never read a book that suggests more helpful and concrete ways of overcoming depression as *Hope Prevails*."
— Pat Wenger, MA, LPC, MFT

John didn't say a word. He was too busy hanging on to every one of mine.

"It was God who reached out to you as you sat hopelessly on that ledge. It was He who plucked you from the hands of the enemy, took you out of the darkness and brought you into the glorious light," I continued. "And now He has given you and I the same commission that He gave to the Apostle Paul. He said that Paul was 'to open their eyes, in order to turn them from darkness to light, and from the power of Satan to God, that they may receive forgiveness of sins and an inheritance among those who are sanctified by faith in Me.'

"John, take that light to the millions who sit helplessly on the edge of eternity, in the darkness of the shadow of death.

"May He use you to reach many."

"And your life would be brighter than noonday.

Though you were dark, you would be like the morning.

And you would be secure, because there is hope.

Job 11:17

Resources

For more on this vital topic, please watch a free movie called *EXIT.*
From Living Waters, creators of the award-winning TV program *The Way of the Master* and the popular movies *180* and *Evolution vs. God,* comes the riveting and hope-inspiring film *EXIT.*

According to the World Health Organization, a massive 800,000 people take their lives every year — one death every 40 seconds. For millions who suffer from depression and despair, *EXIT* points to a better way. This compelling movie shines a powerful light in the darkness and offers true hope to those who think they have none. Someone you know may be secretly considering their final exit. Watch *EXIT,* and share it with those you love.

See theEXITmovie.com to watch *EXIT,* get details on a 4-session Video Study, and find other help.

If you are considering suicide, please, call the "Suicide Prevention Lifeline" and talk with someone right now. It's free, confidential, and available 24/7.
800-273-8255
SuicidePreventionLifeline.org

For Non-Christians

If you would like additional information on Christianity, please check out the following helpful resources:

The Evidence Bible. Answers to over 200 questions, thousands of comments, and 130 informative articles will help you better comprehend the Christian faith.

How to Know God Exists. Clear evidences for His existence will convince you that belief in God is reasonable and rational — a matter of fact and not faith.

Why Christianity? (DVD). If you have ever asked what happens after we die, if there is a heaven, or how good we have to be to go there, this DVD will help you.

If you are a new believer, please read *Save Yourself Some Pain*, written just for you (available free online at LivingWaters.com, or as a booklet).

For Christians

Please visit our website and sign up for our free weekly e-newsletter. To learn how to share your faith the way Jesus did, don't miss these helpful resources:

God Has a Wonderful Plan for Your Life: The Myth of the Modern Message (our most important book).

Hell's Best Kept Secret and *True & False Conversion*. Listen to these vital messages free at LivingWaters.com.

For additional resources and information about Ray Comfort's ministry, visit LivingWaters.com.

Dedicated to Frank and Charri Sutherlin

Contents

Chapter 1

The Depressed Celebrity

For many, it's only the death of a celebrity that reminds them that we all have an appointment. But passing is more common than most think. Since you picked up this book, over 100 people left this life. Every hour, 6,000 move out of the land of the living. Every day, 150,000 breathe their last, and every year a whopping 54 million human beings kick the bucket. They die. It's kind of depressing if you think about it.

Some die quickly in car accidents. Some die slowly as they reluctantly yield to diseases like cancer. Some go in their sleep. Others die drugged beyond consciousness, while others go not so quietly, in the face of our greatest fear — the fear of death. Whatever the case, like it or not, we are all part of the ultimate statistic: ten out of ten die.

But when any human being takes his or her life, it's a double tragedy. Double because a life is not only lost but the loss brings unspeakable and endless pain to friends and loved ones who are left with grief and a sense of guilt that doesn't go away. Author Jeannette Walls said, "When people kill themselves, they think they're ending the pain, but all they're doing is passing it on to those they leave behind."[1]

The suicides that happen daily rarely make national news. But when a celebrity commits suicide, it's international news. It hits the headlines because, in one sense, it doesn't make sense. Riches, success, and fame don't add up to suicide. They don't even add up to depression. But depression is undoubtedly the fast lane on the highway that so often leads to the place of self-destruction. Here are just some of the celebrities who tragically took their own lives:

7

Anthony Bourdain, age 61. Anthony, chef and best known for his show "No Reservations," died from suicide on June 8, 2018.

Kate Spade, age 55. Kate Spade was an iconic fashion designer and mother who died by hanging in her Manhattan, New York, apartment on June 5, 2018.

Chester Bennington, age 41. Chester Bennington was the lead singer of Linkin Park and hanged himself July 20, 2017.

Chris Cornell, age 52. Chris Cornell was the lead singer of Soundgarden who died by hanging in 2017.

Aaron Hernandez, age 27. Former NFL star who died by hanging in his jail cell in 2017.[2]

In August of 2014, ABC News asked, "What's the Deal with Comedians and Depression?"

Robin Williams' apparent suicide has put a spotlight on the dark side of comedy. Williams, like many comedians, lived with long-term depression and addiction. Experts say these mental illnesses are no laughing matter.

He is certainly not the only comedian who has ever lived with depression and addiction. Comedian Marc Maron has spoken publicly about having severe depression. So has stand-up comedian Jim Norton. John Belushi, Chris Farley and Greg Giraldo all died of drug overdoses. And in 2007, Richard Jeni committed suicide by shooting himself in the face.[3]

How could any successful famous person who is rolling in money and surrounded by adoring fans be depressed? Happiness comes from what happens to us and if good things are happening, we should be happy. So why the depression? That is understandably the question that the fans, experts, and the celebrities ask themselves. Why?

And so, mystified doctors call it "clinical" depression. It must be an abnormality that can be treated by drugs to bring normality. It's not rational, so it must be a mental disorder — something that is happening in the brain that has yet to be understood.

Doctors and other experts not only don't understand it, they don't know what causes it:

"It's not known exactly what causes depression."[4]

"It is the leading cause of disability worldwide."[5]

"What Causes Major Depressive Disorder? The exact cause of MDD isn't known."[6]

What are the possible causes of clinical depression? The fact is, despite decades of research into this question, scientists at the U.S. National Institute of Mental Health and research universities around the world still don't really know the cause of depression.[7]

The U.S. Centers for Disease Control and Prevention (CDC) says that one in every ten American adults admit to fighting depression. According to the National Institute of Mental Health (NIMH), 6.7 percent of American adults have MDD, or major depressive disorder, during an average year. It effects as many as 23 million Americans every year, and is called a "most common serious brain disease in the United States." The World Health Organization estimates that approximately 350 million people have depression throughout the world.[8]

Australia is one of the best places to live on this fair earth. They have amazing animals, beautiful beaches, an excellent climate, and friendly people. Yet there is an epidemic of depression that is skyrocketing the suicide rate:

Suicide is the most common cause of death in Australians aged 15–44 years. Australian young people are more likely to take their own life than die from motor vehicle accidents or skin cancer. Every year 400,000 Australians experience suicidal thoughts, 65,000 make suicide attempts,

35,000 are admitted to hospital for suicide-related injuries and 2,500 die.[9]

The United States has the same dilemma:

> Every forty seconds, someone commits suicide. In the United States, it is the tenth most common cause of death in people over ten years of age, far more common than death by homicide or aneurysm or AIDS. Nearly half a million Americans are taken to the hospital every year because of suicide attempts. One in five people with major depression will make such an attempt; there are approximately sixteen non-lethal attempts for every lethal one. The rate of suicide is going up, especially among middle-aged men.[10]

Time magazine said,

> Treating depression is a major challenge, since among the millions of people affected worldwide, only one in five tends to respond well to antidepressants. And for many people who are eventually helped by drugs, it can take months, even years of cycling through the various medications to find the one that works best. In the meantime, their depression persists, and sometimes worsens.[11]

Eighty out of every hundred who are suffering from clinical depression don't find help with drugs. Many even get worse, owing to side effects.

Why the Increase?

Back in 2013, *Newsweek* addressed the epidemic of suicide in America and could give no reason for the increase:

> This year, America is likely to reach a grim milestone: the 40,000th death by suicide, the highest annual total on record, and one reached years ahead of what would be expected by population growth alone.
> This development evades simple explanation. The shift in suicides began long before the recession, for example,

and although the changes accelerated after 2007, when the unemployment rate began to rise, no more than a quarter of those new suicides have been tied to joblessness, according to researchers. Guns aren't all to blame either, since the suicide rate has grown even as the portion of suicides by firearm has remained stable.

Last fall [2012] the World Health Organization estimated that "global rates" of suicide are up 60 percent since World War II. And none of this includes the pestilence of suicidal behavior, the thoughts and plans that slowly eat away at people, the corrosive social cost of 25 attempts for every one official death.[12]

Experts keep insisting that depression is a mental disorder. I disagree and give reasons in this book for why I believe this. I speak in depth about how calling people who are depressed "insane" can only add to their depression, and it may drive them further to suicide. You and I may be able to handle it, but it's not so easy for the famous. After Kate Spade took her life, her sister said,

> I'd come so VERY close to getting her to go in for treatment. . . . We'd get sooo close to packing her bags, but — in the end, the "image" of her brand (happy-go-lucky Kate Spade) was more important for her to keep up. She was definitely worried about what people would say if they found out.[13]

I think it's a huge mistake, but it's all this world has in the face of this Goliath. Plus, the experts are calling for more to be spent on drugs. I don't think that's the answer:

> Drugs, alcohol and suicide could lead to the deaths of more than 1.6 million people over the next 10 years, according to a report released Tuesday that signals a troubling trend in mental health in the U.S.[14]

After a number of celebrity suicides in 2018, Bloomberg.com headlined:

Amid Drastic Rise in Suicide, CDC Says It's Not Just About Mental Health

The nationwide rate increased nearly 30 percent from 1999 to 2016.

There were 44,965 suicide deaths in 2016, according to CDC data. Approximately half of such deaths involve the use of a firearm. While mental health is often a factor, the CDC cautioned that there is no single reason for the nearly 30 percent nationwide increase between 1999 and 2016, pointing to the finding that approximately half of those who died by suicide did not have a known mental health condition.

Suicide prevention largely focuses on addressing mental health treatment, the CDC found, suggesting that a wider variety of preventive measures could be taken. The findings point to the need both to address the circumstances associated with the onset of mental health conditions—such as relationship, financial or criminal problems—and to support those with known mental conditions to decrease the risk of suicide, the CDC said.[15]

There really is such confusion when it comes to this subject. Experts don't know what causes depression. Thankfully, I'm not an expert. The emperor has no clothes. I know the cause. . . .

questions?

1. How many people die every minute, every hour, every year?
2. Why is it a quandary when someone who is rich and famous commits suicide?
3. Name some famous people who took their lives. Share the thoughts you had when you heard of their death.
4. According to *Time* magazine, how many people respond well to antidepressants?
5. Why is it not a good idea to call people who are depressed "insane"?

Endnotes

1. https://www.goodreads.com/quotes/312852-when-people-kill-themselves-they-think-they-re-ending-the-pain.

2. https://thetreatmentspecialist.com/celebrities-who-committed-suicide/.

3. http://abcnews.go.com/Health/deal-comedians-depression/story?id=24945911.

4. https://www.mayoclinic.org/diseases-conditions/depression/symptoms-causes/syc-20356007

5. https://www.psychguides.com/guides/depression-hotline/.

6. http://www.healthline.com/health/clinical-depression.

7. http://psychcentral.com/disorders/depression/depression-causes/.

8. https://adaa.org/about-adaa/press-room/facts-statistics; http://www.who.int/news-room/fact-sheets/detail/depression.

9. https://www.facebook.com/blackdoginst/photos/a.147955009578.143307.1215 87069578/10152745434384579/?type=1&theater.

10. https://www.newyorker.com/culture/cultural-comment/suicide-crime-loneliness.

11. http://time.com/4338947/magic-mushrooms-for-depression/.

12. http://www.newsweek.com/2013/05/22/why-suicide-has-become-epidemic-and-what-we-can-do-help-237434.html.

13. https://people.com/style/kate-spades-family-disgusted-after-designers-sister-claims-suicide-not-unexpected-suffered-mental-illnes/.

14. https://www.usatoday.com/story/news/2017/11/21/deaths-drugs-alcohol-and-suicide-could-hit-1-6-m-over-next-decade-report-says/880887001/.

15. https://www.bloomberg.com/news/articles/2018-06-07/amid-drastic-rise-in-suicide-cdc-says-it-s-not-just-about-mental-health.

Chapter 2

The Depressing Cause

There's good reason not to believe that it is a mental disorder or a brain disease. There is a much more rational explanation and a simpler cure, and it's sitting right under the nose of every human face.

The chronic depression that leads to thoughts of suicide has two major causes. First, it's caused by the hopeless futility of which the wisdom of Solomon spoke 3,000 years ago. And secondly, it's fueled by a *rational* fear, a terrible dread, one spoken of in the Book of Hebrews in the New Testament. There is a persistently depressing fear that haunts *every* human heart, from our early youth through to the day we die:

> Inasmuch then as the children have partaken of flesh and blood, He Himself likewise shared in the same, that through death He might destroy him who had the power of death, that is, the devil, and release those *who through fear of death were all their lifetime subject to bondage* (Hebrews 2:14–15, italics added).

In other words, every human being has an unshakable dread of death, and because of it they are a prisoner — a slave to fear all their lifetime.

There are scores of celebrities who have publicly said they fight serious depression that is so chronic it leads to suicidal thoughts. And because none of the experts know why they have this battle, they are diagnosed as having a chemical imbalance . . . a sort of mental disease. They are therefore treated with chemicals that have horrible side effects, some of which can be depression and suicidal thoughts.

Therefore, I Am

There are, however, many people who don't get depressed. To them, life is just a cycle that's to be pedaled to the destination of death. It happens to all of us. It's nature's way. So be a man, be a woman, accept it and enjoy life's blessings while you can.

But for others, that's a thoughtless copout.

Cogito ergo sum is a well-known Latin philosophical proposition by René Descartes that is translated into English as "I think, therefore I am." I would add one word to his thought:

"I think; therefore, I am *depressed.*"

Creative people *think*, and those who think, think not only about the mysteries of life but they think about the final curtain. They are not happy to just roll over and die. Something in them cries, "Oh, *I don't want to die!*" That's not a weakness. It's a strength. It's not mental illness. It's sanity to want to preserve your most precious possession.

There is an elephant in the room, and it's moving toward you with the intent of taking you out. If you believe that you have to wait for it to kill you, and there's nothing you can do about it, that's a justified depression. The dread of impending doom will steal every ounce of your joy of living, and when the enjoyment has gone, you will contemplate a way to escape the pain and futility.

Think about the successful celebrity who thinks about the elephant. He is rich, famous, happy, and has everything his heart could want. But he is still "through the fear of death . . . [is all of his] lifetime subject to bondage." More money and more fame doesn't make it go away. What once lifted his spirits no longer works because of the elephant. It overshadows everything.

Daily news is depressing. It majors on death. If it bleeds it leads: cancer and who has it, who has been killed in car accidents, terrorism, kids who have cancer, war, plane crashes, fires, murders, tornados, suicides, and of course, highly publicized celebrity deaths.

Life Can Be Depressing

He was born September 25, 1952, in New York City, to a journalist and writer/professor. He came from an upper-class family. His paternal grandfather was CEO of Prudential Financial, and one of his maternal great-grandfathers was a Supreme Court justice.

When he was four, his parents divorced. His mother moved him and his brother to Princeton, New Jersey, and married an investment banker a few years later. After graduating from high school, he studied at Cornell University while at the same time working as a professional actor. In his final year at Cornell (1973) he was one of two students selected (Robin Williams was the other) to study at New York's famous Juilliard School, under the renowned John Houseman. I'm talking of course about Christopher Reeve.

Williams was also the first student that Reeve met at university and he recalls watching Williams "in awe as he virtually caromed off the walls of the classrooms and hallways." Their strong bond lasted way beyond college as their respective careers took off in the late 1970s, with Williams enjoying massive television success in *Mork and Mindy* and Reeve starring in the 1978 blockbuster *Superman*.[1]

> *Newsweek* said of his performance, "Christopher Reeve's entire performance is a delight. Ridiculously good-looking, with a face as sharp and strong as an ax blade, his bumbling, fumbling Clark Kent and omnipotent Superman are simply two styles of gallantry and innocence."[2]

His life was picture-perfect. He was tall, dark, handsome, intelligent, and extremely successful. But one terribly tragic day his wonderful life turned into a hellish nightmare. On May 27, 1995, he became a quadriplegic after being thrown from a horse during an equestrian competition in Culpeper, Virginia. He was confined to a wheelchair and required a portable ventilator for the rest of his life. He couldn't move or even breathe without help. One can't begin to imagine his emotions, or the grief of those who loved him.

He then became a courageous spokesperson for those in a similar plight, and as he did so his loving and faithful wife stood by his side.

In early October 2004, he was being treated for an infected pressure ulcer that was causing sepsis, a complication that he had experienced many times before. On October 10, 2004, Reeve died at the age of 52 from what was believed to be an adverse reaction to the antibiotic that caused his death. Then his sweet, wonderfully faithful and heartbroken wife, Dana Reeve, was diagnosed with lung cancer and died at age 44 in 2006.

Life stinks. But if you think that they were dealt an isolated bad hand, listen to today's news and hear of tragedy after depressing tragedy. For those who have the ability to exercise even the slightest empathy, life is depressing, even when we are able to forget our own unavoidable and miserable demise.

The thinking celebrity thinks about how time will rob him of his looks. Except for expensive transplants he will soon be a wrinkled and bald has-been. Growing old is depressing. But what's the alternative? *Death.* He thinks about the fact that time will also take what pleasure he has left — the pleasures of sex, taste buds, energy, hearing, sight, and it will rip precious loved ones from his grasping hands. Time will come with frightening diseases and the promise of pain. What began as a wonderfully sweet life has slowly turned very bitter. And so the things he achieves in this life are relegated to a place of less importance. Woody Allen understandably said, "I don't want to achieve immortality through my work. I want to achieve it through not dying."[3]

The thinking celebrity decides to try and stay healthy. But he's aware that if he eats right and is able to stay fit and healthy, he is just waiting for a fit and healthy death. *It's unavoidable.* How true are the words of W.H. Auden, "Death is the sound of distant thunder at a picnic."[4] It's the ultimate party-pooper.

Yet yielding to the inevitability of death is against our every instinct. Ecclesiastes 3:11 says that God "*has put eternity in their hearts. . . .*" Everything within us says in the face of death, "Noooo!!! This is not how it should be! Death *cannot* be the end." We know in our hearts that we were made for more. Craig D. Lounsbrough surmised, "If life is nothing more than a journey to death, autumn makes sense but spring does not."[5] And so those who think, find themselves between an immovable rock and a very hard place.

Celebrated Wisdom

These were the thoughts of one enduring celebrity who achieved worldwide fame and fortune in his day, well before the advent of the Internet, television, or film.

Celebrities come and go. Once household names, Cary Grant and John Wayne are largely unknown to today's generation, and even their own contemporary celebrities will become nobodies to coming generations. But this one celebrity not only gained fame is his day, his fame has lasted 3,000 years. He was rich and famous, and his wise words were recorded in a special best-selling book that is read each day daily by millions.

King Solomon spoke about depression and those who thought about life. In chapter 1 verse 18 of his biblical book called Ecclesiastes he put it this way:

> For in much wisdom is much grief, and he who increases knowledge increases sorrow.

So if you think about the reality of life and death and it causes you to be deeply depressed, according to the wisdom of Solomon, you don't have a mental disorder. Your very thoughts and conclusions show that you have "much wisdom."

In speaking of the universality of death, he said,

> All things come alike to all: One event happens to the righteous and the wicked; to the good, the clean, and the unclean; to him who sacrifices and him who does not sacrifice. As is the good, so is the sinner; he who takes an oath as he who fears an oath. This is an evil in all that is done under the sun: that one thing happens to all. Truly the hearts of the sons of men are full of evil; madness is in their hearts while they live, and after that they go to the dead (Ecclesiastes 9:2–3).

Another Solomon

In an interview with *Scientific America*, another Solomon, Sheldon Solomon (professor of psychology at Skidmore College) gives more good reason to be depressed. He said,

Terror management theory (TMT) is derived from cultural anthropologist Ernest Becker's efforts to explain the motivational underpinnings of human behavior. According to TMT, one defining characteristic of human beings is self-awareness: we're alive and we know it. Although self-awareness gives rise to unbridled awe and joy, it can also lead to the potentially overwhelming dread engendered by the realization that death is inevitable, that it can occur for reasons that can never be anticipated or controlled, and that humans are corporeal creatures—breathing pieces of defecating meat no more significant or enduring than porcupines or peaches. Solomon has spent the last few decades studying how thoughts of death can powerfully influence our decisions and judgments.[6]

If you fly regularly and you don't suffer from depression, this may get you started. Statistics tell us that one in eight airline pilots may be clinically depressed:

> Hundreds of commercial airline pilots worldwide may be flying with untreated depression because they fear being grounded or losing their jobs, a new survey suggests. The anonymous survey of about 1,850 pilots from more than 50 countries found that 14 percent of pilots who had worked within the past week had symptoms of depression. Four percent of pilots reported having suicidal thoughts within the past two weeks. The survey offers one of the first snapshots of mental health among commercial pilots, who often don't disclose this type of illness to airline officials or aviation regulators because they fear negative career repercussions, said senior study author Joseph Allen, a public health researcher at Harvard University in Boston.[7]

So 1 in every 25 pilots is tempted to end it all. The figure is probably much higher, because (as is alluded to) those who get depressed while flying aren't going to readily admit it. It's not good for business. It's like a chef admitting that he is often tempted to put poison in patrons' dinners. Who is going to frequent *that* restaurant?

My point is that it's not just celebrities who get depressed, others also think and get suicidal thoughts. Poor and rich people are haunted by the fear of death. It's universal. They are, through fear of death, *all their lifetime* subject to bondage.

Kathy Cronkite, the author of *On the Edge of Darkness: Conversations About Conquering Depression*, said,

> If you have heard John Graden speak, you will know that he firmly believes that depression is a real life long cradle to grave illness.[8]

Anthony Hopkin, whose thoughts led him to the dead end of chronic depression, concluded, "We are dying from overthinking. We are slowly killing ourselves by thinking about everything. Think. Think. Think. You can never trust the human mind anyway. It's a death trap."[9]

Suicide Isn't Painless

Now and then someone addresses the fact that the fear of death is the problem, saying that it is better to take your life and be free of the dread than to have to live with its torment.

In his book, *The Art of Dying*, Robert E. Neale said,

> Chronic anxiety is a state more undesirable than any other, and we will try almost any maneuver to eliminate it. Modern man is living in anxious anticipation of destruction. Such anxiety can be easily eliminated by self-destruction. As a German saying puts it: "Better an end with terror than a terror without end."[10]

I have asked hundreds of people if they are afraid of death, and have found that it's a telling litmus test. The humble will be quick to say that death scares them, but the proud won't because they seek approval, not pity. That's why so few let the deadly cat out of the bag.

My hope is that you're not proud, and that you will allow me to reason with you about this sobering and depressing issue. This is because I want to eliminate suicide as an answer to the question of depression — *To be or not to be*. That is the question. And there is an answer . . . a better way to deal with that haunting fear.

The response to the depressing depression dilemma is not to become a Christian "because Jesus will fix everything and make you truly happy." That popular message just isn't true. Plenty of non-Christians are already happy. That was my dilemma before I came to Christ. I was extremely happy, but I could see that the sharp pin of reality would one day burst my happiness bubble. I sat helpless in the gloomy shadow of impending death. And most come to that sad, hopeless conclusion.

A month before she died, Carrie Fisher said, "I'm not going to enjoy dying, but there's not much prep for that."[11] With due respect to the late Carrie Fisher, there *is* prep for death if you look in the right place.

As a Christian, I would be lying if I said I wasn't fearful of dying. But the fear I have is *controllable*, because of the gift of faith that comes with the new birth of which Jesus spoke in John chapter 3.

Imagine I'm on a plane 10,000 feet in the air. I'm wearing a parachute and I'm about to jump. I've never jumped out of a plane and I'm sure if I had to, I would be fearful. *But I would be able to control that fear by having faith in the parachute.* The more trust I have in it, the less fear there will be. Again, the more confidence, the less fear. I am in control of my fear. I have an antidote because of my ability to trust.

When I pass through death, it will be my first time. I'm not sure what to expect, and that's a little scary. But I have an implicit trust in the risen Savior, and so I will be able to control my fear by my faith, and for the skeptic, this is *not* mind over matter.

The Bible speaks of having a strong confidence in God, and the more confidence or trust I have in Him, the less fear I will have thinking about dying now *and* when death comes. By God's grace, I will be in control of it rather than the fear being in control of me. I can say with the Psalmist, "The Lord is on my side; I *will not* fear" (Psalm 118:6, italics added).

And so I am able to live without the universal dread. The black cloud of the fear of death left the moment I put my faith entirely in Jesus for my salvation. If it seeks to enshroud me, I have my faith in Jesus to dismiss its ghastly influence.

But the person who lives (and dies) without faith in the Savior is like someone who has to jump 10,000 feet out of a plane with no parachute. Put yourself in that person's dilemma for a moment. *Imagine* it. There is no faith, and so there is nothing to control the terror. It will be completely out of control when he faces death. That's why the Bible calls death "the king of terrors" (Job 18:14).

The fear of death torments the ungodly every moment of their faithless existence. And so those who lack faith in the Savior are susceptible to a tormenting fear that leads to chronic depression that, for many, leads to suicide. Between 2–7% of adults with major depression die by suicide,[12] and up to 60% of people who die by suicide had depression or another mood disorder.[13]

Rich, Proud, and Famous

Most of us are proud. We don't want to be seen as being weak and vulnerable. We dress and act for the approval of our peers. Actors are often first to admit that they are driven by their ego. They crave the applause, and so it's difficult for them to publicly admit that they are afraid to die. Depression, yes. That invokes a measure of sympathy. Fear of death, no. That speaks of weakness, and they don't want the scorn of the world or to jeopardize their career by being labeled as mentally ill.

So, as we look at these celebrities, you will have to search for clues as to the cause of their depression. Most hide it. They are not forthcoming about the irrational dread with which they live. Not many of them will say, "I am *terrified* of dying, I always have been, and it is driving me to a depression I can't shake. I've been having suicidal thoughts, and I can't see a glimmer of hope anywhere."

I want to offer you more than a *glimmer* of hope. I want to point you to *sunshine* . . . and for you to let its brilliance shine where there is no hope. To do this, I will give you documented experiences of celebrities to strengthen my case for fear being the cause of their depression. And if you will allow me to, I will present the gospel — God's offer of eternal life in place of death. While this subject is fascinating, it can be a little dark, and so I have therefore put a little light at the end of each chapter — a positive biblical promise of deliverance from fear.

questions?

1. Read Hebrews 2:14–15. Can you personally testify to the truth of those verses, and did it have any influence in your search for God?
2. Give some justifiable reasons (other than the fear of death) that so many are depressed.
3. Explain W.H. Auden's, "Death is the sound of distant thunder at a picnic."
4. Explain why depression shouldn't be called a mental disease.
5. Explain how faith is the antidote to fear.

Endnotes

1. http://www.dailymail.co.uk/news/article-2722888/Closer-brothers-Robin-Williams-extraordinary-friendship-Christopher-Reeve-penniless-roommates-Hollywood-highs-helping-save-friends-life.html#ixzz4XQE7peXn.

2. http://www.boomsbeat.com/articles/106037/20160122/50-interesting-facts-christopher-reeve—fan-favorite-superman.htm.

3. https://www.brainyquote.com/quotes/quotes/w/woodyallen161239.html?src=t_death.

4. https://www.brainyquote.com/quotes/w_h_auden_146088.

5. https://www.goodreads.com/quotes/tag/autumn?page=8.

6. https://www.scientificamerican.com/article/fear-death-and-politics/.

7. http://www.foxnews.com/health/2016/12/15/1-in-8-airline-pilots-may-be-clinically-depressed.html.

8. https://youtu.be/mLHtQ9UyPUU.

9. https://www.brainyquote.com/quotes/quotes/a/anthonyhop359457.html?src=t_death.

10. https://www.goodreads.com/work/quotes/3413732-the-art-of-dying.

11. http://www.justjared.com/2016/12/27/carrie-fisher-spoke-about-dying-a-month-before-her-death/.

12. C.S. Richards and M.W. O'Hara, *The Oxford Handbook of Depression and Comorbidity* (Oxford, UK: Oxford University Press, 2014), p. 254.

13. V.A. Lynch and J.B. Duval, *Forensic Nursing Science* (Elsevier Health Sciences, 2010), p. 453.

Chapter 3

Carrie Fisher

"A human being can survive almost anything, as long as she sees the end in sight. But depression is so insidious, and it compounds daily, that it's impossible to ever see the end." — Elizabeth Wurtzel[1]

Carrie Frances Fisher (October 21, 1956–December 27, 2016) was an American actress, a writer and producer, and a humorist. In an ABC interview, Fisher spoke about living with depression:

"The world of manic depression is a world of bad judgment calls," says Fisher. "Just every kind of bad judgment because it all seems like a good idea at the time. A great idea. . . . So if it's talking, if it's shopping. You can't stop. It's very painful. It's raw. You know, it's rough . . . your bones burn . . . when you're not busy talking and trying to drown it out."[2]

In 2013, *The Daily Mail* published an article entitled, "Carrie Fisher opens up about her manic bi-polar episode which led to a bizarre cruise ship performance." The article said,

Carrie says that warning signs came early in the trip when she started scribbling on everything in sight. "I wasn't sleeping. I was writing on everything. I was writing in books; I would have written on walls. I literally would bend over and be writing on the ground and (my assistant) would try to talk to me, and I would be unable to respond," she recalls. She says that at the time of her manic episode she was on an anti psychotic medication called Seroquel, but it was clearly malfunctioning.[3]

Seroquel is FDA approved and has been prescribed to millions in the United States to treat the depressive lows and manic highs of bipolar disorder and as add-on treatment to antidepressants for major depressive disorder. But here are some of the possible side effects of the drug:

> Side effects of Seroquel may include mood or behavior changes, constipation, stomach pain, upset stomach, nausea, vomiting, drowsiness, dizziness, tiredness, headache, trouble sleeping, dry mouth, sore throat, breast swelling or discharge, missed menstrual periods, increased appetite, or weight gain. Older adults with dementia may have a slightly increased risk of death when taking Seroquel. Call your doctor at once if you have any new or worsening symptoms such as: mood or behavior changes, anxiety, panic attacks, trouble sleeping, or if you feel impulsive, irritable, agitated, hostile, aggressive, restless, hyperactive (mentally or physically), *more depressed, or have thoughts about suicide or hurting yourself* (italics added).[4]

WebMD asked Fisher:

> *"Without the leveling effect of medication: are you more manic or depressive?"*
> Fisher: "Mostly mania. When I got older, depression became more of an issue. Mania is not that unpleasant, but . . . it's a spin of the dial, you don't know what you're going to get. It turned into what they call agitated depression. I would get really impatient. I was going much faster than everything else around me, and it drove me crazy. You feel out of step with the world."
> *"Is there still a stigma attached to mental illness and to seeking help for it? Have we as a society made strides in this arena?"*
> Fisher: "Of course there's still stigma, especially when it comes to shock treatment [which Fisher experienced and

openly discusses in her memoir]. But it's getting better. I think there's more understanding now than there was, depending on what part of the country you're in, or what part of the world."[5]

In another interview, the 60-year-old actress was asked if she was (at that age) happier with life. She responded,

"Yep. Well, I'm not happy about being older, except what are the options? But I've learned a lot. I trust myself. I trust my instincts. I know what I'm gonna do, what I can do, what I can't do. I've been through a lot, and I could go through more, but I hope I don't have to. But if I did, I'd be able to do it. I'm not going to enjoy dying, but there's not much prep for that."[6]

Just a month before her death, Fisher was asked if she feared death. "No. I fear dying," she said. "Anything with pain associated with it, I don't like. I've been there for a couple of people when they were dying; it didn't look like fun. But if I was gonna do it, I'd want someone like me around. And I will be there!"[7]

Years ago I wrote a book called, *What Hollywood Believes*. While researching for it I came across Carrie's quote about her being open to evidence that God existed. I longed to get an opportunity to speak with her, and although that opportunity never presented itself, I will afford it posthumously, in the next chapter.

A Conversation with Carrie Fisher

I don't think you had mental disease. I think you were a normal, witty, intelligent human being and that you thought deeply about life.

You once said, "I love the idea of God, but it's not stylistically in keeping with the way I function. I would describe myself as an enthusiastic agnostic who would be happy to be shown that there is a God. I can see that people who believe in God are happier. My brother is. My dad is, too. But I doubt."[8]

I have never for a moment doubted that someone built my house. Nor do I doubt that *any* painting had a painter. The building is *proof* of a builder; the painting is *proof* of the painter, and creation is proof of the Creator. It is scientifically impossible for nature to have made itself. If it did create itself, it would have had to have been pre-existent *to* create itself *before* it created itself, which is intellectually ludicrous.

It is also outside of the realm of possibility for nature to be eternal — because of the second law of thermodynamics. That says that everything is subject to corruption. It runs down. In 100 million years everything we can see will have turned to dust. If the universe was eternally preexistent, it would have turned to dust 500 trillion plus years ago. Therefore, the universe must have had a beginning, and that prime-mover can't have been itself. It had to be created by something outside of itself — a Designer.

Everywhere we look, from the atom to the universe, we see design, and in the design we see the genius of the Designer. Can anyone really look at the miracle of childbirth and conclude that life is an accident? So we need doubt no longer. We can *know* God exists:

> For since the creation of the world His invisible attributes are clearly seen, being understood by the things that are made, even His eternal power and Godhead, so that they are without excuse . . . (Romans 1:20).

The Power of Faith

Let's say that you are an old friend with whom I have lost contact, and you are in *big* financial trouble. You invested all of your savings in what you were told was a sure scheme, and it fell through. Then you lost your job.

This devastated your spouse, and to your dismay the bank is foreclosing on your home at noon today. You are sick to your stomach with fear that your precious family is going to be living on the streets. Pleading with the bank and seeking help elsewhere fell on deaf ears. Every avenue of hope turned out to be a dead-end street.

A mutual friend informs me of your predicament. I then make contact and assure you that I will meet you just before noon outside of the bank. *I will have in my hand a check for $100,000.* It is a small part of inheritance that my very wealthy father left me. I tell you that it's my joy to gift it to you.

If you trust me, your nightmare is over. You need no longer fear in the slightest, *even though you don't have the money in hand.* You can not only be immediately free from fear, but you can have joy *right now,* even though you don't have the money. That's the power of *trust* or what we sometimes call "faith."

Look closely at the words of Scripture and see faith in action:

> The LORD is my strength and my shield; my heart trusted in Him, and I am helped; therefore, my heart greatly rejoices, and with my song I will praise Him (Psalm 28:7).

Notice the words "My heart trusted in Him, and I *am* helped." It doesn't say I *will be* helped. Faith has the ability to deliver *now.* It is a *present* help in time of need. The moment it's exercised it provides strength and joy.

Think now what would have happened if you hadn't had faith in my word. Instead of trusting me, you said, "How do I know you will keep your word? *I don't trust you.*" The result would be that you are stuck with your fears. No faith, no joy. Not only that, but in your lack of faith you have accused me of lying. You insulted me by not counting me worthy of your trust.

How much more then is lack of faith in God insulting to Him? The Bible warns, "He who does not believe God has made Him a liar" (1 John 5:10). We see this happen with the promised birth of John the Baptist. An angel appeared to his elderly father:

> But the angel said to him, "Do not be afraid, Zacharias, for your prayer is heard; and your wife Elizabeth will bear you a son, and you shall call his name John. And you will have joy and gladness, and many will rejoice at his birth. . . . And Zacharias said to the angel, "How shall I know this? For I am an old man, and my wife is well advanced in years."
>
> And the angel answered and said to him, "I am Gabriel, who stands in the presence of God, and was sent to speak to you and bring you these glad tidings. But behold, you will be mute and not able to speak until the day these things

take place, because you did not believe my words which will be fulfilled in their own time" (Luke 1:13–20).

Zacharias was struck dumb because he insulted Him by his lack of trust.

So there are two good reasons to trust God. The first is that any healthy relationships are established on trust. And the second is that you want to be rid of your fear of death.

The Bible proudly parades those who did great things through trusting God. We are told:

> But without faith it is impossible to please Him, for he who comes to God must believe that He is, and that He is a rewarder of those who diligently seek Him (Hebrews 11:6).

You said, "I would describe myself as an enthusiastic agnostic who would be happy to be shown that there is a God . . . but I doubt." If we want to please God, we must approach Him with trust, not doubt, as we would any person with whom we want to establish a lasting friendship.

Bible Promise

> But the very hairs of your head are all numbered. Do not fear therefore; you are of more value than many sparrows (Luke 12:7).

questions?

1. Elizabeth Wurtzel said, "A human being can survive almost anything, as long as she sees the end in sight. But depression is so insidious, and it compounds daily, that it's impossible to ever see the end." Explain how faith in Jesus solves that problem.
2. Carrie Fisher was an agnostic. She said, "I'm not going to enjoy dying, but there's not much prep for that." What prep can we do?
3. How would you give someone evidence that God exists?
4. How would you prove that creation can't be eternal?
5. Explain how faith in God is a "present" help in time of need.

Endnotes

1. https://www.brainyquote.com/quotes/elizabeth_wurtzel_334889.

2. http://abcnews.go.com/Primetime/story?id=132315&page=1.

3. http://www.dailymail.co.uk/tvshowbiz/article-2292927/Carrie-Fisher-opens-manic-bi-polar-episode-lead-bizarre-cruise-ship-performance.html.

4. http://www.rxlist.com/seroquel-side-effects-drug-center.htm.

5. http://www.webmd.com/mental-health/addiction/features/questions-for-carrie-fisher?page=2.

6. http://www.justjared.com/2016/12/27/carrie-fisher-spoke-about-dying-a-month-before-her-death/.

7. http://www.rollingstone.com/movies/news/carrie-fisher-princess-leia-in-star-wars-dead-at-60-w457713.

8. http://www.christiantoday.com/article/carrie.fisher.and.god.the.star.wars.actress.loved.the.idea.but.never.followed.her.born.again.brother/103393.htm.

Chapter 4

George Michael

"If you know someone who's depressed, please resolve never to ask them why. Depression isn't a straightforward response to a bad situation; depression just is, like the weather. Try to understand the blackness, lethargy, hopelessness, and loneliness they're going through." — Stephen Fry[1]

George Michael (born June 25, 1963 – died December 25, 2016) was an English singer and songwriter who rose to fame as a member of the music duo *Wham!* His solo album, *Faith*, sold more than 20 million copies worldwide.

Michael began his battle with chronic depression when his homosexual partner died in 1993, and then his beloved mother died in 1997. Both deaths left him shattered. He said that he suffered from two afflictions: "grief and self-abuse."

"I lost my partner to HIV then it took about three years to grieve; then after that I lost my mother," he said. "I felt almost like I was cursed."

"So that's 12 years of depression and fear, and lots of other. . . . I swear to God it was like I had a curse on me. I couldn't believe how much God was piling on at once. There was so much death around me, I can't tell you."[2]

"Michael battled depression for most of his life, after losing his first love, designer Anselmo Feleppa, to AIDS in 1993 and his beloved mother four years later. He said, "I struggled with huge depression after my mother died. . . . Losing your mother and your lover in the space of three years is a tough one."[3]

In January of 2017, the *Daily Mail* said,

George Michael is said to have been "living in fear" of history repeating itself after previous suicides in his family. . . .

His maternal grandfather George James Harrison is, according to Michael, also believed to have killed himself in 1960 aged 66. . . .

As previously reported by MailOnline, Michael was "haunted" by his uncle's suicide and feared he might inherit his schizophrenia. . . .

. . . he became so "fixated" over the death of his relative, he even wrote a song about him, called "My Mother Had a Brother."[4]

Michael told the *LA Times in* 1990: "I'm also sure that most people find it hard to believe that stardom can make you miserable. After all, everybody wants to be a star. I certainly did, and I worked hard to get it. But I was miserable, and I don't want to feel that way again."

Michael's comments about stardom making him miserable upset one of the world's most famous singers, Frank Sinatra. Here's what Sinatra wrote (while he was in his mid-70s):

Dear Friends, When I saw your Calendar cover today about George Michael, "the reluctant pop star," my first reaction was he should thank the good Lord every morning when he wakes up to have all that he has. And that'll make two of us thanking God every morning for all that we have.[5]

A Conversation with George Michael

I want to talk about your song about faith, in which you said "'Cause I gotta have faith. I gotta have faith. 'Cause I gotta have faith, faith. 'Cause I gotta have faith, faith, faith."

You are right. You and I have to have faith. Without it we couldn't function. We have to have faith in the pilots, planes, banks, elevators, taxi drivers, doctors, surgeons, and a multitude of other things, from history books to restaurants that prepare our food, and sodas prepared by companies for us to guzzle down without a second thought. We build our human relationships on faith. If you don't trust someone, you have no basis for a relationship. Faith isn't weak, as some would suggest: it is a building block of life.

When I speak of faith in God, I don't mean a faith that He exists. Creation is proof of the Creator. That is intuitive and axiomatic. I mean that faith in God is an implicit trust — the type of trust we may have in a close friend. Yet that friend is fallible. He or she may not be able to keep their word because of some mitigating circumstance. But with God, nothing is impossible. Nothing can stop Him from keeping His Word to us. He is trustworthy. That means we need never doubt His Word.

Doubt Power

Let me now tell you about the power of doubt. If you were on the 80th story of the Empire State building in New York, and you stepped into an elevator doubting that the cables will hold, you would be terrified. Your doubt would rightly produce fear. If, however, I showed you that the elevator was held up by 20 two-inch-thick unbreakable steel cables, as well as having a fail-safe, recently checked automatic emergency braking system, that knowledge would rid you of doubt, explode your faith, and completely eradicate fear. Again, faith is not weak.

Here's my point: Complete faith in God's unbreakable promises can eradicate our fear of death.

You obviously believed in God, but at the same time you had deep-rooted and tormenting fear. Something was hindering your faith, so I'm going to ask you some questions about God and what you believe.

Does He believe in right and wrong? What does He think when a man rapes a teenage girl and then slits her throat and burns her body? Does the God in which you believe have a sense of justice? Or should He let murderers and rapists off the hook? Should He overlook Hitler's slaughter of millions of Jews in World War II? What sort of God do you believe in? I'm asking these questions because it is inherent in human nature to create a god in our own image, one with whom we feel comfortable.

Frank Sinatra was right in calling God "the *good* Lord," and because He is good He must believe in justice. What sort of judge would look the other way and let guilty criminals go? He would be a corrupt judge and should be brought to justice himself. A good judge must do all he can to see that justice is done.

To obtain the sort of faith that delivers us from the fear of death, we have to back up and look at the biblical revelation of the character and nature of the One who gave us life.

The God of the Bible is nothing like the image we have of Him. He certainly is good, and He therefore passionately cares about justice. He has appointed a day in which He will judge the world in righteousness. On that day, perfect justice will be satisfied. Hell is simply God's prison for those who break His law; and all of us have broken it. We are all under the death sentence because we have all violated the moral law. It says, "The soul who sins shall die" (Ezekiel 18:20). Jesus said that if we as much as look with lust, we commit adultery in our hearts (see Matthew 5:27–28) and break the Seventh Commandment. God's moral standards are infinitely higher than ours:

> Do you not know that the unrighteous will not inherit the kingdom of God? Do not be deceived. Neither fornicators, nor idolaters, nor adulterers, nor homosexuals, nor sodomites, nor thieves, nor covetous, nor drunkards, nor revilers, nor extortioners will inherit the kingdom of God (1 Corinthians 6:9–10).

That leaves all of us in big trouble. Fortunately, God is rich in mercy and has made a way for us to be forgiven. That way is through the Cross of Jesus Christ. We broke God's law, and Jesus paid the fine through His suffering on the Cross, and then He rose from the dead. If someone pays your fine in court, even though you are guilty, the judge can let you go. God can let us go — He can commute our death sentence because the fine was paid in full by Jesus. What you and I are commanded to do in response to that is repent and trust in the Savior. The fruit of the new birth will be deliverance from the fear of death.

Bible Promise

Peace I leave with you, My peace I give to you; not as the world gives do I give to you. Let not your heart be troubled, neither let it be afraid (John 14:27).

questions ?

1. Read Matthew 7:22–27. Do you think that George Michael built his house on rock or on sand? Why?
2. Name some everyday things in which we have faith.
3. How would you describe faith in God?
4. Give one reason we need never doubt God's Word.
5. What is inherent in human nature when it comes to our image of God?

Endnotes

1. https://www.telegraph.co.uk/men/thinking-man/stephen-frys-best-quotes/stephen-fry-quotes17/.

2. http://www.nzherald.co.nz/entertainment/news/article.cfm?c_id=1501119&objectid=11773506.

3. http://thenewdaily.com.au/entertainment/celebrity/2016/12/27/george-michael-drugs/.

4. http://www.dailymail.co.uk/news/article-4090230/George-Michael-s-family-haunted-suicides-uncle-grandfather-decades-star-dead-bed-lover.html.

5. http://www.nzherald.co.nz/entertainment/news/article.cfm?c_id=1501119&objectid=11773513.

Chapter 5

Robin Williams

"Whenever you read a cancer booklet . . . they always list depression among the side effects of cancer. But, in fact, depression is not a side effect of cancer. Depression is a side effect of dying." — John Green, *The Fault in Our Stars*[1]

Robin McLaurin Williams (July 21, 1951–August 11, 2014). Williams was an American comedian and actor.

On August 11, 2014, Williams committed suicide at his home in Paradise Cay, California, at the age of 63, after battling depression for many years. Shortly after his suicide, *Time* magazine published an article titled "Robin Williams' Depression Struggles May Go Back Decades."

According to the local sheriff's office, coroners believe Williams may have committed suicide by asphyxia, and the actor's representative said he had been "battling severe depression of late."

While the representative did not elaborate on the potential source of his recent depression, one-third of people with major depression also struggle with alcoholism, and Williams admitted to abusing both cocaine and alcohol during the height of his popularity in the 1970s as alien Mork on Mork & Mindy, which showcased his manic improvisational style.[2]

In an interview with the *Guardian*, Williams said that while he was working in Alaska in 2003, he felt "alone and afraid" and turned to alcohol believing it would help.

Time added,

> Studies suggest that alcoholism and depression may feed each other. People who are depressed are more vulnerable to abusing alcohol than those who don't experience depressive episodes, and those who drink heavily are also more likely to experience depression. The latest evidence also hints that the same genes may be responsible for both conditions, and depression is a strong risk factor for suicide. About 90% of people who take their own lives are diagnosed with depression or other mental disorders.[3]

In September of 2010, Williams spoke to the *Guardian* about his drinking problem:

> "I was in a small town where it's not the edge of the world, but you can see it from there, and then I thought: drinking. I just thought, hey, maybe drinking will help. Because I felt alone and afraid. It was that thing of working so much . . . maybe that will help. And it was the worst thing in the world." What did he feel like when he had his first drink? "You feel warm and kind of wonderful. And then the next thing you know, it's a problem, and you're isolated."

Then he became candid (but was unable to be specific) about the fear that continually tormented him:

> Some have suggested it was Reeve's death that turned him back to drink. "No," he says quietly, "it's more selfish than that. It's just literally being afraid. And you think, oh, this will ease the fear. And it doesn't." What was he afraid of? "Everything. It's just a general all-round arggghhh. It's fearfulness and anxiety."[4]

A Conversation with Robin Williams

As I read your words, I didn't have to try and imagine that feeling of being alone and afraid. I know what it means to be tormented by fear. I was in the middle of the North Island of New Zealand back in the early 1980s. I had spoken at a church in the morning and was the guest at a farmhouse, in a back bedroom, passing the time until the evening meeting. I will never forget what happened. As a small child I would have reoccurring nightmares where I felt as though my fingers were swelling. It sounds strange now to think that the dream terrified me, but it was so fearful I would end up regularly beside my parents' bed, with them dousing me with water to try and snap me out of the feeling of terror. My mom told me that my grandfather spoke of the same dream plaguing him as a child.

As I stood in the farmhouse bedroom, it was as though a thousand demons suddenly invaded my mind, filling me with the same terrible dread I had in those nightmares. *But I wasn't asleep.* I was wide awake. I couldn't wake up, and there were no parents to comfort me. I threw myself to the floor and pleaded with God to help me.

The experience was devastating. I was a Christian who trusted God with all of my heart, yet this was happening!

When I arrived back home and tried to explain to Sue what had happened, I broke down in tears. It was too hard to relate. It was completely irrational.

The experience was so devastating I couldn't have a meal with my family for over a year. It was too traumatic for me to face my wife and children. Yet, I had to continue to travel and speak at churches and conventions.

I had what I now know to be "agoraphobia," commonly called *panic attacks.* Again, these were irrational. They had no explanation. I would lie in bed and feel my heart beating within my chest. I was so filled with a reasonless fear that I didn't even want to get out of bed. It took me about five years to rid myself of that paralyzing terror. So, in a small way, I can empathize with you.

I explained in my book *How to Overcome Panic Attacks* (Bridge Logos) why I believe God allowed me to go through such an experience.

I know that you believe in the existence of God and that you were raised in the Episcopalian faith by your dad. I know this because in one of your stand-up routines you joked, "I'm an Episcopal; that's Catholic Lite. Same religion, half the guilt!" And then when you were 56, you checked yourself into a rehabilitation clinic, and after you came out you said, "You get a real strong sense of God when you go through rehab."[5]

But often in rehab clinics, God is offered as a means of help in life, as a kind of heavenly Buddy. And so, understandably, those with addictions come for help with their addiction problem. The result is that they are able to remove the web, but the spider remains. The *symptom* is addressed, but the *cause* remains. Many who come through that door often experience a *false* conversion to Christianity.

The spider is our sinful nature, and until you deal with that — whether it is manifest in porn, greed, selfishness, rebellion, etc., each of them will be demons you will have to keep fighting.

While secular society points to the symptoms, blaming circumstances, genes or mental issues, the Bible — the ultimate Human Instruction Book, gives insight into who we are and why we react as we do. It says that we are sinners who are guilty before a holy Creator, and even though you may joke about being Episcopalian and halving the guilt, sin is *deadly* serious in His eyes. The Scriptures say that it is so serious, it pays our wages in death (see Romans 6:23). So we must forget the web and instead go for the spider. It's then that your newfound gift of faith will drive out those deep-rooted fears.

The only way you could describe what you thought was an *irrational* fear was to say that it was caused by "Everything. It's just a general all-round arggghhh. It's fearfulness and anxiety." In his book *It's Kind of a Funny Story*, Ned Vizzini asks, "So why am I depressed? That's the million-dollar question, baby, the Tootsie Roll question; not even the owl knows the answer to that one. I don't know either."[6]

Once again, here is the answer to that "million-dollar question," from Hebrews 2:14–15 in the *Living Bible* (a modern paraphrase):

> Since we, God's children, are human beings — made of flesh and blood — he became flesh and blood too by being born in human form; for only as a human being could he die and in dying break the power of the devil who had the power of death. Only in that way could he deliver those who through fear of death have been living all their lives as slaves to constant dread.

When, as mortals, we don't know the answer to some difficult question, we often flippantly say, "*God only knows.*" It is, however, the truth. God is omniscient. He knows. And here in His Word, He tells us why every human being is plagued with an unshakeable dread. The Great Physician gives us the diagnosis *and the cure.*

No Need for Guilt

In looking back at your past, I see that you weren't just a friend of Christopher Reeve, you were like brothers:

> Reeve's widow Dana once described the pair as being "closer than brothers" and it was rumored that Williams had helped pay for Reeves' treatment following his accident. He also became actively involved in Reeve's foundation, The Christopher Reeve Paralysis Foundation.[7]

How could his accident and consequent death not affect you for a lifetime? Add to that tragedy the death of his wife from lung cancer, and for you there was no consolation. It was such a hopeless and dead end. You had nothing to help you control your depressing thoughts. But your words about his dying revealed something deeper than mourning over the death of a close friend. Your answer to the question as to whether or not his dying made you feel "alone and afraid" is very telling. You answered "No" and added, "*it's more selfish than that.* It's just literally being afraid. And you think, oh, this will ease the fear" (italics added).[8]

What did you mean by "it's more selfish than that"? Perhaps there was a feeling of guilt because it wasn't *his* death that was creating your fear. How could it? He had already passed. It was rather the reality of your *own* death that made you afraid. But that's nothing to feel guilty about. It's not selfish. It's okay to fear death. It's a God-given instinct to want to live.

I can't help but wonder how you would have reacted if (instead of being diagnosed as having a mental disorder) you had been told that it was the fear of death that had plagued you all of your lifetime? I think the outcome would have been different if you had been told that *because* you valued your life you were both sane and wise.

Of course, the experts will disagree. They know that 90 percent of people who take their own lives are diagnosed with depression or other mental disorders. Your tragic suicide will confirm in their minds that you were indeed mentally ill, and the blind will continue to lead the blind.

Bible Promise

Be of good courage, and He shall strengthen your heart,
all you who hope in the LORD (Psalm 31:24).

questions **?**

1. What did John Green say about depression?
2. What did a study reveal about the relationship between alcohol and depression?
3. What did Robin Williams say that he was afraid of?
4. When is faith in God (offered in some rehabilitation centers) problematic?
5. What did Ned Vizzini say about depression?

Endnotes

1. https://www.goodreads.com/quotes/465767-whenever-you-read-a-cancer-booklet-or-website-or-whatever.

2. http://time.com/3102414/robin-williams-depression-struggles-go-back-decades/.

3. Ibid.

4. https://www.theguardian.com/film/2010/sep/20/robin-williams-worlds-greatest-dad-alcohol-drugs.

5. http://www.worldreligionnews.com/religion-news/christianity/reflecting-on-the-life-and-spirituality-of-robin-williams.

6. https://www.goodreads.com/quotes/374538-so-why-am-i-depressed-that-s-the-million-dollar-question-baby.

7. http://www.dailymail.co.uk/news/article-2722888/Closer-brothers-Robin-Williams-extraordinary-friendship-Christopher-Reeve-penniless-roommates-Hollywood-highs-helping-save-friends-life.html.

8. https://www.theguardian.com/film/2010/sep/20/robin-williams-worlds-greatest-dad-alcohol-drugs.

Chapter 6

Naomi Judd

"The bravest thing I ever did was continuing my life when I wanted to die." — Juliette Lewis[1]

Diana Ellen Judd (born January 11, 1946) is an American country music singer, songwriter, and activist.

Judd began a 2016 ABC interview by apologizing for the swollen appearance of her face and her shaking hands:

> Naomi said what she describes as the swollen appearance in her face and shaking in her hands are a result of medication to treat her depression. "I really haven't been eating ice cream and candy," she said with a laugh. "I really haven't."
>
> Naomi Judd said her treatment has gotten her to a place where she now finds joy in her everyday life. She writes in her book that she laughs a lot and is "content and at peace."[2]

According to *The Huffington Post*, Judd said,

> "What I've been through is extreme. My final diagnosis was severe depression," Judd told Robin Roberts during the interview. "Treatment resistant because they tried me on every single thing they had in their arsenal. It really felt like, if I live through this I want someone to be able to see that they can survive," the Grammy winner said.[3]

In an interview with *People* magazine, they said,

> Not long after she began writing a memoir about her battle with depression, Naomi Judd called her daughter Wynonna and invited her to lunch at a local restaurant. "It

was just the two of us, and I said, 'I have something to tell you' and she got big tears in her eyes — she expected something dramatic. And I said, 'I'm writing a book,'" Judd tells *People*. "Don't do it, Mom! Don't do it!" Wynonna pleaded with her mother. "People will think you're crazy and I know you're not!"[4]

People continued:

> During her depression, "I literally couldn't leave the house for weeks. I was completely immobilized and every single second was like a day," says Judd, 70, who had to install an elevator in her home because her legs became so weak from lack of exercise. "It's so beyond making sense but I thought, 'Surely my family will know that I was in so much pain and I thought they would have wanted me to end that pain [through suicide].'"
>
> "I'm still recovering myself," says Judd, who chronicles her battle with depression in her new memoir, *River of Time: My Descent into Depression and How I Emerged with Hope.* "I'm still trying desperately to help myself. There's never going to be a pill for it all. I read up on all the scientific literature, I go to courses. I try so hard to stay up on everything that I possibly can to get rid of this horrible curse." Today, she says, "Those thoughts of suicide don't come anymore. But I'm vulnerable. I know I can backslide."[5]

A Conversation with Naomi Judd

Your daughter was right. You are not crazy. You are a brave woman who has been the brunt of clinical experiments for years — experiments that have left you in an emotional and physical mess. And you are still fighting desperately to try "and get rid of this horrible curse."

You probably know the story of the woman in the Bible who had internal bleeding for many years. Doctors had tried to help her, but the Bible says she got worse (see Mark 5:25–34; Matthew 9:20–22; Luke 8:43–48). She was so desperate to get rid of that horrible curse that she pushed into the crowd that surrounded Jesus and touched the hem of His garment. The second she did that the power of God flowed into her, and she was healed.

Many in the country music industry have an intellectual knowledge of God that falls short of conversion. The Bible Belt contains a bellyful of false converts. They have a form of godliness but they haven't received the power of God in their lives. I'm talking about trusting Him for our eternal salvation.

It is when we obey the gospel that God gives us the gift of faith. It is then that you will "rest" in faith and find the antidote to the curse. Here is His promise: "Therefore if the Son makes you free, you shall be free indeed" (John 8:36). If I would suggest anything to you, it would be to go to www.FullyFreeFilms.com and watch our award-winning movies that have been seen by millions. They contain enough condensed biblical truths to, by the grace of God, deliver what you're seeking.

Bible Promise

"The LORD also will be a refuge for the oppressed, a refuge in times of trouble" (Psalm 9:9).

questions ?

1. What did Juliette Lewis say is the bravest thing she ever did?
2. Why didn't Naomi Judd's daughter want her to write a book?
3. What did Naomi say about her own thoughts of suicide?
4. What do many have in common in the country music industry?
5. What is something that God gives us when we obey the gospel?

Endnotes

1. https://www.brainyquote.com/quotes/juliette_lewis_181954.
2. http://abcnews.go.com/Entertainment/naomi-judd-opens-battle-life-threatening-depression/story?id=43988719.
3. http://www.huffingtonpost.ca/2016/12/07/naomi-judd-depression_n_13482928.html.
4. http://people.com/country/naomi-judd-depression-ashley-judd-wynonna-judd-reaction/.
5. http://people.com/country/naomi-judd-suicidal-depression-still-healing/.

Chapter 7

Bruce Springsteen

"Sadness is more or less like a head cold — with patience, it passes. Depression is like cancer." — Barbara Kingsolver, *The Bean Trees*[1]

B ruce Frederick Joseph Springsteen (born September 23, 1949) is an American singer-songwriter. He is best known for his work with the E Street Band.

The Associated Press said of Bruce Springsteen's depression:

> Springsteen has battled his demons out loud, in public and before his fans, contrary to the social isolation stereotypical of depression. Yes, it's still risky to open up about one's vulnerabilities. In terms of choosing between "the closet" and coming out, the stigma of mental illness is most closely analogous to LGBT status. . . . The champion of numerous underdogs, Springsteen has now taken on depression, to the benefit of us all.[2]

Of his depression, detailed by Bruce in his recently published memoir *Born To Run*, he said it stems from coming from a family of mental illness sufferers. Asked how he comes back from moments that he previously described as being "close to the abyss," Bruce said: "Patti's very helpful, and sometimes just time. Or sometimes the correct medication, you need the right drugs. That can really help also."[3]

"It sneaks up on you," he said. "It's like this thing that engulfs you. I got to where I didn't want to get out of bed, you know? And you're not behaving very well at home, and you're tough on everybody — hopefully not the kids; I always tried to hide it from the kids. Patti really had to work with me through it and . . . her strength and the love she had was very important as far as guiding me through it. She was, 'Well, you're gonna be okay. Maybe not today, maybe not tomorrow but it's gonna be alright.'"

While depression has affected his home life, he was somehow always able to switch it off when it came time to make music.[4]

The biggest revelations from the book concern his battle with depression, something he's been quietly treating with medication for years. It came late in life and caused him much agony. "I couldn't get out of bed," he writes. "H-ll, I couldn't even [manage sex]. It was like all my notorious energy, something that had been mine to command for most of my life, had been cruelly stolen away. I was a walking husk."[5]

So why am I jumping on the bandwagon and adding yet another voice to the coverage? Because when the Boss talks about struggling with suicidal thoughts, a painful childhood, a family history of mental illness, and a decades-long struggle with clinical depression, it opens doors. Doors to a discussion that for some reason America is still having trouble having.[6]

The Boss's treatment regimen has included both decades of therapy and antidepressants, the latter eschewed by many artists who fear they will inhibit creativity. But he has also said that touring was the best therapy of all: "You are free of yourself for those hours; all the voices in your head are gone. Just gone. There's no room for them. There's one voice, the voice you're speaking in."[7]

> Baby I've been down, but never this down
> I've been lost, but never this lost.
> — Bruce Springsteen, *This Depression*

He was 60 years old, and in the jaws of a blackness without end, and his old friends were dying, and one autumn morning Bruce Springsteen found himself alone on a beach in New Jersey with his paddle board and his tears. Not just any tears, either: "*Bambi* tears," as he writes in his new autobiography, *Born to Run.* "*Old Yeller*[8] tears. . . . *Fried Green Tomato* tears."[9]

A Conversation with Bruce Springsteen

I did a lot of research about your depression and (as usual) nowhere did I find an explanation for its existence. Also, as usual, I don't believe that you have a mental illness. Rather, that you are normal. But just like every other normal human being with a love of life, you fear death, and if the disease you have isn't diagnosed for what it is, you will never find a cure. Whatever the case, you're not alone in your depression:

> An estimated 350 million people in the world suffer from depression, according to the World Health Organization, and Springsteen is far from the first artist to open up about his or her struggles — artists are statistically more likely to suffer from depression.[10]

Neither do I believe that artists are statistically more likely to suffer from depression, unless there are 350 million artists in the world. Rather, *every* human being who thinks deeply about life, and particularly about death, is a candidate for depression.

Your experience is similar to mine. You cried on that beach, not necessarily because you were depressed. It's deeper than that. Rather, you were depressed because your friends were dying, and an unstoppable death was also was coming for you and those you cherish most in life.

Back on a dark night in 1971, I wept those same bitter tears. I cried at the futility of life because of death. Let me tell you what happened. . . .

In 1999, a Chicago businessman called, said that he had listened to an audio tape I had produced [HellsBestKeptSecret.com] and asked if I would like to take a team to Israel. He would cover the cost if I would do a little teaching on the side.

Fast forward a few months. I was in a large tour bus on the way back to Jerusalem after visiting Jericho. While the rest of the passengers were in the back of the bus chatting, I was like a wide-eyed little kid, up in front on the right side with my nose up against the window.

I could see across a massive valley thousands of feet below. I was deep in thought, wondering if perhaps I was looking at the very spot where the Good Samaritan helped the beaten stranger. *Suddenly the bus went over the edge of the three-thousand-foot cliff!* I was so terrified I couldn't even draw a breath. It was as though my heart literally stopped for fear of what was happening. *I was a dead man.* Even now, as I relive that experience, I can feel those *dreadful* emotions. I can't express the terror that gripped me.

Just as suddenly, the bus turned left and we were moseying along the road as though nothing had happened. *But something had happened!* I had been as good as dead and returned from the grave.

To turn left on the road, the driver had swung the large bus to the right to accommodate the sharp corner, putting me and the front right side over the massive cliff edge, while the rest of the bus remained safely on the road. But I didn't know that.

I looked at the passengers who were still chatting down the back. Everyone was oblivious to the terror I had experienced. In a second, I went from being paralyzed by fear to exploding with joy — an unspeakable joy that I was going to stay in the land of the living.

Six months before my conversion to Jesus Christ, I found myself over a deep and dark chasm. It was the valley of the shadow of death. With all my success as a young businessman, I had the breath-taking and terrifying revelation that death was going to swallow me, and I was utterly helpless to do anything about it. I was as good as dead. It was just a matter of time.

It was on that dark night in 1971 that I sat on the end of our bed as a newly married man, looked at my sleeping bride, and shed bitter tears at the futility of life and the reality of impending death.

I came to that realization at the age of 22. You, Mr. Springsteen, took a little longer — probably because you have had the distraction of fame.

But six months after that experience, life took a radical turn. I was suddenly on the straight and narrow knowing that death had been conquered by the Savior. God rescued me from its power through the everlasting gospel, and granted me eternal life! Now I have joy unspeakable that I am going to live, but at the same time I shed tears for people like you, who are still being hung over the edge of futility — hopeless and helpless.

So there you have it, Mr. Bruce Springsteen. God offers you everlasting life, freedom from the fear of death and the hopelessness that comes with it. Are you going to stay with depression and those seductive suicidal thoughts? May I suggest, sir, that you don't.

Bible Promise

God is our refuge and strength, a very present help in trouble. Therefore we will not fear (Psalm 46:1–2).

questions?

1. How did Barbara Kingsolver describe the difference between sadness and depression?
2. To what did Bruce Springsteen liken "the stigma of mental illness"?
3. According to the World Health Organization, how many people are estimated to suffer from depression?
4. What does God offer Bruce Springsteen and every other lost sinner?
5. Finish this verse: "God is our refuge and strength, a very present help in trouble. Therefore. . . ." (See Psalm 46:1–2.)

Endnotes

1. https://www.goodreads.com/quotes/206045-there-is-no-point-treating-a-depressed-person-as-though

2. http://bigstory.ap.org/article/4e1c322c7b1d4733b09299d191915b91/why-bruce-springsteens-depression-revelation-matters.

3. http://www.breakingnews.ie/showbiz/bruce-springsteen-hails-very-beautiful-relationship-with-wife-and-talks-about-depression-769055.html.

4. http://ultimateclassicrock.com/bruce-springsteen-depression/.

5. http://www.rollingstone.com/music/lists/bruce-springsteens-new-memoir-10-things-we-learned-w442001.

6. http://www.forbes.com/sites/melaniehaiken/2012/07/25/bruce-springsteen-discusses-clinical-depression-and-gives-the-rest-of-us-permission-to-discuss-depression-too/#3d35d57efbf6.

7. http://bigstory.ap.org/article/4e1c322c7b1d4733b09299d191915b91/why-bruce-springsteens-depression-revelation-matters.

8. *Old Yeller* was a 1957 Disney movie about the death of a faithful dog.

9. http://www.theglobeandmail.com/arts/music/once-upon-a-time-in-bruce-springsteens-america/article32469925/.

10. http://www.ibtimes.com/famous-quotes-depression-bruce-springsteen-6-other-celebrities-battling-mental-2412480.

Chapter 8

Ernest Hemingway

"I don't want to see anyone. I lie in the bedroom with the curtains drawn and nothingness washing over me like a sluggish wave. . . . I have done something wrong, something so huge I can't even see it, something that's drowning me. . . . I might as well be dead." — Margaret Atwood, *Cat's Eye*[1]

Ernest Hemingway (July 21, 1899–July 2, 1961) was an American novelist, short story writer, and journalist. The Nobel and Pulitzer Prize-winning author committed suicide at the age of 61.

Hemingway suffered from bipolar disorder, then known as manic depression, and was treated with electroshock therapy at the Menninger Clinic. The therapy he claimed, had destroyed his memory. . . .[2]

Just a few months before Mariel Hemingway was born, her famous grandfather, Ernest Hemingway, committed suicide in the Idaho home where Mariel later grew up. The Nobel Prize-winning novelist had struggled with depression, and the Hemingway family as a whole has been plagued by a legacy of addiction, mental illness, and suicide across generations. In fact, just one day before the anniversary of Ernest Hemingway's suicide in 1996, Mariel's older sister Margaux also took her own life in what was ruled an intentional overdose.[3]

A Conversation with Ernest Hemingway

You once said, "Fear of death increases in exact proportion to increase in wealth."[4] I would perhaps qualify your quote by saying that the more we have in this life, the harder it is to leave. A homeless person leaves little. A billionaire leaves his mansion, his yacht, his Rolex, his beloved family, and of course his big bank account. So his grip is tight on these things. He feared thieves would take them from him in this life, but the Grim Reaper is taking them from him for the next.

Psychologists have said that "death anxiety is not only real, but it is humanity's most profound source of concern." One psychologist said that the anxiety is so intense "that it can generate fears and phobias of everyday life — fears of being alone or in a confined space. Based on the theory, many of people's daily behavior consist of attempts to deny death and to keep their anxiety under strict regulation."[5]

One of your most famous quotes was, "All thinking men are atheists." It is more truthful to say that all thinking men live in a constant state of depression. That was true in your case.

An atheist wrote the following words on my Facebook page: "Your bible says 'lean not on your own understanding,' which is why you lack reason and accept absurdities. You have a brain and reason, for a reason. It filters out nonsense."

The context of the Bible verse he quoted, was, "*Trust in the Lord with all your heart* and lean not to your own understanding" (Proverbs 3:5).

What the secular world doesn't understand is that God chose a *foolish* message that would only be received by the humble. The proud and arrogant *cannot* see the gospel. It is hidden from them:

> At that time Jesus answered and said, "I thank You, Father, Lord of heaven and earth, that You have hidden these things from the wise and prudent and have revealed them to babes" (Matthew 11:25).

One sure way to have a hit movie is to create conflict between a quiet kid and a bully, and then have it end with the bully getting what's coming to him and the kid winning. That's the story of the gospel.

God did this by using "foolish things . . . to shame the wise" (1 Corinthians 1:27). This seeming foolishness is consistent in the

Scriptures from Noah and the Ark to Jonah and the whale, right through to Jesus being born in a cowshed and riding on a donkey.

The foundation of the "foolishness" that God has used as the means to grant everlasting life is childlike "faith," something that is despised by the proud. And yet as we have seen, faith or "trust" is the basis of every healthy human relationship — from a relationship with our spouse to our pilots, taxi drivers, doctors, drug companies, surgeons, government institutions that regulate food and drugs, banks, those who write history books, politicians, chefs, and every other area of society. God chose trust over human reasoning, and there was at least two reasons for this.

First, the human mind isn't reliable. This is why pilots deliberately ignore their easily fooled reasoning and *trust* their trustworthy instruments. They are trained to do that, because their lives and the lives of their passengers depend on it.

Back in July of 1999, the *Washington Post* reported:

> The cause of John F. Kennedy Jr.'s apparent fatal plane crash may not be known for some time, if ever, but it is clear he was flying into conditions that have lured many other pilots to their deaths. . . .
>
> Human beings tend to become disoriented when they are suspended in blackness and have almost no "visual cues." It is easy to believe that up is down. That is why planes have instruments, and pilots are told to believe their instruments rather than go with their senses.
>
> Nonetheless, the flight into Martha's Vineyard should not have been beyond Kennedy's capabilities as long as he followed that basic rule of "trust your instruments."[6]

The second reason God chose faith over reason is that reasoning comes from the human intellect. Reasoning takes ability. If God granted eternal life to those who were able to attain it by their ability, then those who were less intelligent wouldn't qualify. But *anyone* can exercise faith. All of us do it every day. And that gives a level playing field to humanity. The Kingdom of God is not made up of those who are powerful and rich and who got that way by their own ability. It is made up of the poor and the humble, simply because of the principle of childlike faith. This is the teaching of the Bible:

> Notice among yourselves, dear brothers, that few of you who follow Christ have big names or power or wealth. Instead, God has deliberately chosen to use ideas the world considers foolish and of little worth in order to shame those people considered by the world as wise and great. He has chosen a plan despised by the world, counted as nothing at all, and used it to bring down to nothing those the world considers great, so that no one anywhere can ever brag in the presence of God (1 Corinthians 1:26–29, TLB).

Bible Promise

> Yea, though I walk through the valley of the shadow of death, I will fear no evil; for You are with me; Your rod and Your staff, they comfort me (Psalm 23:4).

questions ?

1. What was it that Ernest Hemingway said destroyed his memory?
2. At what age did the Nobel and Pulitzer Prize-winning author commit suicide?
3. What was it that he had been plagued by across generations?
4. One of his most famous quotes was, "All thinking men are atheists." Do you think that's true?
5. What is it that God has chosen that is despised by the proud of heart?

Endnotes

1. https://www.goodreads.com/quotes/104390-i-don-t-want-to-see-anyone-i-lie-in-the.
2. https://www.imdb.com/name/nm0002133/bio.
3. http://www.huffingtonpost.com/2014/04/28/ernest-hemingway-suicide-mariel-hemingway-childhood-home_n_5215399.html.
4. https://www.brainyquote.com/quotes/ernest_hemingway_383489.
5. https://en.m.wikipedia.org/wiki/Death_anxiety_(psychology).
6. http://www.washingtonpost.com/wp-srv/national/longterm/jfkjr/stories/crash071899.htm.

Chapter 9

Stephen Fry

"I start to think there really is no cure for depression, that happiness is an ongoing battle, and I wonder if it isn't one I'll have to fight for as long as I live. I wonder if it's worth it." — Elizabeth Wurtzel[1]

Stephen John Fry (born August 24, 1957) is an English comedian, actor, writer, atheist, presenter, and homosexual activist.

The Huffington Post UK published an article with the title: "Atheist Stephen Fry Delivers Incredible Answer When Asked What He Would Say If He Met God."

Interviewed in 2015 by veteran Irish broadcaster Gay Byrne, Fry was asked what he would say if he came face-to-face with God. Fry said: "Bone cancer in children, what's that about? How dare you? How dare you create a world where there is such misery that's not our fault? It's utterly, utterly evil." Within days, the video was viewed over five million times.[2]

"I always heard voices in my head saying what a useless b-st-rd I am, but the voice is my own," says Stephen Fry. "It is my own voice, telling me what a worthless $#!#% I am. . . . I'm actually kind of sobbing and kind of tearing at the walls inside my own brain while my mouth is, you know, wittering away in some amusing fashion," he says. . . . The 49-year-old actor has been tormented by mental illness for much of his life.

Fry came close to gassing himself in his car. "I had this image of my parents staring right in at me while I sat there for at least, I think, two hours in the car with my hands over the ignition key," he says. "And so I decided not to do it. When you feel you can't go on — it's, it's not just a phrase, it is a . . . it's, it's a reality. I could not go on, and I would have killed myself if I didn't have the option of disappearing because it was that absolute."[3]

> "I suppose this was the first time I had ever felt an urge not to be. Never an urge to die, far less an urge to put an end to myself — simply an urge not to be. This disgusting, hostile and unlovely world was not made for me, nor I for it." Stephen Fry, *Moab Is My Washpot*[4]

> "Nowadays a lot of what was wrong with me would no doubt be ascribed to Attention Deficit Disorder, tartrazine food coloring, dairy produce and air pollution. A few hundred years earlier it would have been demons, still the best analogy I think, but not much help when it comes to a cure." Stephen Fry, *Moab Is My Washpot*[5]

In June of 2013, author Alastair Campbell published an insightful article entitled, "I feel for Stephen Fry. Nobody would wish depression on their worst enemy":

> I remember several years ago, a leading politician telling me a friend had taken his own life, and the politician had harsh words for this act of "cowardice and cruelty." We ended up having a row. "Who are you to say he was a coward?" Back came the answer. "He had a good job, a nice house, great wife, two lovely sons — what did he have to be depressed about?" We hear it less than we used to, but hear it we do. Stephen Fry is often called a national treasure. He is clever, witty, hugely successful, massively popular. So "what does he have to be depressed about?" Nothing. He just is.[6]

A Conversation with Stephen Fry

I've watched some of your interviews and read many of your quotes. I can see why you are so popular. There is something likable about you. You are clearly intelligent and very witty.

It's well-known that you're an atheist, so the bone cancer in children argument is either irrelevant or disingenuous. You don't believe

He exists. So He didn't do anything wrong. And if God *does* exist and He is responsible for kids with bone cancer, you can't accuse Him of "evil" because there's no such thing as good and evil in an atheist's worldview.

You remind me of how the average church treats its sound man. He is only noticed when something goes wrong. No one thinks of him while the sound is perfectly sound, but as soon as a microphone dies or screeches, there is indignation. *"Where is that stupid sound man?"*

God gave you the warmth of the sun and life-giving rain, eyesight and hearing, sunrises and sunsets, color and beauty, puppies and kittens, butterflies and music, and love and laughter. He gave you friends and family. . . . He gave a brain with which to think, and the gift of life itself. *Are you at all thankful?* Do you love your Creator with your heart, mind, soul, and strength? That is the greatest Commandment — to love the One who gave you your life. From what I see, you are like the rest of us. I never gave God one second of serious thought before I was a Christian. I wasn't an atheist, but I certainly didn't keep that Commandment, even though I knew that God should have been first in my affections.

You said, "Bone cancer in children, what's that about? How dare you! How dare you create a world where there is such misery that's not our fault? It's utterly, utterly evil."

But let's broaden your indignation a little to include the many children who are killed in car accidents, mauled to death by dogs, crushed in earthquakes, are killed in war, drown in floods or swimming pools, die from other horrific diseases, are molested and murdered, or die in tornadoes. Or how about including teenagers who get cancer? How about the millions of *adults* who get cancer — mothers and fathers, brothers and sisters, or friends who suffer and die? It is understandable that you say, "This disgusting, hostile, and unlovely world was not made for me, nor I for it." Stop the world, I want to get off. Life is a matter of going from one sickness to another, many ending in death:

> Worldwide, about one out of every five cases of acute gastroenteritis (diarrhea and vomiting illness) is caused by norovirus. Globally, norovirus is estimated to be the most

common cause of acute gastroenteritis. It is responsible for 685 million cases every year, 200 million of these cases are among children younger than 5 years old. This leads to an estimated 50,000 child deaths every year, nearly all of which occur in developing countries.[7]

How about the fact that *every* human being will die? *What's with that?* Let me answer that question.

Each of these terrible sufferings stands as evidence that the Bible is true when it says that we live in a *fallen* creation. Sin entered by one man, and with it came disease and death. It was passed on to all men. You can become angry and say that you didn't ask to be born, let alone born a sinner, and therefore you are not responsible for wrongdoing. But that defense doesn't even work in our courts, let alone the courtroom of God. No judge will let a criminal go because he said that he was made a criminal by being born a sinner, and that the robbery and rape were therefore God's fault. The criminal is morally responsible for his crimes, and so are we before God. We deserve the death penalty and the pain that comes with it, both before and after death.

But there is another reason for us to lay our accusing hand over our sinful mouths. Guilty though we are, God has graciously made a way for us to be instantly forgiven for our sins and granted everlasting life. The Judge will dismiss our case and let us live. So to rail at Him in blasphemy would be the ultimate biting of the hand that feeds you.

An indignant atheist is like a man who walks into a lighted room, turns out the light, and then complains about the darkness. The Bible gives light on this and other subjects, but if you refuse to believe it you are left in darkness, with the irony of an indignation against the God you don't believe exists.

Your Unusual Book Title

I found it intriguing that, as an atheist, you took the title of your book, *Moab is my Washpot* from the Bible (Psalm 60:8). Maybe it was in mockery because it's such a seemingly meaningless verse. Perhaps you have a better reason. Whatever the case, it is interesting to know that Moab was a deadly enemy to Israel, but after their defeat they became a lowly wash pot to Israel. I guess our equivalent would be that the Allies so defeated Germany in the Second World War that after the war they became our water boy.

I also noticed that in your book you create a number of straw man arguments, something often done by atheists when it comes to the Scriptures. You said,

> And if the best you can do is quote the Bible in defense of your prejudice, then have the humility to be consistent. The same book that exhorts against the abomination of one man lying with another also contains exhortations against the eating of pork and shell-fish and against menstruating women daring to come near holy places. It's no good functionalistically claiming that kosher diet had its local, meteorological purposes now defunct, or that the prejudice against ovulation can be dispensed with as superstition, the Bible that you bash us with tells you that much of what you do is unclean: don't pick and choose with a Revealed Text — or if you do, pick and choose the good bits, the bits that say things like "Let he who is without sin cast the first stone," or "Love thy neighbor as thyself." Stephen Fry, *Moab Is My Washpot*[8]

You make the mistake of equating universal moral Law (lying, theft, murder, rape, adultery, homosexuality, etc.) with Israel's dietary laws. Eating shellfish and pork were clearly forbidden for health reasons (they are scavengers), and those laws were unique to the Hebrew nation. The moral Law was given *universally* — to leave the "whole world guilty before God" (see Romans 3:19–20). So there is nothing morally wrong with eating pork or shellfish.

Also, the "good bits" to which you refer aren't good *for us,* because they condemn us. For example, you quoted the words of Jesus: "Let he who is without sin cast the first stone" (John 8:7), and you're right about each of us being in a moral position to cast stones. None are without sin. Only God is sinless and He warns that a big stone is coming, which Jesus said will "grind to powder" (Matthew 21:44). The Bible warns of a day in which God will judge the world in righteousness. When something is "ground" to powder, a thorough job has been done. God's justice will be so thorough on Judgment Day that He will punish all sin, including the thoughts and intents of every human heart, and every idle word that has ever been spoken.

You also quoted "Love thy neighbor as thyself." In context, the full quote is, "You shall love the Lord your God with all of your heart, mind, soul, and strength. And you shall love your neighbor as yourself" (Deuteronomy 6:5; Luke 10:27).

Have you obeyed that command? Have you loved the God who gave you life? Have you loved your neighbor (every other person) as much as you love yourself? Or have you lied to, stolen from, or even hated others? So in retrospect, the good bits aren't good bits at all when they leave all of us guilty. The Living Bible puts it this way:

> That is why I felt fine so long as I did not understand what the law really demanded. But when I learned the truth, I realized that I had broken the law and was a sinner, doomed to die. So as far as I was concerned, the good law which was supposed to show me the way of life resulted instead in my being given the death penalty (Romans 7:9–10).

The Law was given as a mirror so that we could see ourselves as we are: self-righteous, God-hating sinners, who have fallen woefully short of the moral perfection demanded by the Commandments. Only God's mercy in Christ can save us from death and a very real and just hell.

The Voices

In reference to the tormenting voices you hear in your head, I assume that you said the following in jest:

> A few hundred years earlier it would have been demons, still the best analogy I think, but not much help when it comes to a cure.[9]

When people say "He had his demons," they of course don't mean it literally. Nor do they mean it when they say "As sure as hell" or "I will be damned." However, the Bible says that the god of this world is real, that he blinds minds to the gospel, and that he came to "kill, and to steal, and to destroy" (John 10:10). The Scriptures also tell us we are in a state of hostility toward God and that we don't want His moral government over us. So your tirade against your Creator is in keeping with the Scriptures. You were able to eloquently say what most only think. You pointed out what you thought was some dirt on God, and that is why you were so applauded.

The Scriptures teach that a Christian is inhabited by the Holy Spirit, while "unsaved" people have an unholy spirit . . . that there is a *spirit* "that works in the sons of disobedience" (see Ephesians 2:2). So your thought is correct, in that demonic possession is "still the best analogy," but then you dismiss it with but it's "not much help when it comes to a cure." To say there's no cure confirms that you are indeed blinded by the god of this world, and to the power of the gospel to free you from death.

In 2016, I had a hernia operation. The surgeon told me beforehand that it was major surgery, and that I would be debilitated for some weeks. But just a few days after the surgery I was running up stairs with no problems. What I didn't realize was that I was on pain-killing opiates. When I did realize that, I decided to get off them as soon as possible, but when I did, I found that I could hardly walk. I was in agony. The drugs gave me a false sense of reality. Pride does the same thing. It blinds us to reality. Fear humbles us. It shows us how weak and vulnerable we are. It strips us of our precious pride. Look at these words of Scripture:

> "Put them in fear, O LORD, that the nations may know
> themselves to be but men" (Psalm 9:20).

The Psalmist implores God to put the nations in fear "that they may know themselves to be but men." Fear takes those who are famous household names and reminds them that they are nobody special, that they are nothing but weak and ordinary mortals who in time will die. Frightening though that may be, such a sobering revelation is a wonderful wake-up call *if it leads us to the Savior.* Tragically, it drives many to suicide. Please don't let that happen to you.

Back in 2006, it was said of you, "Fry fears the growing intensity of his attacks of depression and says he is 'in a very sort of black state' but remains undecided about whether he needs medical treatment."[10]

I don't believe that you need medical treatment, because I don't believe you have a mental disease. You are not insane. You are intelligent, and because you *think* you have a reasonable, natural, and perfectly understandable fear of death, dread covers you like a cloud. So how can you have peace when you sit in the shadow of the Great Reaper? You don't *stand* in the shadow of death. The Bible says that you "sit" in it (see Luke 1:79). You are not going anywhere. Without the Savior you are both helpless and hopeless. The guillotine is on its way down.

In speaking of a friend who had everything going for him but took his own life, author Elizabeth Wurtzel wrote:

> So here is the miserable truth that those of us who are given to depression are forced to face when David Foster Wallace commits suicide: It didn't and doesn't turn out well. There is no happy ending to the story of sorrow if you are born with a predilection for despair. The world is, after all, a coarse and brutal and cruel place. It's only a matter of how long you can live with it.[11]

And so you have a fear that the depression will get worse, and that will more than likely happen as each heartbeat brings you closer to death. Please, forget your atheism, soften your heart, and seek earnestly after the God who can free you from your fears. He did it for me and millions of others. We can say, "I sought the Lord, and He heard me, and delivered me from all my fears" (Psalm 34:4).

Bible Promise

> And you will seek Me and find Me, when you search for Me with all your heart (Jeremiah 29:13).

questions**?**

1. Elizabeth Wurtzel said, "I wonder if it's worth it." To what was she referring?

2. To what did Stephen Fry attribute the things that were wrong with him?

3. How is an indignant atheist like a man who walks into a lighted room?

4. What is a "straw man" argument?

5. Where in the Bible does it tell us that the moral Law is universal?

Endnotes

1. https://www.brainyquote.com/quotes/elizabeth_wurtzel_334890.

2. http://www.huffingtonpost.co.uk/2015/01/30/atheist-stephen-fry-delivers-stunning-answer-when-asked-what-he-would-say-if-he-came-face-to-face-with-god_n_6581710.html.

3. http://www.independent.co.uk/life-style/health-and-families/health-news/stephen-fry-my-battle-with-mental-illness-416386.html.

4. https://www.goodreads.com/quotes/713944-i-suppose-this-was-the-first-time-i-had-ever.

5. https://citaty.net/citaty/1537650-stephen-fry-nowadays-a-lot-of-what-was-wrong-with-me-would-no/.

6. http://www.independent.co.uk/voices/comment/alastair-campbell-i-feel-for-stephen-fry-nobody-would-wish-depression-on-their-worst-enemy-8649425.html.

7. https://www.cdc.gov/norovirus/worldwide.html.

8. https://www.goodreads.com/work/quotes/2951429-moab-is-my-washpot?page=3.

9. Ibid.

10. http://www.independent.co.uk/life-style/health-and-families/health-news/stephen-fry-my-battle-with-mental-illness-416386.html.

11. http://nymag.com/news/intelligencer/50515/.

Chapter 10

Amy Winehouse

"Depression . . . is flat, hollow, and unendurable. . . . You're frightened, and you're frightening, and you're 'not at all like yourself but will be soon,' but you know you won't." — Kay Redfield Jamison, *An Unquiet Mind: A Memoir of Moods and Madness*[1]

Amy Jade Winehouse (September 14, 1983–July 23, 2011) was an English singer and songwriter. Her album *Back to Black* (2006) led to five 2008 Grammy Awards.

Amy, who this year admitted drinking too much, said she refuses to take medication, even though clinically diagnosed as a manic depressive. Of her visit to rehab, she said: "The fella in charge said: 'Why are you here?' and I said: 'Well, I think I've come here because I'm drinking a lot. But I'm in love and the drinking is symptomatic of my depression. I'm not an alcoholic.' "[2]

In a 2007 interview following her first highly publicized overdoses, she spoke candidly about her depression. "Since I was 16, I've felt a black cloud hangs over me," she said. "Since then, I have taken pills for depression. I believe there are lots of people who have these mood changes."[3]

Just after her death, the *Telegraph* reported:

Amy Winehouse had "prescribed drug" in system when she died. The father of singer Amy Winehouse said that his daughter had the prescription medication Librium in her system when she died of a seizure in July, according to media reports.[4]

Here are the "Common Side Effects of Librium":

> Call your doctor at once if you have any of these serious side effects: confusion, depressed mood, thoughts of suicide, or hurting yourself.[5]

The *Washington Post* wrote:

> Cobain, Winehouse, Joplin and Hendrix all were 27 when they died. In each of their cases, the symptoms of manic depression were mistaken for youthful wildness and artistic angst, when something much more serious was lurking beneath.[6]

Super-talented British singer-songwriter Amy Winehouse suffered from substance abuse and bipolar disorder. She was not known to have sought treatment for her bipolar disorder. By one estimate, 30–60% of people who suffer from manic depression also have substance abuse problems. Winehouse herself linked her drinking to depression.

> The illness, formerly known as manic depression, affects hundreds of thousands of people in the UK. Although it can be managed successfully with drug and psychological therapies, 15 per cent of sufferers — about 2,000 people a year — kill themselves.[7]

> Recording her verdict, the coroner said Winehouse had died from "alcohol toxicity," adding that it was "a level of alcohol commonly associated with fatality." She said Winehouse "voluntarily consumed alcohol" and added that "two empty vodka bottles were on the floor" beside her bed when her body was discovered.[8]

The *Washington Post* said,

> About 1 out of 5 people with manic depressive disorder commit suicide.

What a confounding disorder of the mind, this melancholia mated with mania, the driving force behind creative genius.

Mental illness — the subject shows up in all kinds of music, from "19th Nervous Breakdown" by the Rolling Stones, to "Lithium Sunset" by Sting, to "Down on Me," by Janis Joplin, a manic depressive who died of a drug overdose in 1970. And yet, there is so much more to understand.

"I do drink a lot. I think it's symptomatic of my depression," Winehouse said in an interview on a British TV show. "I'm manic depressive, I'm not an alcoholic, which sounds like an alcoholic in denial."[9]

A Conversation with Amy Winehouse

Amy, like millions of others, you suffered from debilitating depression, and once again, there was no cause given. Something made you despair about life, and so you found refuge from your fears in the toxin alcohol. It seems that you literally drank yourself to death.

I know that you were Jewish. You said the following in July 2011:

> In 10 years' time I'm gonna be looking after my husband and our seven kids. I'd really like to get everyone in one place and sit down and eat a meal together. I would like to uphold certain things, but not the religious side of things, just the nice family things to do. At the end of the day, I'm a Jewish girl.[10]

With all your wild living, you wanted the normality of a happy family. You had millions of adoring fans, and as appealing as that may be to the human ego, fans are just a superficial reality of the modern era. Media makes ordinary people famous overnight. But as much as the crowd roars, and the applause explodes, you go home and end up alone with your thoughts and fears. The echoes of praise have gone. You can't live on them. But you could live on the promise of a stable family. And that was your dream.

But you made plans to exclude the One who gave you life and could free you from the fear of death. Had you opened the Jewish Scriptures you would have read:

Who has woe? Who has sorrow? Who has contentions?
Who has complaints? Who has wounds without cause?
Who has redness of eyes? Those who linger long at the wine,
those who go in search of mixed wine. Do not look on the
wine when it is red, when it sparkles in the cup, when it
swirls around smoothly; at the last it bites like a serpent,
and stings like a viper (Proverbs 23:29–32).

Your last words were, "I don't want to die," spoken to your doctor
over the phone two hours prior to your death.[11]

Bible Promise

There is no fear in love; but perfect love casts out fear,
because fear involves torment. But he who fears has not
been made perfect in love (1 John 4:18).

questions ?

1. Just before she died of a seizure, Amy Winehouse was taking
   Librium. What are its common side effects?
2. What was her cause of death?
3. Where did Amy see herself in ten years' time?
4. Why do you think she didn't want the religious side of being
   Jewish?
5. What were her last words?

Endnotes

1. https://www.goodreads.com/quotes/180984-others-imply-that-they-know-what-it-is-like-to.

2. http://www.independent.co.uk/life-style/health-and-families/health-news/stephen-fry-my-battle-with-mental-illness-416386.html.

3. http://lynncinnamon.com/2015/05/amy-winehouse-and-the-loneliness-of-running-away-in-plain-sight/.

4. http://www.telegraph.co.uk/news/celebritynews/8754374/Amy-Winehouse-had-prescribed-drug-in-system-when-she-died.html.

5. http://www.rxlist.com/librium-side-effects-drug-center.htm.

6. https://www.washingtonpost.com/local/amy-winehouse-another-tragic-victim-of-manic-depression/2011/07/24/gIQAW3FJXI_story.html?utm_term=.d5ba694e2c2c.

7. http://www.independent.co.uk/life-style/health-and-families/health-news/stephen-fry-my-battle-with-mental-illness-416386.html.

8. https://www.theguardian.com/music/2013/jan/08/amy-winehouse-alcohol-poisoning-inquest.

9. https://www.washingtonpost.com/local/amy-winehouse-another-tragic-victim-of-manic-depression/2011/07/24/gIQAW3FJXI_story.html?utm_term=.40f59defa713.

10. http://hollowverse.com/amy-winehouse/.

11. https://en.m.wikiquote.org/wiki/Last_words.

Chapter 11

Rita Ora

"Depression is the most unpleasant thing I have ever experienced. . . . The absence of hope. That very deadened feeling, which is so very different from feeling sad. Sad hurts but it's a healthy feeling. It is a necessary thing to feel. Depression is very different." — J.K. Rowling[1]

Rita Ora (born 26 November 1990) is a British singer and actress. She was the artist with the most number-one singles on the U.K. singles chart in 2012.

In an article titled "Rita Ora Is Afraid of Dying . . ." by Matthew Scott Donnelly August 25, 2015, he said,

> The topic of death has never sat particularly well with Ora, who explained she's suffered from a fear of dying for years. "Death is my biggest phobia," Ora confessed. "I used to have panic attacks when I was little, saying, 'Mum, I don't want to die.' I've been to therapy and still try to go every week."[2]

Does the article's writer know anyone on whom the topic of death sits well? No sane person wants to die, and it takes courage to admit to having a fear of death. This young lady loves life and desperately wants to keep it. She doesn't need therapy. She needs to hear the gospel — that "Jesus Christ . . . has abolished death and brought life and immortality to light through the gospel" (2 Timothy 1:10). The odds are she's never heard it and, like most, thinks that the gospel and religion are one and the same.

Journalist Daisy Buchanan, in writing for *The Telegraph* also had a fear of death. She wrote of an experience when she was just four years old. Her dad had been playing a game with her and her sister, jokingly chasing them, saying, "You're going to die!"

After one particularly dramatic game, I said to Dad, conspiratorially, "I'm glad people don't really die, aren't you?" He looked a bit panicked, summoned Mum, and I had my first mortality chat. Everyone died? How come we were all so calm?

She took great consolation when she read that Rita Ora and actor Lena Dunham spoke openly about a fear of death. She said that Dunham said,

> "It could be tomorrow. It could be 80 years from tomorrow. But it was coming for us all, and I was no exception," she writes. "I asked my father . . . 'How are we supposed to live every day if we know we're going to die?' "

> Until I read this, I'd tried to forget my own fears, and I was stunned to learn that, growing up, Dunham felt exactly as I did.

> But anxiety isn't rational, and its progress isn't slowed down by success or security. It simply seeks out something bigger to work with. When your life is going well, death will always be around for you to worry about.[3]

A Conversation with Rita Ora

I understand that your mother is Catholic and your father is Muslim, and that you don't consider yourself to be religious, saying instead that you are more of a spiritual person.

I can also understand why you make that difference. Most young people nowadays say they believe in some sort of higher power, but they are not committed to any particular religion. There's a difference between being religious and being spiritual.

There is also a difference between being religious and being a Christian. That difference is something called "works of righteousness." Most religions say that you must *do* something to get to heaven. You have to *work* at it to obtain righteousness; and that is your ticket into heaven. Christianity maintains that there is nothing you can you do to save yourself from death and hell. It says that we can be saved by "grace."

Let me try to explain the difference with a story about a young man who was into a lifestyle of partying and visiting prostitutes, when something went terribly wrong:

A certain man had two sons. And the younger of them said to his father, "Father, give me the portion of goods that falls to me." So he divided to them his livelihood. And not many days after, the younger son gathered all together, journeyed to a far country, and there wasted his possessions with prodigal living. But when he had spent all, there arose a severe famine in that land, and he began to be in want. Then he went and joined himself to a citizen of that country, and he sent him into his fields to feed swine. And he would gladly have filled his stomach with the pods that the swine ate, and no one gave him anything.

But when he came to himself, he said, "How many of my father's hired servants have bread enough and to spare, and I perish with hunger! I will arise and go to my father, and will say to him, 'Father, I have sinned against heaven and before you, and I am no longer worthy to be called your son. Make me like one of your hired servants.'"

And he arose and came to his father. But when he was still a great way off, his father saw him and had compassion, and ran and fell on his neck and kissed him. And the son said to him, "Father, I have sinned against heaven and in your sight, and am no longer worthy to be called your son."

But the father said to his servants, "Bring out the best robe and put it on him, and put a ring on his hand and sandals on his feet. And bring the fatted calf here and kill it, and let us eat and be merry; for this my son was dead and is alive again; he was lost and is found." And they began to be merry.

Now his older son was in the field. And as he came and drew near to the house, he heard music and dancing. So he called one of the servants and asked what these things meant. And he said to him, "Your brother has come, and because he has received him safe and sound, your father has killed the fatted calf."

But he was angry and would not go in. Therefore his father came out and pleaded with him. So he answered and said to his father, "Lo, these many years I have been serving you; I never transgressed your commandment at any time; and yet you never gave me a young goat, that I might make merry with my friends. But as soon as this son of yours came, who has devoured your livelihood with harlots, you killed the fatted calf for him."

And he said to him, "Son, you are always with me, and all that I have is yours. It was right that we should make merry and be glad, for your brother was dead and is alive again, and was lost and is found" (Luke 15:11–32).

This is the story of the human race, and how much God loves us despite what we have done.

Notice how the young man went to a *far* country. His hormones had kicked in, and he wanted to have sex. Nothing new there. No doubt there were local ladies who could have helped him out, but he went to a *distant* country, no doubt to get away from his father, to get away from his standards. He knew that his dad frowned on fornication.

That's a picture of why you and I want to stay away from God — from His moral standards. As we have seen, the Bible says that we are in a state of hostility toward Him, and particularly His moral Law — the Ten Commandments (see Romans 8:7). We don't want God telling us what to do. So, we show our contempt for Him by using His Name as a cuss word. We want to party, but we know that He frowns on a lifestyle of blasphemy, lust, fornication, drunkenness, lying, stealing, gossip, and hatred. We love the darkness and hate the light. And so, like the Prodigal Son, we distance ourselves from Him . . . some even denying His existence. It is no coincidence that young men become atheists around the same time that their hormones kick in.

But there's a deathly famine in the life that is devoid of faith. There is a gnawing fear that eats away at the soul. It is the dread of death. It is the knowledge that you are going to die. There's nothing you can do about it, and that thought is terrifying and unbearable.

You try and blot it out with other things, but it remains. You go to therapists for help. Doctors give you deadly drugs. You're afraid to tell anyone that you are fearful of dying. But you do, and they say, "Rita Ora Is Afraid of Dying!"

Let such sobering thoughts cause you to think about God and His claims. We are all living in a moral pigsty. We are doing things that we know are shameful. Our language and thought-life are in the gutter.

Come to your senses. Get up out of the filth of sin, humble yourself and go to the Creator who gave you life. Make your way to the One you have been avoiding and apologize to Him. Say that you are sorry and want to turn from sin — "God, be merciful to me, a sinner." And wonder of wonders! The Father, who has been waiting for this moment, will run toward you, fall on you, and kiss your neck. He will call, "Kill the fatted calf!" He will call for a robe to cover your sin and a ring for your finger! For you were once dead, and now you have been made alive!

That's what Jesus was saying in this story — that while you are away from God, you are dead in your sins. You belong to death. It has the legal rights to you because you serve sin. That's the deadly wages it pays.

Here now is the difference between being religious and being a Christian. Did the son *do* anything to *earn* his father's love? Of course not. The father took the son back because he loved him. His son was guilty of sinning against him, and the father forgave him freely.

The Bible paints us as guilty sinners, and God as a morally per-fect Judge who has seen everything we have done, and every time we sinned we stored up His wrath. Just like a freeway chase through the streets of Los Angeles, every time the lawbreaker breaks the law he makes it worse for himself. Every time we violated God's Law we made it worse for ourselves.

So picture yourself standing guilty in front of the Judge of the universe. What can you do to save yourself? Religion says that you can fast, pray, do good works, etc. But a criminal who offers a judge something in exchange to have his case dismissed is guilty of an attempt to bribe him. That will just add to his crimes. The only thing a guilty criminal can do is throw himself on the mercy of the court.

Religion tries to bribe the Judge, and God will not be bribed. His Word says that *any* sacrifice we offer Him is an abomination to Him. *So don't become religious.* It can't save you from the justice of God. Instead, throw yourself on the mercy of the court, and God can be rich in mercy toward you, because of what happened on the Cross two thousand years ago. You need not offer any sacrifice, because God made the sacrifice Himself, once and for all. Jesus was the sacrificial Lamb who took the punishment for the sin of the world. You and I broke God's Law, and Jesus paid the fine in full. That means that God can legally dismiss your case. Your sins can be forgiven.

When a sin-stained sinner gets up out of the pigsty and goes to the Father, something amazing happens. When you are born again, God gives you His Holy Spirit to help you. But He gives you even more than that. He gives you a new heart with new desires. You will find that you don't *have* to please God. Instead you *want* to please Him.

Hundreds of years before Christ, God spoke of the new birth experience through the prophet Ezekiel. This is what He said:

> I will give you a new heart and put a new spirit within you; I will take the heart of stone out of your flesh and give you a heart of flesh. I will put My Spirit within you and cause you to walk in My statutes, and you will keep My judgments and do them (Ezekiel 36:26–27).

Do you see that? "I will put my Spirit within you and *cause* you to walk in My statutes." That's the miracle of being born again! You *want* to please God. You delight to do His will.

That's called "grace." He saves us because He's good and kind. We don't deserve eternal life, but it is freely given to us because of God's favor — His amazing grace.

Bible Promise

> So we may boldly say: "The LORD is my helper; I will not fear. What can man do to me?" (Hebrews 13:6)

questions ?

1. J.K. Rowling said that depression was the absence of what?
2. Why does Rita Ora have weekly therapy?
3. Finish this verse: "Jesus Christ . . . has abolished . . ." (2 Timothy 1:10).
4. What's the difference between being religious and being a Christian?
5. How would you describe God's grace?

Endnotes

1. https://www.goodreads.com/quotes/388617-depression-is-the-most-unpleasant-thing-i-have-ever-experienced.

2. http://popcrush.com/rita-ora-afraid-of-death/.

3. http://www.telegraph.co.uk/women/womens-life/11824975/Death-anxiety-Feel-stressed-Think-about-how-youre-going-to-die.html.

Chapter 12

Jane Fonda

"I thought depression was the part of my character that made me worthwhile. I thought so little of myself, felt that I had such scant offerings to give to the world, that the one thing that justified my existence at all was my agony." — Elizabeth Wurtzel[1]

Jane Fonda, born December 21, 1937, is an American actress, writer, political activist, former fashion model, and fitness instructor. To her credit, Fonda has been open about her family's depression. Her mother committed suicide when Fonda was 12 years old.[2]

In February of 2014, the *Daily Mail* wrote:

"I have so little time left!" Jane Fonda, 76, reveals she can't stop crying as she comes to terms with her own mortality. She may not look anywhere near her 76 years but Jane Fonda says she is well aware of her age. The Hollywood legend — who has made her career in an industry which isn't exactly kind to aging actresses — admits she has been brought to tears on more than one occasion recently as she comes to terms with her own mortality.

In a thoughtful blog post entitled "Crying," which has since been removed, Jane wrote: "[I've been thinking], how come my tears are so close to the surface? And I've come to feel it has to do with age. I have become so wonderfully, terribly aware of time, of how little of it I have left; how much of it is behind me, and everything becomes so precious."[3]

The whole of humanity is quietly crying about death. But we hide our tears from others because we are proud. But Jane's tears and words (that didn't stay online for long), speak volumes.

Chronic depression comes as a gloomy black cloud, not because life is bad, *but because life is good.* With all of its problems and pain, life is wonderful . . . with its friends and family, its love and laughter, sunrises and sunsets, playful puppies and cute kittens, with its beautiful birds and colorful flutter-by butterflies. Life is more than good. And so the more it is loved and its blessings are appreciated, the greater the wrenching will be as death rips this precious possession from our unwilling hands. That's why there are such bitter tears. That's why there is sorrow beyond words. That's why I wept in 1972 and Bruce Springsteen wept Old Yeller tears alone on the beach.

Simone de Beauvoir, in *Memoirs of a Dutiful Daughter,* spoke of this:

> The fear of death never left me; I couldn't get used to the thought; I would still sometimes shake and weep with terror. By contrast, the fact of existence here and now sometimes took on a glorious splendor.[4]

A Conversation with Jane Fonda

Aging can be cruel. Particularly for famous women, and for famous pretty women who are admired for their beauty. I not only think of you, but I think of stars such as Lucille Ball. As the lines of time did their painful work and carved into her stunning natural beauty, the contrast between the young and the old was very public. And so we had the phenomenon of the Hollywood recluse, hiding from her once-adoring fans.

I once read the words, "You know that you're getting old when you walk around a puddle rather than through it." From that day until now I deliberately walk through puddles — defiant of the aging process. So I empathize with every bitter teardrop that falls from your face.

Ask any of the elderly how they feel, and they will often widen their eyes and tell you that they still *feel* that they are same person they were in their teenage years, except that they can't move at the same speed. They put their foot on the accelerator, but the car is out of gas.

The question is, Why? Why would God shower us with all of these wonderful things and then have time cruelly take them away with such painful permanency?

The Bible says it's all because of sin . . . and because of such, we should never think of the pleasures of sin without thinking of the pain of death. The two go hand-in-hand: "The wages of *sin is death*" (Romans 6:23), "The soul who *sins* shall *die*" (Ezekiel 18:20), "The Law of *sin* and *death*" (Romans 8:2). If we want to be free from death, what started out with a passionate embrace must part because of irreconcilable differences. Our love affair with sin has to end.

Time shows us the effects of sin. It ravages the ravishing. But the *real* result of sin can be seen in the *spiritual* realm. When we sin, we sin against God, and in His morally perfect eyes the sight is more than ugly, it's *abominable*. Those who deny the ugliness of sin and cling to self-righteousness (saying that man is basically good) have either never seen themselves in the moral mirror, or any gaze has been with the light turned down low.

But for us to live, the light dimmer mustn't be used. We have to see what we look like, and that takes the light of a tender conscience. I must ask myself, have I ever lied? Even once? Have I stolen anything, irrespective of its value? Have I ever used God's Holy Name in vain — as a cuss word to express disgust? Have I looked with lust, and in doing so committed adultery in my heart (see Matthew 5:27–28). The truth is that each of us have done these things, and loved it. The Book of Job, when speaking of mankind, said, "If God puts no trust in His saints, and the heavens are not pure in His sight, how much less man, who is abominable and filthy, who drinks iniquity like water!" (Job 15:15–16).

The only way any human being can be free from death is to be free from sin, and how could that ever happen? None of us are morally perfect. All of us have sinned and fallen woefully short of the glory of God. Jesus said, "Blessed are the pure in heart, for they shall see God" (Matthew 5:8), and it doesn't take a rocket scientist to figure out that if that is the criteria, none of us will then see God.

I saw where you once said,

> I was stunned when I read in William Bridges's *The Way of Transition*, that in Matthew 5:48 when Jesus tells his disciples, "You, therefore, must be perfect, as your heavenly Father is perfect," it was a mistranslation of the Greek adjective *teleios* which actually means "whole, fully formed, fully developed." Jesus wasn't telling his disciples to be perfect like God, he was telling them to be whole like God.[5]

But this isn't a mistranslation. Deuteronomy 18:13 says, "Thou shalt be perfect with the LORD thy God" (KJV). We are told that God is morally perfect, His Law is perfect (see Psalm 19:7), and God's perfect Law demands moral perfection. This is why we are to preach Christ and Him crucified:

> "Him we preach, warning every man and teaching every man in all wisdom, *that we may present every man perfect in Christ Jesus*" (Colossians 1:28, italics added).

The mirror of the moral Law leaves us hopeless and helpless. It reflects our utter moral depravity. We are all "as an unclean thing" (see Isaiah 64:6). And so it sends us to the font of mercy. It sends us to the water of God's grace for cleansing.

And that's the miracle of God's grace. Because of the suffering death of Jesus of Nazareth, He can justify us. "Justification" is the process by which God washes away our sins and clothes us with the purity of the righteousness of Christ, making it as though we have never sinned. He makes us pure in His eyes, because of His amazing grace. We are made perfect in Christ.

Until we come to the Savior, sin has us chained to death, and every movement we make, we will hear the rattle of those deathly chains. And that reminds us of the fearful day of our execution. That's the reason for universal chronic depression.

Back in 1738, Charles Wesley wrote the famous words:

> Long my imprisoned spirit lay,
> Fast bound in sin and nature's night;
> Thine eye diffused a quickening ray —

I woke, the dungeon flamed with light;
My chains fell off, my heart was free,
I rose, went forth, and followed Thee.[6]

The new birth is like the miracle of metamorphosis. God takes the helpless and lowly caterpillar and makes it into a beautiful butterfly. He takes us in our sinful and helpless state, and hides us in the cocoon of Jesus Christ. The Scriptures say, "If anyone is in Christ, he is a new creation" (2 Corinthians 5:17), and that new creature will one day become glorified. We will receive a new body, and it will happen in a moment of time: "in the twinkling of an eye . . . we shall be changed" (1 Corinthians 15:52). This is the teaching of Holy Scripture. It is the glorious hope of the Christian, and our trusting that it is true is the effective means of banishing the fear of death.

Bible Promise

For I am persuaded that neither death nor life, nor angels nor principalities nor powers, nor things present nor things to come, nor height nor depth, nor any other created thing, shall be able to separate us from the love of God which is in Christ Jesus our Lord" (Romans 8:38–39).

questions?

1. At 76, Jane Fonda can't stop crying. Why?
2. What does it mean that "chronic depression comes as a gloomy black cloud, not because life is bad, but because life is good"?
3. What did Simone de Beauvoir say about the splendor of life?
4. With what should we always pair the pleasures of sin?
5. According to Romans 8:38–39, what can separate us from the love of God?

Endnotes

1. https://www.brainyquote.com/quotes/elizabeth_wurtzel_334895.
2. http://www.etonline.com/news/186813_why_jane_fonda_went_to_therapy_after_filming_grace_frankie/.

3. http://www.dailymail.co.uk/tvshowbiz/article-2566899/Jane-Fonda-76-reveals-stop-crying-comes-terms-mortality.html.

4. https://www.goodreads.com/quotes/8092283-the-fear-of-death-never-left-me-i-couldn-t-get.

5. http://www.janefonda.com/about-my-faith/.

6. "And Can It Be That I Should Gain," words by Charles Wesley, music by Thomas Campbell.

Chapter 13

Amanda Peet

"The pupil dilates in darkness and in the end finds light, just as the soul dilates in misfortune and in the end finds God." — Victor Hugo, *Les Misérables*[1]

Amanda Peet (born January 11, 1972) is an American actress and author who has appeared in film, stage, and television. In February of 2016, Amanda Peet appeared on "The Late Show" with Stephen Colbert and put him into a very awkward moment. Things got real, soon after the *Late Night* host asked Peet about her HBO show *Togetherness*. On the show, many of the characters struggle through mid-life crises as they attempt to cope with where they are without losing sight of where they'd like to be. Given that premise, Colbert talked with Peet, who recently had another child with her highly successful husband David Benioff (one of the producers on *Game of Thrones*).

Here is a transcript of the interview:

> Stephen Colbert: "You've got a lovely life. What do you know from the mid-life crisis, is this a stretch for you?"
>
> Amanda Peet: "*No!* Forty-four is really . . . it's quite something."
>
> SC: "You don't look like a personal crisis to me. What is your crisis?"
>
> AP: "It's on-going."
>
> SC: "I'm catching your mid crisis right now?"
>
> AP: "Yes. But you know how some men hit middle-age and they go get a motorcycle? I had a baby. . . ."
>
> SC: "What do you worry about?"

AP: *"I fear death!"*

SC: "Death?"

AP: "Yes!"

SC: "Okay. Well . . . maybe. What's . . . we all die . . . we all die."

AP: "Right."

SC: "Keep it light. We all die. It's the late night talk show, keep it light, keep it light. Maybe you'll go to heaven. You'll die and go the heaven."

AP: "Okay. That's where I need help. You're Catholic, right? I'm Jewish."

SC: "What do you believe?"

AP: "I need to know what to believe in!"

SC: "Like, what happens when you die?"

AP: "Yes. I don't want to be a bag of dust!"

SC: "I don't really know . . . I don't know what happens. I kind of believe, I kind of want the pearly gates and all that.

AP: "This is not inspirational."

SC: "Not helping?"[2]

A Conversation with Amanda Peet

I admire your bold humility in admitting *on international television* that you fear death. My heart breaks for you and for the millions, who just like you, are groping for truth. The Bible describes us as being like the groping blind until the eyes of our understanding are enlightened:

> And He has made from one blood every nation of men to dwell on all the face of the earth, and has determined their pre-appointed times and the boundaries of their dwellings, so that they should seek the Lord, in the hope that they might grope for Him and find Him, though He is not far from each one of us (Acts 17:26–27).

Allen Atzbi (the General Manager of Living Waters) has Jewish roots. You may identify with him in his search for the truth:

> I'm a skeptic. I always have been. I question things. I have a need to understand before I make big decisions.

So as a teen with a Jewish father named Mordecai and a Muslim stepfather named Mohammed, and a bunch of druggy friends who were atheists, agnostics, or thought they were God, when it came to religion I sure didn't abandon my skepticism. I did some serious critical thinking.

When I died, common sense dictated that I wasn't going to stand before 50 Gods and just pick the one I liked. Either there was one God or no God at all, and I needed to know.

I knew I was dirty. I was stained by my sins, and no amount of joking around or entertaining distraction could erase it. I could taste it in my darkest moments. I had broken the Ten Commandments like a neighbor's windowpane and needed forgiveness. I needed to be clean again.

I knew I was guilty, I knew I needed forgiveness, but what is the right path to God? Who can forgive me? Jehovah, Buddha, Allah, karma, Zeus? I had pieced together the message of Jesus Christ from two friends and Christian TV, and somehow I knew He was true. Faith came in me. But being the natural skeptic, I knew people believed in all sorts of crazy things because of a convincing, charismatic leader, peer-pressure or mob mentality, or a dozen other mental processes. So I struggled quite a bit. I wanted to intellectually "know" that I was following the true path to God.

I discovered that there are ancient supernatural prophecies about a coming Savior that reveal many specific details about Him, so when He came all who wanted the truth would be able to recognize Him.

I didn't realize it until some years later, but when the good news of Jesus Christ was shared in the first century, in the book of Acts, they always shared about these treasured Jewish prophecies of the coming Messiah. They expected people to be skeptical, they expected there to be honest questions — their whole way of life would change if they followed Jesus (many would even die in severe persecution if they believed). In fact, God Himself wanted these prophecies heard, it's part of the good news; He embedded them within His Holy Scriptures for truth seekers to find. These predictions are spread like breadcrumbs throughout the entire Jewish Bible to lead us to the Savior. God used these to intellectually convince me that Jesus was the truth path to God.

Let me share just two:

* Isaiah 53. The entire chapter is about the Messiah. It explains that He would be a man of suffering, who would be wounded and bruised for the sins of the people, die with criminals, and be buried in a rich man's tomb.

Not long ago I saw a YouTube video of people on the streets being asked to read this passage, and then asked who it was referring to, without mentioning where it was in the Bible. People immediately knew it was speaking of Jesus. Read the chapter, forgetting that it was written 700 years before Jesus' birth, and see what you think. Ancient Jewish rabbis and scholars, including the Babylonian Talmud, saw Isaiah 53 as a prophecy about their Messiah.

* Daniel 9:24–26. A prophecy that predicts, 500 years before Jesus' birth, the exact year the Messiah would die for the sins of the people (right when Jesus died). It also says He would come before the destruction of the Second Temple, which happened in 70 A.D.

There are several others, but you can Google them.

Peter Stoner, in his book *Science Speaks,* determined the probability of one man fulfilling eight of the prophecies of the Old Testament for the Messiah to be 1 in 10 to the 17th power.

Try to imagine that. If we took that many silver dollars (100,000,000,000,000,000) and laid them over the State of Texas, they would cover the entire state two feet deep. Now draw a black X on one of the silver dollars, stir the whole mass thoroughly, blindfold a person, and tell him that they can travel as far as they want but they can only pick up one silver dollar and that must be the marked one. What chance would they have of picking up the right one? It would be the exact same odds of anyone fulfilling just eight of the Messianic prophecies by chance alone.

Peter Stoner then goes on to consider the possibility of any one person fulfilling 48 of the prophecies by chance. Here the odds jump to 1 in 10 to the 157th power. That number would look like this:

1 out of 100,000,000,000,000,000,000,000,000,000, 000,000,000,000,000,000,000,000,000,000,000,000,000 ,000,000,000,000,000,000,000,000,000,000,000,000,00 0,000,000,000,000,000,000,000,000,000,000,000,000,0 00,000,000,000,000.[3]

I encourage you to be an honest skeptic too, and ask the hard questions, and don't settle until you have the answers. Thank you for listening to a little of my spiritual journey.

Bible Promise

For you did not receive the spirit of bondage again to fear, but you received the Spirit of adoption by whom we cry out, "Abba, Father" (Romans 8:15).

questions ?

1. Stephen Colbert asked, "What do you worry about?" What did Amanda Peet reply?
2. What do you think of her for being so open?
3. According to Acts 17:26–27, what is the five-letter word the Scriptures use to show our helplessness in coming to God?
4. To what physical disability does the Bible allude?
5. Explain Ephesians 4:18.

Endnotes

1. https://www.goodreads.com/quotes/10397-the-pupil-dilates-in-darkness-and-in-the-end-finds.
2. https://youtu.be/6RWWq5_wZy8; http://dev30.denisonforum.org/main-articles/entertainment/2405-actress-describes-her-fear-of-death.
3. https://goodfishbadfish.wordpress.com/2016/12/24/im-a-skeptic-allen-atzbi/.

Chapter 14

Rodney Dangerfield

"He has turned his life around. He used to be depressed and miserable. Now he's miserable and depressed." — David Frost[1]

Rodney Dangerfield (November 22, 1921– October 5, 2004) was an American stand-up comedian, actor, producer, and screenwriter.

The veteran comedian known for his "I get no respect" line of jokes is opening up about his lifelong battle with depression in "Health Week," a PBS medical show. "People think comedians are never depressed — that they're always happy, but depression has been with me all my life," Dangerfield says on the program. "I was writing jokes when I was 15 — not out of happiness, but to escape."

Fearing the stigma of mental illness and convinced change was impossible, Dangerfield suffered in silence for years.

"Some see the glass half-empty, others half-full," he said. "The way I see it, it's always empty."[2]

Dangerfield said,

My life is nothing but pressure. All pressure. This pressure is like a heaviness. It's always on top of me, this heaviness. It's always there since I'm a kid. Other people wake up in the morning, "A new day! Ah, up and at 'em!" I wake up, the heaviness is waiting for me. Sometimes I even talk to it. I say [adopts cheerful voice] "Hi, heaviness!" and the heaviness looks back at me, [in an ominous growl] "Today you're gonna get it good. You'll be drinking early today."[3]

In considering the cause of chronic depression, we could look at Dangerfield's "My life is nothing but pressure. All pressure," and wonder if it is caused by the pressure of our modern way of living. However, this doesn't seem to be the case:

It is a myth that depression is something that predominantly affects Western societies. Researchers from the University of Queensland, who claim to have made the most comprehensive study of depression and anxiety, concluded that depression and anxiety exist in every society in the world today.[4]

He once said, "My fan club broke up. The guy died." And, " I got lost on the beach. A cop came and helped me look for my parents. I asked him, 'Do you think we'll find them?' He said, 'I don't know kid, there are so many places they could hide.' "

A Conversation with Rodney Dangerfield

Almost everyone loves your self-deprecating humor. I have often used it when an audience may not know me. It quickly melts the coldest of ice. I was once looking at my physique in the mirror and mumbled, "Could be worse," when I heard my wife say, "Not much."

That sort of humor endears an audience to a speaker, and that's what your humor did for you. Rabbi Joseph Telushkin, author of *Jewish Humor: What the Best Jewish Jokes Say About the Jews*, calls it the "distressed optimist." If there is one hallmark of Jewish humor, says Rabbi Telushkin, it is the absurd ability to keep us "laughing in order not to cry."[5]

As I read of your battle with depression, there is a sadness. Not just for you, but for the millions like you who appreciate humor and love laughter despite their daily battle with depression.

Bible Promise

Whenever I am afraid, I will trust in You. In God (I will praise His word), In God I have put my trust; I will not fear. What can flesh do to me? (Psalm 56:3–4).

questions **?**

1. Why was Rodney Dangerfield writing jokes at the age of 15?
2. Why did he suffer in silence for many years?
3. What did researchers from the University of Queensland discover about depression and anxiety?
4. What is self-deprecating humor?
5. What did Rabbi Telushkin say of Jewish humor?

Endnotes

1. https://www.goodreads.com/quotes/355012-he-s-turned-his-life-around-he-used-to-be-depressed.

2. http://www.deseretnews.com/article/584113/Dangerfield-standing-up-in-fight-with-depression.html?pg=all.

3. https://film.avclub.com/rodney-dangerfield-s-it-s-not-easy-bein-me-a-lifetime-1798225298.

4. http://www.medicalnewstoday.com/articles/251300.php.

5. http://www.beliefnet.com/entertainment/2004/10/rodney-dangerfield-jewish-everyman.aspx.

Chapter 15

Rosie O'Donnell

He: What's the matter with you?
Me: Nothing.
Nothing was slowly clotting my arteries. Nothing slowly numbing my soul. Caught by nothing, saying nothing, nothingness becomes me. When I am nothing they will say surprised in the way that they are forever surprised, "but there was nothing the matter with her." — Jeanette Winterson, *Gut Symmetries*[1]

Roseann "Rosie" O'Donnell (born March 21, 1962) is an American comedian, actress, author, and television personality. She says that she fights off depression through medication and yoga — and by hanging upside down for up to 30 minutes each day.

O'Donnell, 44, says she first began treatment for depression after the Columbine massacre in 1999. "I couldn't stop crying," she says in an episode of *The View*. "I stayed in my room. The lights were off. I couldn't get out of bed, and that's when I started taking medication."[2]

> The Columbine High School massacre was what pushed her over the edge, O'Donnell said. She became obsessed with the idea that there was danger everywhere, and that no one was safe. She worried about her three adopted children. She would wake up in the middle of the night four or five times, gripped by fear. It got to the point that she considered leaving her talk show and checking into a hospital.
>
> O'Donnell says she was depressed even as a child, feeling that there was a darkness in her home but not knowing what

99

it was. In fact, depression runs in her family. . . . O'Donnell's aunt was severely depressed and attempted suicide when she was a child. O'Donnell remembers watching her aunt at parties, sluggish from the lithium she was taking, unable to remember the names of her nieces and nephews. It scared her.[3]

Speaking further, on *The View*, she said,

But in life, you have two choices always, faith or fear. A government should lead by faith, never by fear.

And faith is not Christianity, faith in humanity, faith in equality.[4]

A Conversation with Rosie O'Donnell

Patrick Swayze tragically died of cancer with his family at his side on September 14, 2009, at the age of 57. He said, "The longer your life goes on, the more death you face."[5] That is true for most of us. I reached 20 years of age before I lost any friends. It was because of the prevalence of drug abuse in the surfing world in the early 1970s that five of them tragically died.

One of my friends managed to avoid death through drug abuse, but he told me that he believed life wasn't worth living over 50. Rodney said that he would kill himself when he reached that age. He kept his word.

But life need not be a depressing downhill slide leading to a hopeless dead end, if we look to our Creator and are born again (see John 3:3).

The odds are that you will never read this. But there are millions of others out there that are just like you. They are thinkers. When they see death around them, they continue to live, but in a quiet despair because of the futility of life and because of the fear of death.

Hollywood's Assumption

Hollywood rarely fails to use the death psalm — Psalm 23 — at a funeral in the movies. This is probably because they assume it's speaking about death when it says, "Yea, though I walk through the valley of the shadow of death I will fear no evil" (verse 4). But it's not talking about death. It's talking about the opposite.

If I am in the *shadow* of a building, I'm not *in* the building, I'm just in close proximity to it. When the Bible speaks of the shadow of death, it's not speaking of our coming death — it is speaking of this life. The shadow of death is in close proximity to us. It hangs over each of us every day. In speaking of the living, the Bible says,

> The people who sat in darkness have seen a great light, and upon those who sat in the region and shadow of death Light has dawned (Matthew 4:16).

This life is called "the shadow of death," and the Scriptures tell us that all humanity "sits" in the shadow of death. We are not going anywhere. As condemned prisoners, we are held captive, awaiting execution because we are guilty of violating an eternal Law. In the next 24 hours, 150,000 human beings, people who are just like you and me, with a love of life and a fear of death, will die. If there was ever a justified cause for chronic depression, that is it.

Bible Promise

> Fear not, for I am with you; be not dismayed, for I am your God. I will strengthen you, yes, I will help you, I will uphold you with My righteous right hand (Isaiah 41:10).

questions?

1. How does Rosie O'Donnell fight off depression each day?
2. What was it that pushed her "over the edge" to take medication?
3. What did Patrick Swayze say about life?
4. What is the "shadow of death"?
5. How many people die every 24 hours?

Endnotes

1. https://www.goodreads.com/quotes/442131-he-what-s-the-matter-with-you-me-nothing-nothing-was.

2. http://people.com/celebrity/rosie-says-she-hangs-upside-down-for-depression/.

3. http://abcnews.go.com/GMA/Depression/story?id=126783&page=1.

4. http://www.crosswalk.com/1424194/.

5. https://www.brainyquote.com/quotes/patrick_swayze_450360.

Chapter 16

Rod Steiger

"I am living in a nightmare, from which from time to time I wake in sleep." — Ursula K. Le Guin[1]

Rodney Stephen "Rod" Steiger (April 14, 1925–July 9, 2002) was an American actor, noted for his portrayal of offbeat, often volatile and crazed characters.

"It's difficult for the public to realize how powerful the mind is, and how much pain the mind can give you. When you're depressed, it's as though this committee has taken over your mind, leaving you one depressing thought after the other. You don't shave, you don't shower, you don't brush your teeth. You don't care." Rod Steiger, *On the Edge of Darkness*[2]

"When you're depressed, there's no calendar. There are no dates, there's no day, there's no night, there's no seconds, there's no minutes, there's nothing. You're just existing in this cold, murky, ever-heavy atmosphere, like they put you inside a vial of mercury." Rod Steiger, *On the Edge of Darkness*[3]

Steiger suffered from depression throughout much of his life. He described himself as "incapacitated for about eight years with clinical depression" before his Oscar win for *In The Heat of the Night*.[4]

In one of his final interviews, he stated that there was a stigma wrongfully attached to sufferers of depression and that it was caused by a chemical imbalance, not a mental disease. He commented:

"Pain must never be a source of shame. It's a part of life, it's part of humanity."[5]

I believe that Steiger was right in saying that depression isn't a mental disease. Yet "experts" insist on calling it such:

> Robin Williams' apparent suicide has put a spotlight on the dark side of comedy. Williams, like many comedians, lived with long-term depression and addiction. Experts say these mental illnesses are no laughing matter.
>
> "Comedy can often be a defensive posture against depression," said Deborah Serani, a clinical psychologist who treats performers with depression and other mental health problems. Serani, author of the book *Living with Depression*, said that for many comedians, humor is a "counter phobic" response to the darkness and sadness they feel. Their intelligence, she said, helps them put a funny spin on their despair."[6]

The problem with the experts is that they have no absolute standard by which to judge mental health. Who is mentally imbalanced — someone who really believes that they are a primate? How about those who drink a toxin (poison) called alcohol? Is someone sane who is self-destructive by breathing poisonous smoke into their lungs in the form of a cigarette?

> So 100,000s of readers now know that scientifically, it's not alcohol that causes people to live longer, but it is simply being with others and that they are less socially isolated when they drink that prolongs their lives. After all, alcohol is a toxin.[7]

Is a man sane who believes he's a woman and therefore should frequent women's restrooms? A generation ago he would have been put in prison or diagnosed as having serious psychiatric problems. How about a mother who insists on her legal right to pay someone to kill her unborn child? Is that sane? We can't definitively say what is normal or perverted, truth or error, right or wrong, without an absolute standard by which to measure. If there is no unchanging reference, then there can be no "normal."

The Test

There are three main criteria that are commonly used to determine whether a person might have a psychological disorder. These are:

The person's behavior violates culturally determined standards or acceptability.

The person's behavior is maladaptive or harmful to that person or others.

The person suffers from distress.[8]

A. What are "culturally determined standards or acceptability"? Are these standards determined by the majority? If the 350 million people who WHO says are suffering from depression say that their depression is justified in today's culture, does depression then become culturally acceptable, and qualify as normal and sane? Or are normalities determined by a few elite, self-appointed, professing non-depressants?

B. Are sufferers from depression deemed as being sane if they don't aspire to harm themselves or others? Who makes that determination?

C. If the criteria for mental disease is that the person "suffers from distress," then add millions of Los Angeles freeway drivers to the client list.

According to *Newsweek*, "Nearly 1 in 5 Americans Suffer from Mental Illness Each Year."[9] That means that 65 *million* Americans suffer from mental disease. Spreading such a wide net may be good business for psychologists and drug companies, but it's unethical and perhaps cruel. While some may get a sense of relief when they are diagnosed as being mentally ill, others who are suicidal may be pushed in that direction because of the social stigma. That last straw may be enough to break the already weak camel's back.

Do we seriously think that people such as Carrie Fisher, Stephen Fry, and Bruce Springsteen are mentally imbalanced? Rather, millions of sane people aspire to be like them.

Again, those who are depressed about life and death are not mentally ill. They are realists who understand that life is deeply depressing and almost intolerable, because they see no hope.

Bible Promise

Be strong and of good courage, do not fear nor be afraid of them; for the LORD your God, He is the One who goes with you. He will not leave you nor forsake you (Deuteronomy 31:6).

questions **?**

1. Ursula K. Le Guin said, "I am living in a nightmare, from which from time to time I wake in sleep." What does she mean?
2. Does the above quote motivate you to reach out to the lost?
3. How long was Rod Steiger "incapacitated with clinical depression"?
4. What did Rod Steiger say about the "pain" of depression?
5. According to *Newsweek*, "Nearly 1 in 5 Americans Suffer from Mental Illness Each Year." How many million is that?

Endnotes

1. https://www.goodreads.com/quotes/100043-i-am-living-in-a-nightmare-from-which-from-time.

2. http://www.wingofmadness.com/reflections-on-depression/.

3. Ibid.

4. Chris Sullivan, "Never Meet Your Hero. Unless it's Rod Steiger," *Sabotage Times*, https://sabotagetimes.com/life/interview-with-a-legend-rod-steiger.

5. "Rod Steiger Interview by Matias A. Bombal," MAB Archives, October 2000; https://sabotagetimes.com/life/interview-with-a-legend-rod-steiger.

6. Liz Neporent, "What's the Deal with Comedians and Depression?" ABC News, 8-12-2014; https://abcnews.go.com/Health/deal-comedians-depression/story?id=24945911.

7. https://www.psychologytoday.com/blog/addiction-in-society/201011/science-is-what-society-says-it-is-alcohols-poison.

8. http://www.sparknotes.com/psychology/psych101/disorders/study.html.

9. http://www.newsweek.com/nearly-1-5-americans-suffer-mental-illness-each-year-230608.

Chapter 17

Woody Allen

"I am young now and can look upon my body and soul with pride. But it will be mangled soon, and later it will begin to disintegrate, and then I shall die, and die conclusively. How can we face such a fact, and not live in fear?" — Jack Kerouac[1]

W oody Allen (born December 1935) is an American actor, author, filmmaker, comedian, playwright, and musician, whose career spans more than six decades.

After the suicide of Robin Williams, Woody Allen said,

Everybody feels that pain and existential loneliness and terror. When you see it in a comic persona, you tend to think it's special because the person is so funny and seems to be the very antithesis of gloom. How ironic that that person is sad. But he's no sadder than the guy who drives a cab. It just looks more ironic on him as he makes his living as a funnyman.[2]

"I wish I had grown up sanguine and buoyant and not obsessed with these questions, but I didn't," he told *Time Out*. "My mother said that I was a very happy kid until about five years old and then I turned sour."

Nothing happened: I had no traumas in the family, nobody died. I never missed a meal. Everything was fine. I think the trauma was that I realized: my G-d [blasphemy], this ends! It comes to a point where one day you vanish. You totally vanish for ever. You're gone. Period."[3]

He also said:

> Maybe it's because I'm depressed so often that I'm drawn to writers like Kafka, Dostoyevski, and to a film-maker like Bergman. I think I have all the symptoms and problems that their characters are occupied with: an obsession with death, an obsession with God or the lack of God, the question of why we are here. Almost all of my work is autobiographical — exaggerated but true.[4]

The following exchange is from another interview.

> *Interviewer:* Like Colin Firth's character Stanley in this film, you've always said you don't believe in God, just in cold, hard reason. But if you look at Stanley, that doesn't seem like much fun.
>
> *Woody Allen:* I know, that's the problem. Years ago I was on television with [evangelist] Billy Graham and we were debating this in a friendly way, and he said to me, "Even if I'm wrong and you're right, then when I die and there's nothing, I'll still have had a better life than you." And I'm thinking: Yes, you're right.'
>
> *Interviewer:* So were you exploring that same conundrum when writing Colin Firth's character?
>
> *Woody Allen:* Yes, he is like a character in an Ingmar Bergman film, who wants to believe but can't because his common sense, his intelligence, his logic and rationality tell him clearly: what you see is what you get. There is no after-life, heaven, God, Santa Claus. We live for a while, then everything is over. Eventually the universe will be gone. Everything will be gone. All the works of Shakespeare and Beethoven. The sun will burn out, the Earth will be gone. Eventually the entire universe — the entire universe — will be gone. There will be nothing, no light, no air. Nothing![5]

Other quotes by Allen include:

You need to tell yourself a couple of lies to get through life," he said. "Otherwise it's too grisly. If you don't have a stong denial mechanism, try waking up in your bed at 3am when there are no distractions. You get a cold chill.[6]

I'm not afraid of death; I just don't want to be there when it happens.[7]

But your back hurts more, you get more indigestion, your eyesight isn't as good and you need a hearing aid. It's a bad business getting older and I would advise you not to do it if you can avoid it.[8]

One must have one's delusions to live. If you look at life too honestly and too clearly life does become unbearable because it's a pretty grim enterprise.[9]

This is my perspective and has always been my perspective on life. I have a very grim, pessimistic view of it. . . . I do feel that it is a grim, painful, nightmarish, meaningless experience and that the only way that you can be happy is if you tell yourself some lies and deceive yourself.[10]

A Conversation with Woody Allen

I admire both your dry humor, and your honesty about death. Most don't admit that they're afraid of dying. To openly talk about it is perhaps too personal, too humbling, or too fearful.

A young lady named Gillian was also honest when she wrote the following letter to a hypnotist therapist:

Fear of death. I forget about it sometimes; I might be at a party or having dinner with friends, and then it hits me all over again. I'm going to die! I don't know when, but I do know it will happen sometime. One day I won't be here, none of us will. I feel frightened, sad, and immediately stop enjoying myself — what's the point because I'll be dead one day anyway! It happens at night sometimes, too — I become acutely aware, not just a thought, but a strong *feeling* that one day I'll be gone . . . forever. I just want to forget about it like other people seem to do; after all, I'm young and, as far as I know, healthy.[11]

Like you, she was frighteningly honest. Life *is* dark and scary. In one interview you use the word "grim" three times to describe it. Life is grim because we all know we have to face the you-know-what reaper. You began thinking about that at the age of five. Most of us have a measure of that level of thinking at a young age, but death is for the elderly. As we mature, and death takes our beloved pets, then our friends and family, and we hear of young people and celebrities dying, it dawns on us that it is universal and can come to any of us at any moment. Grim indeed. However, there is one positive spark of light when it comes to the darkest of subjects. It may cause us to listen to reason. So I want to reason with you . . . if you will let me.

You have come to the age where your kids leave the nest, and in time, you and your bride enter what is referred to as your golden years. But placing a "g" at the front of *olden* years does little to change them. Menopause and equipment malfunctions take the sweetness out of the honeymoon. Among other things, you get upbeat mail from undertakers and crematoriums who offer exciting sales, deep discounts and deathly deals. The vultures are hovering.

Murphy's Law proves to be a reality: *What can go wrong will go wrong.* The knees go, the memory goes, so does the hair, eyesight, memory, steadiness of the hands, and hearing. On top of that, we even shrink and, of course, the memory goes. *Or did I already say that?* Everything wonderful about life dissipates: youthful looks, healthy skin, bright eyes, white teeth, energy, sharpness of mind, and up comes the heartburn, along with insomnia, vertigo, shortness of breath, and the joy of acid reflux. And all that is just the tip of the cold elderly iceberg. There's also Parkinson's disease, multiple sclerosis, stroke, Lou Gehrig's, Alzheimer's, and a long list of other horrors. Then again, the odds are that cancer will get in first and take us out. So what will it be — skin cancer, brain cancer, lung, esophagus, kidney, or liver? There's also the big kill-joy of heart disease. Then again, cancer may not take us out. Check America's accidental death statistics: Death by texting: 6,000. Falling off the Grand Canyon: 12. Falling at home: 6,000. Traffic lights: 2,000.

Choking on food: 3,000. High School football: 12. Contaminated food: 5,000. Bee stings: 100. Falling off horses: 20. Falls from ladders: 355.

That's not the complete list. From 2005–2014, there were an annual average of 3,536 fatal drownings in the United States.[12]

Depressed even further? This isn't a pretty picture. So, is there no God? Or is life some sort of divine comedy? If God exists, where is He in all this misery? Is this the way He planned it?

The answer to that question, is "No," not according to the Bible. We have all these horrible things (as we have seen earlier) because of the Curse that God put on Adam and his descendants.

Despite all these gloomy, depressing, and grim thoughts, it's in the interest of every atheist for Him to exist, if He is indeed merciful. If He is the reservoir of life as the Bible says, it's in your highest interest to see if you can negotiate some sort of deal before you are swallowed by this monster.

As an atheist, I would assume that certain beliefs you have about God shape your worldview. So let me see if I can broaden the context to some of the more common atheist convictions.

You more than likely think that there's no solid scientific evidence for God's existence and that it is just a matter of *believing* or having a blind faith. So let's see is there is scientific evidence.

The Evidence

Could you believe that this book happened by accident? The paper formed itself into pages, and the ink fell from nowhere and formed itself into coherent sentences with commas, exclamation points, periods, and capital letters? Could you believe that ink also fell onto the paper and formed itself into page numbers on the appropriate corners of each page in sequential order? *Of course you couldn't.* It's foolish talk. It is not within the realm of possibility.

I'm sure that you are familiar with DNA. It is the information that instructs your cells on how to form your skin, muscles, hair, eyes, ears, nose, teeth, and even your personality. Everything about you was in your DNA from the moment you were conceived. There is so much information and amazing programming in DNA that scientists call it "The book of life."

What would you think of the mentality of some who could believe that a physical book could make itself? I'm sure that if you yourself are sane, you would say that they have serious mental problems. And what would you think of the mentality of someone who believed that DNA made itself . . . an atheist? To believe that DNA made itself is *beyond* insane. It is without the realm of possibility. It is not even remotely possible. DNA could not make itself. Atheism is a stretch of the imagination, way beyond the breaking point.

So there you have irrefutable evidence for intelligent design and the Intelligent Designer.

Perhaps you're saying that God can't exist because we see suffering everywhere. But that's like saying, "My house has developed really serious cracks in the walls. *Therefore there was no builder.*" That's an illogical leap. *Every* house has a builder. Structural problems don't get rid of the builder. They merely show that there is *something wrong* with the building. If you then want the building fixed, you should go back to the builder and find out why it's like it is.

Your building is falling apart and is about to be demolished. You need to go back to the Maker and have all things made new. You need to be born again if you want to keep your life.

Someone once said that the difference between God and humanity is that God is never so confused that He thinks He's us. We do think we are like God. We think that we are eternal and that death is only what happens to others. But we are finite. We are weak. We are mortal. That's why we need His help.

Your Worth

No one is sure how many millions you have in your piggy bank. Some say 60 million; others say it's more like 80 million. Whatever the case, the film industry has been good to you. Despite the confusion about how much you have, I know *exactly* how much you are going to leave when you die. *All of it.*

When Jesus spoke of a certain rich man, He said,

> "The ground of a certain rich man yielded plentifully. And he thought within himself, saying, 'What shall I do, since I have no room to store my crops?' So he said, 'I will

do this: I will pull down my barns and build greater, and there I will store all my crops and my goods. And I will say to my soul, "Soul, you have many goods laid up for many years; take your ease; eat, drink, and be merry."' But God said to him, 'Fool! This night your soul will be required of you; then whose will those things be which you have provided?' So is he who lays up treasure for himself, and is not rich toward God." Luke 12:16–21

So, what are you going to do? Stay under the shadow of the guillotine or move away? Do you like the fear in which you live? Some try to escape it by taking their own lives. Is that the future path you plan? If you think that that is how you are going to be in control of your death, it's not. You are surrendering to it.

What have you got to lose by trusting in Jesus? Your pride? Is His very Name an offense to you? It's not offensive when it's said in vain. It is one of the most popular cuss words. Have you ever wondered why? Look at what the Bible says Jesus did 2,000 years ago and see how pin-pointedly accurate it is in describing your situation:

Therefore, since [these His] children share in flesh and blood [the physical nature of mankind], He Himself in a similar manner also shared in the same [physical nature, but without sin], so that through [experiencing] death He might make powerless (ineffective, impotent) him who had the power of death — that is, the devil — and [that He] might free all those who through [the haunting] fear of death were held in slavery throughout their lives (Hebrews 2:14–15; AMP)

Woody, you can be delivered from the *fear* and the *power* of death. Repent today. Trust in Jesus, and you will pass from death to life. You have God's Word on it. I wouldn't lie to you, sir.

Bible Promise

Praise the LORD! Blessed is the man who fears the Lord, Who delights greatly in His commandments (Psalm 112:1).

questions ?

1. Woody Allen's mother said that he was a very happy kid until about five years old and then he turned sour. Why?
2. What did Woody Allen say about his death?
3. What word did he use three times to describe life?
4. Why is the thought that DNA made itself beyond insanity?
5. The Bible promises "Blessed is the man who . . . (see Psalm 112:1).

Endnotes

1. https://www.goodreads.com/quotes/605283-i-am-young-now-and-can-look-upon-my-body.

2. http://www.independent.co.uk/news/people/woody-allen-on-depression-and-tears-of-clowns-the-comedian-is-no-sadder-than-the-guy-who-drives-a-9721971.html.

3. Ibid.

4. https://jewsforjesus.org/issues-v08-n08/god-and-carpeting-the-theology-of-woody-allen.

5. https://www.timeout.com/paris/en/cinema/film/woody-allen-interview.

6. https://www.independent.co.uk/news/people/woody-allen-on-depression-and-tears-of-clowns-the-comedian-is-no-sadder-than-the-guy-who-drives-a-9721971.html.

7. https://www.brainyquote.com/quotes/authors/w/woody_allen.html

8. http://the-talks.com/interview/woody-allen/.

9. Ibid.

10. Ibid.

11. http://www.uncommonhelp.me/articles/dealing-with-a-fear-of-death/.

12. https://www.cdc.gov/homeandrecreationalsafety/water-safety/waterinjuries-factsheet.html.

Chapter 18

William Shatner

"When the game is over, the king and the pawn go into the same box." — Italian Proverb

William Shatner (born March 22, 1931) is a Canadian actor, author, producer, and director.

William Shatner hopes to drop dead of a heart attack on stage. Shatner's not joking about his planned stage exit either — he's given the matter a lot of thought. The following article was called "William Shatner Reveals Death Wish." It was published in August of 2015 while Shatner was touring Australia.

> "I don't want to be anticipating my death thinking I can't breathe and what's going to happen and where's my family and all the thoughts that must come to you when you realize you're in your last breath," he says. "How much fear must you feel? How much better would it be to die suddenly doing something that you love or being with someone that you love . . . but you don't go through the pain of it."[1]

It would seem that the iconic star is alluding to the recent frightening death of his friend and fellow actor, Leonard Nimoy. The memory of someone you care about dying in such a horrible way isn't easily shaken. He later said, "I was thinking of Leonard. He couldn't get his breath, he was drowning in his own fluids. What a difficult way of passing. His death affected me a great deal. . . . no matter how famous you are, it's dust, it's over in the blink of an eye so nobody remembers your name."[2]

In another interview, he shared the following:

"I was afraid of dying," he says, noting that the fear of dying is supposed to open one to joy, making one more conscious of life. And so it did. "Day after day . . . I'm looking around and I'm smelling life, the sweetness of cut grass, cattle cars going by, and seeing the horizon and feeling the wind and the heat and the cold, every sensation," Shatner recalls. "The immediacy of life, and how fragile life is, stayed with me."[3]

A Conversation with William Shatner

In wanting to enjoy every moment you have left, you are like a man on a plane who has to jump, who is deliberately engrossing himself in a good movie because he doesn't want to leave the plane. There's a parachute available and you're ignoring it.

What then is the best thing that I can do for you? It is to talk to you about what a fearful thing it would be to jump ten thousand feet without a parachute. It is to talk about the unseen force of gravity and what it will do to you when you hit the ground. That will hopefully produce a healthy fear, one that acts as your friend. It will give you the incentive to put on the parachute.

Although the effects of gravity are terrifying, they can be nullified with a parachute. That's what the Savior will do to with the terrifying law of sin and death. The Apostle Paul said, "The law of the Spirit of life in Christ Jesus has made me free from the law of sin and death" (Romans 8:2). Trust alone in Jesus frees us from the power of death. It removes the sting from the beast: "O Death, where is your sting?" (1 Corinthians 15:55).

In law, a *summons* is "a call or citation by authority to appear before a court or a judicial officer."[4] Death is a summons. It is the arresting officer, and it will take us before the ultimate Judge for our court case. Hebrews 9:27 says, "And as it is *appointed* for men to die once, but after this the judgment" (italics added). On that day there will be no insanity plea or pleading the fifth. Nothing is hidden from the eyes of Him to whom we have to give an account.

The Scriptures also warn us that it is a "fearful thing to *fall* into the hands of the living God" (Hebrews 10:31, italics added). When we say that a criminal *falls* into the hands of the police, we are saying that he is being held, not that he waits for the law to take its course.

But the Bible tells us that even though God loves justice, He wants the criminal to *escape* its clutches — "Mercy rejoices over judgment" (James 2:13). We are told to *flee* from the wrath that's to come. Thank God there is a place to which we can flee. The Scriptures ask the rhetorical question, "How shall we escape if we neglect so greater a salvation?" (Hebrews 2:3).

It Never Rains in California

Early in 2017, a long drought was broken in Southern California. We often take rain for granted but without it, like a tender plant without water, humanity would soon wither and die.

How many drops of rain do you think have fallen since the beginning of time? God not only created each one, but He's intimately familiar with every hydrogen and oxygen atom of which every drop was made. That's what it means to be omniscient. He has *all* knowledge. He also created every ray of light that has burst from the exploding face of the sun — since the beginning of time, as it traveled to the earth at 93,000,000 miles at 186,000 miles per second. How many rays of sunlight do you think have taken that journey? Then think about how God created each one and how He is intimately familiar with every photon particle. He is nothing like we imagine Him to be, and we have offended Him to a point of awaiting personal wrath for our sin. That's why we need the Savior. Don't quash fear. Let it be your friend and bring you to faith in Jesus. Once you fully realize the danger that you were in, you'll be eternally grateful for His mercy.

Bible Promise

Draw near to God and He will draw near to you. Cleanse your hands, you sinners; and purify your hearts, you double-minded. Lament and mourn and weep! Let your laughter be turned to mourning and your joy to gloom. Humble yourselves in the sight of the Lord, and He will lift you up (James 4:8–10).

questions ?

1. What was William Shatner's "Death Wish"?
2. What did Shatner say stayed with him?
3. What did he say of Leonard Nimoy's death?
4. What do the Scriptures say to those who humble themselves before God?
5. According to James 4:8–10, if we draw near to a God, what will happen?

Endnotes

1. http://www.news.com.au/entertainment/celebrity-life/william-shatner-reveals-his-ideal-exit-ahead-of-the-australian-tour-of-his-oneman-show-shatners-world/news-story/756f86493fe9ad558891ea0c343ea560.

2. Ibid.

3. http://www.smh.com.au/entertainment/tv-and-radio/variety-the-spice-of-life-in-william-shatners-world-20151005-gk1f1z.html.

4. Dictionary.com.

Chapter 19

David Bowie

"I wish I was in a full body cast, with every bone in my body broken. . . . Then, maybe, people would stop minimizing my illness because they can actually see what's wrong with me." — Sally Brampton, *Shoot the D-mn Dog: A Memoir of Depression*[1]

David Robert Jones (January 8, 1947–January 10, 2016). David Bowie was an English singer, songwriter, and actor.

In October 2003, David Bowie spoke of the depression he had back in the 1980s:

"I hated every minute of it and I lost every ounce of energy and enthusiasm for the deal. There were several times when I was really going to throw in the towel and give it up."

The DIAMOND DOGS star continues, "Maybe I was in recovery from all the drugs and booze that I had done. I was in a very bad psychological state and as near to defeat as at any time in my life — and there I was, having really big albums and tours."

"I felt all so empty and none of it meant anything to me. It was depression, it is not unknown to my family."[2]

In a *Daily Mirror* interview with Richard Wallace, Bowie said,

I used to slip easily into deep, deep depressions, really manically depressed. I'd then swing the other way and become incredibly euphoric. I wasn't in control of it at all. I OFTEN get pangs of isolation and all that, particularly in the very early morning, but it doesn't haunt me as such any more.[3]

After overcoming his addictions, Bowie came to terms with the depression that he had been hiding from for many years. He continued to make music, underwent counseling sessions and went on to make a full recovery until his death, even gaining custody of his son.

An article from January 2016 titled "Did Depression lead David Bowie to Addiction?" said:

David Bowie's public battle with co-occurring disorders has become worldwide news. With his death at 69, his previous struggles show that through admitting a problem with substances, people with addictions can go on to make full recoveries and live healthy, successful lives. One essential key to Bowie's recovery from a co-occurring disorder was admitting himself to an inpatient rehab clinic and addressing the underlying mental issues beyond the addictions.[4]

David Bowie and God

In an unaired interview with *60 Minutes* from 2003, Bowie discussed his search for a higher spiritual meaning.

"Searching for music is like searching for God," he said. "They're very similar. There's an effort to reclaim the unmentionable, the unsayable, the unseeable, the unspeakable, all those things, comes into being a composer and to writing music and to searching for notes and pieces of musical information that don't exist."

"Questioning my spiritual life has always been germane to what I was writing. Always," he told Beliefnet.com.

"It's because I'm not quite an atheist and it worries me. There's that little bit that holds on: Well, I'm almost an atheist. Give me a couple of months."

He added: "That's the shock: All clichés are true. The years really do speed by. Life really is as short as they tell you it is. And there really is a God — so do I buy that one? If all the other clichés are true. . . . H-ll, don't pose me that one."[5]

David Bowie reportedly sought solace in spirituality during the final months of his life. The legendary artist, 69, died on a Sunday after a secret 18-month battle with cancer, and while he had questioned organized religion throughout his career, according to close friends it had been a great source of comfort and strength toward the end.

"Despite some of the comments David made during his career from talking about dabbling with Christianity, Buddhism and Satanism, he reassessed everything when told he was terminally ill a year ago," a source told *The Sun*.

They continued: "He concluded there was something greater than all of us and it may be some version of what others might call God. This was probably quite comforting. He certainly wasn't scared of death." It was also to religion that his wife Iman appeared to turn on Sunday, posting a poignant message to her Instagram page on the day her husband passed away. It read: "The struggle is real, but so is God"[6]

Bible Promise

You who fear the LORD, trust in the LORD; He is their help and their shield (Psalm 115:11).

questions ❓

1. What did Sally Brampton want when she said, "I wish I was in a full body cast, with every bone in my body broken"?
2. What did David Bowie say about his career while he was suffering from depression?
3. What helped him come to terms with his depression?
4. To what did He believe searching for music was like?
5. While discussing his spirituality, he said that he was almost an. . . .

Endnotes

1. Sally Brampton, *Shoot the Damn Dog: A Memoir of Depression* (London: A&C Black, 2011), chapter 9.

2. http://www.contactmusic.com/david-bowie/news/david-bowie.s-.80s-depression.

3. http://www.bowiewonderworld.com/press/00/0206interview.htm.

4. https://www.thecabinchiangmai.com/did-depression-lead-david-bowie-to-addiction/.

5. http://www.mirror.co.uk/3am/celebrity-news/david-bowie-didnt-fear-death-7169844.

6. Ibid.

Chapter 20

Lady Gaga

"Perhaps depression is caused by asking oneself too many unanswerable questions." — Miriam Toews, *Swing Low*[1]

Stefani Joanne Angelina Germanotta (born March 28, 1986), known professionally as Lady Gaga, is an American singer, songwriter, and actress.

In a *Billboard* article she said,

> I've suffered through depression and anxiety my entire life, I still suffer with it every single day. I just want these kids to know that that depth that they feel as human beings is normal. We were born that way. This modern thing, where everyone is feeling shallow and less connected? *That's* not human.[2]

Following the release of her 2013 album ARTPOP, Lady Gaga shocked fans when she revealed that she was taking medication on a daily basis to deal with mental illness. And after her triumphant return to the charts with the unveiling of her new single *Perfect Illusion*, the star has admitted that she's still getting pharmaceutical help.

> "I needed a moment to stabilize," she told the *Daily Mirror* of her overwhelming rise to fame. "When my career took off, I don't remember anything. It's like I'm traumatized. I needed time to recalibrate my soul."
>
> "I take medication," she said. "I'm not saying I feel good because of the medication — I wouldn't encourage

young people to take anti-depressants or mood stabilizers. I admit to having battled depression and anxiety and I think a lot of people do."[3]

Lady Gaga and God

In a 2010 interview she said,

> "I pray very much but at the same time there is no one religion that doesn't hate or speak against or is prejudiced against another racial group or religious group or sexual group and for that I think religion is also bogus. So I suppose you could say I'm quite a religious woman but very confused about religion," she admitted. "I dream and envision a future where we have a more peaceful religion or a more peaceful world or a more peaceful state of mind for the younger generation. That's what I dream for."[4]

A Conversation with Lady Gaga

I appreciate that you said that you were confused about religion. So was I for many years. Your contempt for religion is certainly justified. Everywhere we look, we see religious hypocrisy. But that's nothing new for human nature. We see hypocrisy in politics, business, sports, and human relationships. Life is filled with people who are pretending to be something that they are not. John Lennon had similar thoughts about religion. His famous song, *Imagine*, was written as a prayer to God. Imagine how good things would be if there was no infighting about religion . . . with all the people living as one. But as time goes on, such a thought is a mere imagination. Human beings fight like cats and dogs, whether it be in marriage, politics, or religion, because we have a sinful nature. We hardly agree about anything. I'm sure you would disagree with that.

A quote often attributed to G.K. Chesterton, although his authorship is contested, is: "It is often supposed that when people stop believing in God, they believe in nothing. Alas, it is worse than that. When they stop believing in God, they believe in anything."[5] And so we have a generation who thinks that they are nothing but primates, with no purpose for existence, and that nothing is right or wrong, outside of what they believe. So, if I had your undivided attention for a moment, I would encourage you to not only cry out to God but to read the New Testament with an open and humble attitude of "Please, show me the truth." He will.

Bible Promise

> For God has not given us a spirit of fear, but of power and of love and of a sound mind (2 Timothy 1:7).

questions ?

1. How prevalent has depression been for Lady Gaga?
2. What did she say about religion?
3. What did G.K. Chesterton say happens when people stop believing in God?
4. What should someone do who is confused about religion?
5. According to 2 Timothy 1:7, what sort of mind do we receive in Christ?

Endnotes

1. https://www.goodreads.com/quotes/325446-perhaps-depression-is-caused-by-asking-oneself-too-many-unanswerable.

2. http://www.billboard.com/articles/news/magazine-feature/6730027/lady-gaga-billboard-cover-born-this-way-foundation-depression-philanthropy.

3. http://www.dailymail.co.uk/tvshowbiz/article-3784980/Lady-Gaga-admits-s-taking-medication-cope-depression-reveals-plans-include-tales-real-life-betrayal-new-album.html.

4. http://www.christianpost.com/news/lady-gaga-moved-by-sermon-about-communion-gods-gift-to-believers-163719/.

5. https://www.chesterton.org/ceases-to-worship/.

Chapter 21

Rod Stewart

"I have studiously tried to avoid ever using the word 'madness' to describe my condition. Now and again, the word slips out, but I hate it. . . . That word is too exciting, too literary, too interesting in its connotations, to convey the boredom, the slowness, the dreariness, the dampness of depression." — Elizabeth Wurtzel, *Prozac Nation*[1]

> I got a fear of death that creeps on every night.
> I know I won't die soon, but then again I might.
> Water down the drain, I'm wasting away.
> Doctors can't help the ghost of a man that's me, no,
> no, no. (Rod Stewart's "Plynth")[2]

A Conversation with Rod Stewart

I wonder if you identify with those lyrics. Have you ever laid your head on a pillow and heard your heartbeat in your ear, and wondered what will happen to you when it stops? That is the most profound question any of us can ask. The day we die is the most breath-taking day of our lives. Someone once said that the last thing we do is the last thing we want to do.

While most celebrate birthdays, we would be wise to give great consideration to that other day we would rather not talk about. But we can, because God has provided us with a *living* hope through the gospel. We can look death in the face and call it a defeated enemy, one that is soon to be destroyed:

The last enemy that will be destroyed is death (1 Corinthians 15:26).

Jim Morrison, songerwriter, poet, and lead singer for the Doors,
said just before his death, "People fear death even more than pain.
It's strange that they fear death. Life hurts a lot more than death.
At the point of death, the pain is over. Yeah, I guess it is a friend."[3]
R.C. Sproul addresses the thought:

> So is death now our friend? Or is it still our foe? For
> believers, death is a friend insofar as it ushers us into the
> immediate presence of Christ. But insofar as it is still cou-
> pled with much suffering, it remains the last enemy that
> must be totally vanquished. However, our problem with
> death is not with death itself but with the process that leads
> up to it. It is *dying* that is still feared by Christians. What
> Christian would be afraid of death if we could just shut our
> eyes and wake up in heaven? We know that the other side of
> death is glory and that death is but the portal or threshold
> to that glory.[4]

Faith and Fear

Earlier, we spoke of the power of faith to completely deliver us from
the fear of death. If we have one hundred percent faith in God,
we will have zero fear. If we have any fear, the fear is a barometer
that we lack faith in God. This is exemplified in the following and
famous portion of Scripture:

> Now when He got into a boat, His disciples followed
> Him. And suddenly a great tempest arose on the sea, so
> that the boat was covered with the waves. But He was
> asleep. Then His disciples came to Him and awoke Him,
> saying, "Lord, save us! We are perishing!"
> But He said to them, "Why are you fearful, O you of
> little faith?" Then He arose and rebuked the winds and
> the sea, and there was a great calm. So the men marveled,
> saying, "Who can this be, that even the winds and the sea
> obey Him?" (Matthew 8:23–27).

If you fully trust in God (and in the Savior He provided), you will have peace when the ultimate storm comes your way. And that storm will be in the form of winds of fury and the rain of wrath.

Sniper Fire

If you came under sniper fire, I'm sure that you would you hide yourself. You would seek shelter behind or under anything that would protect you from the rain of bullets. The famous song "Rock of Ages" speaks of being "hidden" in the cleft of a rock. The reason we need hiding is seen in the biblical story of Moses asking to see God. God told him that he couldn't see Him and live. This is because the justice of God would spill on him in an instant. So God hid Moses in the cleft of a rock, passed by the rock, and then He let Moses look upon where He had been (see Exodus 33:18–23). That's a picture of us being hidden in the "Rock" of Jesus Christ. He shelters us from the wrath that is to come. Because of your sin, justice will come for you if you refuse to come to the shelter that is in the Savior. Physical death is just the first installment. There is more to come.

Bible Promise

> The LORD is on my side; I will not fear. What can man do to me? (Psalm 118:6).

questions?

1. "What word did Elizabeth Wurtzel studiously try to avoid ever using to describe her depression?
2. What lyrics did Rod Stewart sing about death?
3. What type of "hope" do we have in the gospel?
4. What did Jim Morrison say about the fear of death?
5. According to Psalm 118:6, why should we not fear?

Endnotes

1. https://www.goodreads.com/quotes/301041-i-have-studiously-tried-to-avoid-ever-using-the-word.

2. "Around the Plynth" by Rod Stewart; http://songmeanings.com/songs/view/13593/.

3. https://www.brainyquote.com/quotes/jim_morrison_109347.

4. R.C. Sproul, *The Last Enemy*, http://www.ligonier.org/learn/articles/the-last-enemy/.

Chapter 22

Kristen Bell

"Dead, but not allowed to die. Alive, but as good as dead." — Suzanne Collins[1]

Kristen Anne Bell (born July 18, 1980) is an American actress and singer.

In an essay in *Time* in May 2016, actress Kristen Bell detailed her experiences with depression and stressed the importance of ending the stigma surrounding the illness.

"I didn't speak publicly about my struggles with mental health for the first 15 years of my career," Bell wrote. She described how, as a college student at New York University, she felt there was something "intangible dragging [her] down."[2]

The article in *Time* was called "There's nothing weak about struggling with mental illness," in which she further said,

Here's the thing: For me, depression is not sadness. It's not having a bad day and needing a hug. It gave me a complete and utter sense of isolation and loneliness. Its debilitation was all-consuming, and it shut down my mental circuit board.

Then she spoke of the stigma that comes with mental health issues:

There is such an extreme stigma about mental health issues, and I can't make heads or tails of why it exists. Anxiety and depression are impervious to accolades or achievements. Anyone can be affected, despite their level of success or their place on the food chain. In fact, there is a good chance you know someone who is struggling with it since nearly 20% of American adults face some form of mental illness in their lifetime. So why aren't we talking about it?[3]

The reason that there is a stigma is because it wasn't too long ago that mental disease was synonymous with being crazy, insane, and mad. We called the places that housed those with mental disorders "the crazy house," "the nut house," and "the mad house."

Quietly being diagnosed as being mentally ill may be okay for those who aren't in the public eye. Who is going to look at you a little weirdly besides your family and friends? But if you are a *public* figure and it gets out, West Chester University may put you on their list of "Famous People with Mental Illness," and the tabloids will be chasing you to see what strange thing you're going to do next.[4]

One reason for the change in thinking is that there has been a *redefining* of "insanity" to include those who are depressed:

> For decades there has been increasing evidence that psychologists can't reliably diagnose or treat mental illnesses, or mental illnesses aren't objective illnesses as that term is understood, or that psychology has no testable scientific content. Psychologists' reaction to this long-term trend has been to add more human behaviors to the "mental illness" category, in order not to lose more ground to medicine. *The Diagnostic and Statistical Manual of Mental Disorders* (DSM), what many call the "Bible" of psychology and its single most important guide to practice, shows this trend clearly — each new edition contains more conditions thought to merit the label "mental illness.
>
> Here is a count of "mental illnesses" included in the DSM by year: In 1952 there were 112 mental illnesses. In 1980 this number had been increased to 224, and by 1994 it had jumped to 374.[5]

So as of 2016, 44.7 million American adults were included in the category of being mentally ill.[6] The reality is that most of the 44 million know that they aren't mentally ill. They are depressed. That's why they object to the label.

A Conversation with Kirsten Bell

You opined "So why aren't we talking about it?" Okay, let's talk about it. Let's talk about the cure to the "disease." To do this, we will go where Hollywood is reluctant to go — to the Bible. It says that when someone is born again, they receive a "sound mind":

> For God has not given us a spirit of fear, but of power and of love and of a sound mind (2 Timothy 1:7).

The inference is that until we come to Christ, we don't have a sound mind. That makes sense, in the light of God offering everlasting life as a free gift to the dying human race, and the majority ignoring it. That *is* insane!

Self-mutilation

In February of 2012, *Psychology Today* published an article entitled "Depression and Non-Suicidal Self Injury." It said,

> What do these high profile individuals have in common? Singer, Fiona Apple; Comedian, Russell Brand; Actress, Drew Barrymore; Actor, Johnny Depp; Actor, Colin Farrell; Actress, Megan Fox; Actress, Angelina Jolie; Singer, Demi Lovato and Princess Diana.
> Before finding emotional health, they struggled with self-injury. Self-Injury is a deliberate, non-suicidal behavior that inflicts physical harm on one's body to relieve emotional distress. Self-injury has a paradoxical effect in that the pain self-inflicted actually sets off an endorphin rush, relieving the self-harmer from deep distress. . . . This kind of self-injury can take many forms from cutting, picking, burning, bruising, puncturing, embedding, scratching or hitting one's self, just to name a few.[7]

Research has revealed that this self-injury is practiced by as many as 4% of the adult population the United States.[8]

The New Testament tells the story of a man who had his demons, and was self-destructive. He lived an isolated existence. He spent most of his time "crying and cutting himself." The man came to Jesus with a humble heart and pleaded with Him for help.

Jesus cast out his demons. The Scriptures say that the change was so dramatic that a crowd came out to see this man, and when they saw him he was "sitting and clothed and in his right mind: and they were afraid" (see Mark 5:2–15).

Notice that once this man was free from that which terrorized him, he was said to be "in his right mind." If any of us, knowing that we are going to die, and yet refuse to come to Christ, we are not in our right mind.

Bible Promise

> The LORD is my light and my salvation; whom shall I fear? The LORD is the strength of my life; of whom shall I be afraid? (Psalm 27:1).

questions ?

1. Who said, "Dead, but not allowed to die. Alive, but as good as dead"?
2. Why do you think Kristen Bell said, "There's nothing weak about struggling with mental illness"?
3. Of what couldn't she make heads or tails?
4. As of 2016, how many Americans have been diagnosed with mental illness?
5. What percentage of the adult American public practice self injury?

Endnotes

1. https://www.goodreads.com/quotes/588580-dead-but-not-allowed-to-die-alive-but-as-good.
2. http://www.livescience.com/56342-celebrities-depression.html.
3. http://time.com/4352130/kristen-bell-frozen-depression-anxiety/.
4. https://www.wcupa.edu/_admin/social.equity/documents/MentalIllnessFacts.pdf.
5. http://arachnoid.com/psychology/myth.html.
6. https://www.nimh.nih.gov/health/statistics/prevalence/any-mental-illness-ami-among-us-adults.shtml.
7. https://www.psychologytoday.com/blog/two-takes-depression/201202/depression-and-non-suicidal-self-injury.
8. http://www.mentalhealthamerica.net/self-injury.

Chapter 23

Michael Jackson

"I spend a lot of time wondering what dying feels like. What dying sounds like. If I'll burst like those notes, let out my last cries of pain, and then go silent forever." — Jasmine Warga, *My Heart and Other Black Holes*[1]

Michael Joseph Jackson (August 29, 1958–June 25, 2009) was an American singer, songwriter, record producer, dancer, and actor.

When asked about death and immortality, Michael Jackson said,

> Who wants mortality? Everybody wants immortality. You want what you create to live! Be it sculpting, painting, music, composition. That is why to escape death I attempt to bind my soul to my work because I just want it to live forever and just give all that I have.[2]

In a candid interview with a rabbi, he said,

> I think growing old is the ugliest, the most, the ugliest thing. When the body breaks down and you start to wrinkle, I think it's so bad. I don't . . . that's something I don't understand. . . . And I never want to look in the mirror and see that. I don't understand it. I really don't. And people say that growing old is beautiful and this and that. I disagree.
> Rabbi: So do you want to die before that happens?
> Michael Jackson: Um . . . I don't want to grow old.
> Rabbi: Are you afraid of death?

Michael Jackson: Yes.

Rabbi: We all are.[3]

A Conversation with Michael Jackson

You said that you don't understand why we grow old and ugly. It *is* a mystery to those who reject the light of Scripture. It says that we are under "the curse of the Law" (Galatians 3:13), and the Law says "The soul who sins shall die" (Ezekiel 18:20). Everything fell when Adam fell. In time, the most vibrant and cutest of little puppies becomes a deaf, blind, slow-moving, and smelly old dog. Leaves fall and die, roses lose their petals, trees bend and crack, elephants wrinkle, horses sag, and frogs croak. Everything grows old, dies, and turns to dust.

Most of us protest. We fight the curse. We go vegan, work out, juice, Botox, use moisturizers, and try to slow down the process by using so-called anti-aging products. But we can't beat the curse. There's more chance of a flea drinking the oceans of the earth, than of us reversing the curse. There is only one avenue of escape. The Bible says, "Christ has redeemed us from the curse of the Law, being made a curse for us" (Galatians 3:13). If you won't turn onto the straight and narrow path of trust in Jesus, you will be stuck on a dead end street of sin, in the City of Destruction. That means aging, death, and then damnation. Life is depressing if you think about it.

You once wrote, "Who am I? Who are you? Where did we come from? Where are we going? What's it all about? Do you have the answers?"[4]

I found the answers. Let me share them with you.

Trip to the Inlaws

There was hardly a moment of my life when I was depressed. Of course there were the usual ups and downs when things didn't go my way and I felt a little melancholy, but I had a very happy child-hood. I lived near the beach and spent most of my youth soaking in the sun and the surf.

The only thoughts of death that came my way were when my grandmother died, the lady next-door died of cancer, someone drowned at the beach, and my dog was killed in front of me by a car.

But, in time, the reality of death got my attention, and by the age of 20 I was feeling a sense of futility because of its inevitability. And yet, like Solomon, I was able to hold onto my sanity and sense of personal happiness. I had everything in the world that anyone could want, and I loved it. Life was wonderful. But something strange happened just after I was married that had a profound effect on me.

A number of my surfing buddies were experimenting with LSD and raving about it. Most of them didn't have what I had, so had little to lose. But I had a wonderful wife, my own home, a child, my own business, a car, and was well enough off financially to do anything I wanted. So I had no inclination to experiment with an illegal drug, and I told them so. Because I wouldn't play their game, they put me on the sidelines. But that didn't worry me.

One day a strange thing happened. It was as though all my convictions about not taking LSD left me. I suddenly decided that I would check it out. Even to this day I have no idea why.

When I told a friend that I would like to try LSD he was excited for me, went into his parents' house, climbed up to a high cupboard, and retrieved something he called "clear light." He said that because it was my first time, I should cut the tiny flake in half and share it with a friend. So that's what I did. I found a surf buddy named Kevin, had him cut the clear light in half, and I placed my half on my tongue.

I had decided not to tell Sue what I had done. It was about 2 o'clock in the afternoon and I had to pick her up at about 4 p.m. and go to her parents' place for dinner. That shows how naïve I was. An LSD trip can last for many hours, and mine certainly did.

I hardly remember a thing about the ten-mile drive to pick her up from her work. However, I do remember stopping on the way to let some pedestrians walk across the road. As they did so, I was listening to Frank Sinatra sing "My Way," a famous reflective song about life and death. As I watched them cross the road, tears filled my eyes. *They were going to die.* And there was nothing they could do about it.

As I parked outside Sue's place of work, I redetermined not to tell her anything about the LSD trip. But when she opened the passenger side door and sat down, I said, "I took some LSD." I couldn't believe what I had just said. It was as though I had no control over my mouth. She went quiet for a moment, looked me in the eyes, and said a devastating, "I'm disappointed in you. . . ."

As her father opened their front door to let us in, I began the first of a number of hallucinations. Dinner went down in lumps, and during the evening I burst out laughing for no reason. But Sue was extremely supportive and made excuses for my weirdness.

When we got home I continued to hallucinate. Sue had gone to sleep, and so I sat on the edge of our bed and looked at her. This was my beautiful bride . . . and an evil monster called "death" was waiting in the shadows to take her from me. It could happen in 50 years or it could happen that night. But it *was going* to happen.

Why did life have to end?

Why don't people talk about death? Why doesn't science find out what causes death and put a stop to it? Why was it going to rip from my hands *everything* I held dear? As I sat there I saw a hallucination of the word "Why?" stacked on top of many other *whys* going up above me like a ladder into the ceiling. That's when *Old Yeller* tears began to flow down my cheeks. The LSD had given me the ability to reach right into the depths of my soul and bring to the surface something I couldn't put into words.

I was very fortunate that I had a good trip. Others weren't so fortunate. A few years later a friend named Janet threw herself off a cliff to her death while on the drug. Five of my surfing friends died through drug abuse.

A few months after that experience, Sue and I visited a minister friend and his wife. When we arrived I took my jacket into a room to put it on a bed. I remember sitting on the bed and wanting him to come in and speak to me about something, but I didn't know what or why. Looking back, I was a blind man groping for a guiding hand. That hand came a few months later when a surfing buddy explained the gospel. He led me to the Cross where I found everlasting life! In Christ I also found freedom from futility and was delivered from the fear and power of death. I learned that night that, outside of Jesus Christ, death wins.

Bible Promise

For I am persuaded that neither death nor life, nor angels nor principalities nor powers, nor things present nor things to come, nor height nor depth, nor any other created thing, shall be able to separate us from the love of God which is in Christ Jesus our Lord (Romans 8:38–39).

questions?

1. What did Michael Jackson say about life and death?
2. What did he say about growing old?
3. What was said in his interview with the rabbi?
4. What fell when Adam fell?
5. How do people often try to fight the curse?

Endnotes

1. https://www.goodreads.com/author/quotes/7224009.Jasmine_Warga.

2. http://www.truemichaeljackson.com/on-death-and-immortality/.

3. Ibid.

4. Ibid.

Chapter 24

Prince

"Almost everyone is overconfident — except the people who are depressed, and they tend to be realists." — Joseph T. Hallinan[1]

Prince Rogers Nelson (June 7, 1958–April 21, 2016) was an American singer-songwriter, multi-instrumentalist, and record producer.

The below are lyrics from Prince's *Let's go Crazy:*

> We're all excited
> But we don't know why
> Maybe it's 'cause
> We're all gonna die
> And when we do, what's it all for
> You better live now
> Before the Grim Reaper come knocking on your door.
> Dr. Everything'll be alright
> Will make everything go wrong
> Pills and thrills and daffodils will kill

In addition to his physical challenges, the "Purple Rain" singer by his own admission struggled with mental illness as well. "During the *Dirty Mind* period I would go into fits of depression and get physically ill," he told *Rolling Stone* back in 1985.[2]

But all that paled beside the anguish of the death of his baby son Gregory in 1996. Prince had set his heart on starting a family with his first wife, dancer Mayte Garcia.

Seven days after their child was born the child died from a genetic disorder of the skull called Pfieffer syndrome. More heartbreak and soul-searching followed with the death of both the star's parents.. . . Prince grappled with depression and something approaching a midlife crisis.[3]

A Conversation with Prince

There's nothing like the death of a child and beloved parents to stop us in our tracks and make us ask what life is all about. Such experiences can drag us into the depths of depression as we think about our own mortality. The fear of death is often referred to as a more congenial "midlife crisis."

In October of 2009, Dr. Alex Lickerman, MD, penned an article called "Overcoming The Fear Of Death — A Physician Confronts His Own Mortality" for *Psychology Today*.

With a wonderful humility, he related how a series of serious illnesses made him confront his own mortality. He said,

> I'm always surprised by people who say they're not afraid to die. Most are usually quick to point out they *are* afraid to die *painfully* — but not of the idea of no longer being alive. I continue to be mystified not only by this answer but by the number of people who give it. Though I can imagine there are indeed people who, because of their age, character, or religious beliefs, truly do feel this way, I've always wondered if that answer hides a denial so deeply seated it cannot be faced by most.

How perceptive of the honest doctor. I have confronted many people who say that they're not afraid of death. When I enquire as to why, they almost always reply, "I don't think about it." The doctor continued,

> I've always spoken openly of my fear of death to anyone who's ever asked (not that many have — I suppose even the question is uncomfortable for most), but I've rarely experienced moments where I actually felt afraid. Whenever I've tried wrapping my mind around the concept of my own

demise — truly envisioned the world continuing on without me, the essence of what I am utterly gone forever — I've unearthed a fear so overwhelming my mind has been turned aside as if my imagination and the idea of my own end were two magnets of identical polarity, unwilling to meet no matter how hard I tried to make them.

I was expecting him to have diagnosed his own mental illness, and prescribe himself a medical solution. He didn't. He instead said,

I felt like one of my long-time patients who for as long as I've known him has been consumed by an anxiety so great he'd become like a child in his need for constant reassurance that he would be all right. His anxiety had made him inconsolable and his life a joyless nightmare.

As the article came to a conclusion, I was expecting it to turn philosophical and speak about how his fear had made him a better person who appreciated life so much more because of it. He did no such thing. Instead, he said,

I've tried to resolve my fear of death intellectually and come to the conclusion that it can't be done, at least not by me. Some kind of practice that actually has the power to awaken me to the truth is required (assuming, of course, the truth ends up being what I hope it to be).[4]

Bible Promise

In the multitude of my anxieties within me, Your comforts delight my soul (Psalm 94:19).

questions **?**

1. What did Joseph T. Hallinan call depressed people?
2. What caused Prince to grapple with depression?
3. What did Dr. Alex Lickerman say about people who say that they are not afraid of death?
4. What did he frankly say about his own fear of death?

5. He concluded: "I've tried to resolve my fear of death intellectually and come to the conclusion that it can't be done, at least not by me." Who can resolve it?

Endnotes

1. https://quotefancy.com/quote/41555/Joseph-T-Hallinan-Almost-everyone-is-overconfident-except-the-people-who-are-depressed.

2. http://www.wetpaint.com/prince-death-health-issues-epilepsy-hip-1487793/.

3. http://www.mirror.co.uk/3am/celebrity-news/prince-how-rock-legend-turned-233415.

4. https://www.psychologytoday.com/blog/happiness-in-world/200910/overcoming-the-fear-death.

Chapter 25

Mindy McCready

"Depression is like a bruise that never goes away. A bruise in your mind. You just got to be careful not to touch it where it hurts. It's always there, though." — Jeffrey Eugenides, *The Marriage Plot*[1]

Malinda Gayle "Mindy" McCready (November 30, 1975–February 17, 2013) was a popular American country music singer.

In an article entitled "The Tragic Life, Depression and Suicide of Mindy McCready," the *Journal of Psychiatric Orgone Therapy* related details of her tragic suicide and her fight with depression:

> More recently, in 2013, she entered a court-ordered rehabilitation center, checked herself out one day later and shortly thereafter, she shot herself in the mouth, on the porch of her home where her boyfriend, Wilson, had committed suicide.[2]

After her death, CNN lamented about the lyrics of one of her albums:

> They seemed so triumphant at the time, the lyrics to country music star Mindy McCready's hope-filled title track to her most recent album, "I'm Still Here."
> "On a cold dark cloud, with nowhere to fall but down, like a single, naked, unrelenting tear . . . I'm still here."
> Now, those words sound like a cry for help.[3]

Chronic depression *is* a cry for help, from those who are helpless in the face of certain death. Most of us battle the fear of death, but if we witnessed the violent death of someone we loved, we would be no doubt be susceptible to an even greater fear. *USA Today* did a piece headed, "In the end, Mindy McCready couldn't shake her demons." It quoted the chief medical officer at the drug and alcohol treatment center Cumberland Heights in Nashville:

> Becoming a reality television star didn't help, and her boyfriend's death may have pushed her over the edge. "Acute grief increases the risk," he said.[4]

And so Mindy masked her fear with drug and alcohol abuse, and because she was chronically depressed, psychologists told her that she was mentally ill. That didn't sit well. She, of course, felt the stigma of being diagnosed as being insane. The thought that a thinking person may be uncomfortable with that diagnosis didn't enter the mind of the psychologist who penned another article:

> It's odd, sad, and slightly contradictory that Ms. McCready recently checked out of a psychiatric hospital before completing treatment because, according to Dr. Drew, she feared the stigma.[5]

The father of Mindy's eldest son told the *Today* show: "As sad as it is, it didn't come as a major shock, because she's just been battling demons for so long. . . . The demons that she hasn't beaten were still there, and until she was going to face them, something was going to happen."[6]

Some busy themselves and ignore the fear. Others, like Mindy, try to drown the fear with alcohol and dull it with drugs. But when they wear off, the dread is still there and the cloud of depression returns. And so the unthinkable begins to be entertained. Suicide becomes a viable and final option to escape that terrible dread. And the medical profession can't heal a disease it can't diagnose:

> In spite of many years of conventional treatment, Mindy McCready and thousands of others like her suffered from severe depression and ultimately committed suicide, a clear indication that conventional psychiatry fails in many cases.[7]

For psychology, the diagnosis of mental illness is a self-fulfilling prophecy. This person committed suicide, *therefore* that is the evidence that they had mental problems:

> Sometimes all the treatment in the world is just not enough. Mindy McCready's death was a tragedy to be sure, but there is no one and nothing to blame — except the mental illness.[8]

In commenting about her death, a leading doctor said,

> But let me be clear. Mindy's tragic situation is about mental illness. Chronic mental illness.
>
> We have a wrongly perpetuated notion that people who are mentally ill can somehow "conquer their demons." There is no such thing. Mental illness is not a weakness or moral failing. It is a sickness for which people need ongoing treatment.
>
> About a week ago, Mindy was at a facility getting care for herself. But she left prematurely. I believe that the stigma surrounding mental illness caused her to resist treatment. We need to think about this: Public figures are scrutinized, even jeered, for admitting a problem such as mental illness and getting help. We should be cheering for them instead.[9]

Again, it doesn't enter their minds that calling someone *insane* could possibly contribute to their depression and consequent suicide. If being depressed about death is grounds for having a mental disease, then there are around seven billion people, including doctors, who have mental disease. They are insane. Some just don't know it yet, but as the grave nears, they will.

Here is a study case on depression from the *AMA Journal of Ethics* from June of 2016:

> Ms. G is a 55-year-old white female who is treated in Dr. C's office for bipolar affective disorder. A lifetime of relapsing mood episodes resulted in failures at school, limited capacity to hold steady employment, and an inability to sustain intimate relationships or friendships. She lives

with her father, who is currently ill and unlikely to survive long. Her mother died recently, and Ms. G has no siblings.

Over the years, Ms. G's depressions varied in severity but she never fully recovers. She survives in a state of chronically depressed mood. Dr. C's treatment for Ms. G over the last 10 years has covered the range of pharmacotherapy, psychotherapy, electroconvulsive therapy (ECT), and experimental agents offered through a number of clinical trials and second opinions. In a session one day, Ms. G states to Dr. C that she will live as long as her father is alive, but, after his death, she will elect to stop her medications and commit suicide. When asked by Dr. C to explain this more fully, she states, "I see no hope for my future. After he dies, no one, other than you, Dr. C, will be left to grieve for me."[10]

This poor woman is surrounded by death, is understandably chronically depressed, and has been an experimental pin cushion for years … to no avail. The doctor can offer her nothing for her depression, no deliverance from her fear of death, nor hope in place of her hopelessness. All she can see is an end to the pain through suicide. Yet in Christ she would find:

1. God is the lover of her soul,
2. purpose for her existence,
3. freedom from the fear of death,
4. a hope that the Bible says "is both sure and steadfast, an anchor for the soul."

As we have seen, hope is oxygen for the soul, and is perhaps the most misunderstood word in the English language. When it runs out, the soul suffocates and dies:

The power of hope to keep the human body going is truly remarkable and well documented. Hopes can vary: hope for a cure, hope for improvement in condition, hope for relief of pain, hope for an easy death. But hope for a cure as an end in itself might not be useful, and like all therapeutic interventions, it is accountable to the truth.[11]

Bible Promise

"I sought the LORD, and He heard me, and delivered me from all my fears" (Psalm 34:4).

questions ?

1. What did a psychologist find "odd" about Mindy McCready?
2. For psychology, why is the diagnosis of mental illness a self-fulfilling prophecy?
3. What did a leading doctor say about her death?
4. What would hopeless sinners find in Christ?
5. According to Psalm 34:4, from what are we delivered if we seek the Lord?

Endnotes

1. Depression is like a bruise that never goes away. A bruise in your mind. You just got to be careful not to touch it where it hurts. It's always there, though.

2. More recently, in 2013, she entered a court-ordered rehabilitation center, checked herself out one day later and shortly thereafter, she shot herself in the mouth.

3. http://www.cnn.com/2013/02/18/showbiz/mindy-mccready-death/.

4. http://www.usatoday.com/story/life/music/2013/02/19/mindy-mccready-demons/1930859/; http://www.usatoday.com/story/life/music/2013/02/19/mindy-mccready-demons/1930859/.

5. https://www.psychologytoday.com/blog/reading-between-the-headlines/201302/mccreadys-suicide-no-one-blame-much-learn.

6. http://www.dailymail.co.uk/news/article-2281888/Mindy-McCreadys-death-confirmed-suicide-father-eldest-son-says-believes-killed-children-her.html.

7. https://www.psychorgone.com/?s=Mindy&x=22&y=9.

8. http://drdrew.com/2013/guest-blog-1/.

9. http://www.hlntv.com/video/2013/02/18/dr-drew-reacts-mindy-mccreadys-death/.

10. http://journalofethics.ama-assn.org/2016/06/ecas4-1606.html.

11. J. Groopman, *The Anatomy of Hope: How People Prevail in the Face of Illness* (New York, NY: Random House; 2004), http://journalofethics.ama-assn.org/2016/06/ecas4-1606.html.

Chapter 26

Joan Rivers

"I did the only thing I knew how to do: I built my own walls of silence to disguise my desperation and what later came to be recognized and diagnosed as depression." — Sharon E. Rainey, *Making a Pearl from the Grit of Life*[1]

Joan Alexandra Molinsky (June 8, 1933–September 4, 2014), widely known as Joan Rivers, was an American comedian, actress, writer, producer, and television host.

"Only my really good friends know. And even my daughter I don't show it to. You cannot take a twenty-two-year-old girl and burden her with 'I'm so down, I'm so depressed, I'm so scared, I'm so worried.' " — Joan Rivers[2]

"I was alone upstairs. I opened a drawer and there was a gun. I took the gun and sat down in my dressing room, with the gun in my lap, and I thought, 'It would be so easy. I want to be out of all this pain. I just want to be out of it.' It's not even so much pain, but the aching weariness of the whole thing; I just wanted to be out of it all. Oh, I was so down. I thought, 'I can't fight anymore. I can't go on anymore. I'm so weary, G-d, what's the point?' But when my dog came in and sat in my lap, I thought, 'Who's going to take care of Spike?' " — Joan Rivers[3]

"I think actual death will be a lot easier than dying on stage." — Joan Rivers[4]

Joan Rivers and God

"I'm Jewish. I don't work out. If God had wanted us to bend over, He would have put diamonds on the floor." — Joan Rivers[5]

A Conversation with Joan Rivers

Someone once sent me a link to an article by a woman from Texas. As I read what she had written, I was horrified. It so disturbed me that I had my wife read it. As she read it out loud, I was embarrassed. This is what the woman said:

> A few years ago I met Ray in person while attending a dinner with Governor Perry in Houston. . . . When we first met and he heard our story, he impulsively took my hand and rubbed it along his mustache, not wanting me to miss the fact he could grow facial hair. . . . This fall, I was a guest at a large event in Dallas where Ray was the speaker. I waited in line to talk with him, and when he saw me he grabbed me and gave me a big hug. I reminded him of our first meeting, and he remembered it well. He once again grabbed my hand and said, "You have to feel my face. I now have a beard."

I looked at Sue and said, "Darling, you know me. I don't grab the hands of women and hug them, let alone have them touch my mustache and beard."

I decided to find out who this woman was. I found that she was an author and speaker and that she had a website. I began searching for some sort of clue as to why she would say such things about me. Suddenly, my eyes filled with tears. *She was blind.*

Just as quickly, the memory of meeting this dear woman flooded my mind. As I continued to read her testimony, she said how she became pregnant and visited her doctor because she was having trouble with her eyes. The doctor said, "You have a choice to make. If you go ahead with this pregnancy, you will go blind." She immediately said, "I choose to go blind." The doctor said, "You stupid woman" and walked out, leaving her alone.

In a moment of time I went from suspicion and indignation to weeping at her wonderful courage. I also read that she had died six weeks earlier.

Like me, you may have preconceived thoughts about God, shaped by what the Bible calls a "darkened understanding." My hope is that light is giving you a paradigm shift, and that the love of God in Christ will bring tears to your eyes as you find out the truth.

Bible Promise

"Are not two sparrows sold for a copper coin? And not one of them falls to the ground apart from your Father's will. But the very hairs of your head are all numbered. Do not fear therefore; you are of more value than many sparrows" (Matthew 10:29–31).

questions ?

1. What did Joan Rivers hide from her daughter?
2. What stopped her from shooting herself?
3. Does your heart go out to Joan Rivers? If so, does this concern extend to your neighbors?
4. How does it make you feel — to know that God is intimately familiar with you, even knowing every hair on your head?
5. In Matthew 10:29–31, after telling us of God's great love for us, what did Jesus tell us not to do?

Endnotes

1. https://www.goodreads.com/work/quotes/14472987-making-a-pearl-from-the-grit-of-life.
2. Joan Rivers, *On the Edge of Darkness*; http://www.wingofmadness.com/reflections-on-depression/.
3. Ibid.
4. http://www.azquotes.com/quote/1233209.
5. http://hollowverse.com/joan-rivers/.

Chapter 27

Jim Carrey

"I enjoy almost everything. Yet I have some restless searcher in me. Why is there not a discovery in life? Something one can lay hands on and say 'This is it'? My depression is a harassed feeling. I'm looking: but that's not it — that's not it. What is it? And shall I die before I find it?" — Virginia Woolf, *A Writer's Diary*[1]

James Eugene "Jim" Carrey (born January 17, 1962) is a Canadian-American actor, comedian, impressionist, screenwriter, and producer.

Jim Carrey and Prozac

"Although you may not know it, Jim Carrey has dealt with major depression for a significant portion of his life. In fact, at one point, his depression became so debilitating, that he didn't know how he would overcome it. Like many people, he sought out help from a doctor and was prescribed Prozac."[2]

"I was on Prozac for a long time and I'm not sure, it may have helped me out of a jam a little bit. . . . it feels like a low level of despair you live in, where you're not getting any answers, but you're living OK and you can smile at the office. But it's a low level of despair." — Jim Carrey[3]

A Conversation with Jim Carrey

You once said, "I'm a Buddhist, I'm a Christian, I'm a Muslim, I'm whatever you want me to be. It all comes down to the same thing.

You're in a loving place or you're in an unloving place, if you're with me right now you cannot be unhappy, it's not possible."[4]

Your "I'm whatever you want me to be" is not in the context of your amazing facial expressions. It's in reference to your spiritual convictions, and they do matter. There are huge differences between Buddhism, Islam, and Christianity that have eternal repercussions.

In reference to those repercussions, let me address the amazing words of Virginia Woolf. She said,

> I enjoy almost everything. Yet I have some restless searcher in me. Why is there not a discovery in life? Something one can lay hands on and say "This is it"? My depression is a harassed feeling. I'm looking: but that's not it — that's not it. What is it? And shall I die before I find it? — Virginia Woolf, *A Writer's Diary*[5]

I so identify with what she is saying, because I didn't realize that I was "groping" for God as the Bible says we are. The night that I cried "Why?" I wasn't praying to God. Neither was I thinking of Him, let alone seeking Him. However, a few days after I came to Christ, I watched a movie that ended with a Bible verse that left me dumbfounded. This is what I read: "And you shall know the truth, and the truth shall make you free" (John 8:32).

I sat and stared at the verse. This was that for which I had been searching! This was the answer to my desperate cry that night! I was lost in my darkness, groping for the light. The only way I can try to explain it is with an inadequate analogy.

Imagine you're holding a newborn in your arms and he's crying. You ask him what his problem is and he says that he doesn't know. There is just a cry within him that he can't explain. Then you put that newborn onto his mother's breast. As he quietly suckles, you ask him how he's now doing. He smiles and says that he has found that for which he was yearning.

Every human being has a cry in their heart for truth, a "restless searcher" within them. Everyone is whispering with Virginia Woolf "What is it? And shall I die before I find it?" Is that all there is . . . is that all there is? There must be more than death. . . .

Please, don't die without finding it.

Bible Promise

Then Jesus said to those Jews who believed Him, "If you abide in My word, you are My disciples indeed. And you shall know the truth, and the truth shall make you free" (John 8:31–32).

questions?

1. Do you identify with Virginia Woolf's, "I enjoy almost everything. Yet I have some restless searcher in me"?
2. She said of the search in her life, "What is it? And shall I die before I find it?" For what do you think she was groping?
3. What did Jim Carrey say about Prozac?
4. What did he call his depression?
5. He said, "I'm a Buddhist, I'm a Christian, I'm a Muslim, I'm whatever you want me to be. It all comes down to the same thing." What does this show about his understanding of Christianity?

Endnotes

1. https://www.goodreads.com/quotes/389428-i-enjoy-almost-everything-yet-i-have-some-restless-searcher.
2. https://mentalhealthdaily.com/2014/11/16/jim-carreys-battle-with-depression-and-how-he-overcame-it/.
3. https://www.youtube.com/watch?v=KfWN5EW5eo4&feature=youtu.be.
4. http://www.cbsnews.com/news/carrey-life-is-too-beautiful/.
5. https://www.goodreads.com/quotes/389428-i-enjoy-almost-everything-yet-i-have-some-restless-searcher.

Chapter 28

Kurt Cobain

"It feels like you've swallowed a bag of stones. A heavy feeling somewhere between your heart and stomach." — Kyla Dale[1]

Kurt Donald Cobain (February 20, 1967–April 5, 1994) was an American musician, artist, songwriter, guitarist, and poet.

I'm constantly confused. I am as confused as anybody if not more. Everyone deals with themselves in different ways. Everyone feels insecure at times and depressed. Sure, it happens to me all the time. I can't think of the exact reasons. That's why people feel really vulnerable and confused because they can't understand why they feel that way. . . . when I'm not stable, I'm not way down low, like, death.[2]

When Kurt Cobain took his life — [he was] the third member of the Cobain family to do so. . . .[3]

Rolling Stone said,

Cobain's clinical depression had been diagnosed as early as high school. . . . "Over the last few years of his life, Kurt saw innumerable doctors and therapists."[4]

From *Newsweek*:

As Cobain biographer Charles Cross shows in his 2014 book *Here We Are Now: The Lasting Impact of Kurt Cobain,* the rock star had a serious family history of suicide and depression. He was at an increased risk to take his own life long before he found commercial success.[5]

Why did Kurt Cobain kill himself?

The most likely answer is that suicidal depression was just a part of life in Kurt Cobain's family. If you read *Heavier Than Heaven: A Biography of Kurt Cobain* by Charles Cross, you'll see that Kurt Cobain thought constantly about suicide all the way back to his teens. Kurt's great uncle, Burle Cobain, committed suicide by shooting himself in the head and stomach, the same method of suicide that Kurt would choose years later. In addition, the biography recounts an incident, from when he was in eighth grade, of Kurt Cobain discovering the swinging corpse of a classmate who committed suicide by hanging.[6]

A Conversation with Kurt Cobain

When I was a child I saw a movie where there was a mere shadow on a wall of someone who had hung themselves. That image gave me nightmares, so I can't imagine how discovering "the swinging corpse of a classmate who committed suicide by hanging" affected you. It would be a horror you could never shake, and an image that probably put your natural fear of death on steroids. Add to that, three people in your family who had tragically killed themselves, and you became a magnet for depression. It seems that you had already been trying to talk yourself out of your intuitive fear of dying:

> "If you die you're completely happy and your soul somewhere lives on. I'm not afraid of dying. Total peace after death, becoming someone else is the best hope I've got." — Kurt Cobain[7]

Rolling Stone magazine said of you:

> In his lyrics, Cobain dealt with the thorny discomfort of growing up and railed about his inner demons. Like Bob Dylan, he hated the notion of being dubbed "the voice of a generation" — in Cobain's case, Generation X — but got it anyway.[8]

"Inner demons" often come in the form of jealousy, bitterness, lust, envy, pride, greed, anger, or hatred. While the medical profession has treatments of what they say are mental disorders, the Bible says that this is deeper, that it's spiritual. Here is what the Scriptures say about this battle:

> For we are not fighting against people made of flesh and blood, but against persons without bodies — the evil rulers of the unseen world, those mighty satanic beings and great evil princes of darkness who rule this world; and against huge numbers of wicked spirits in the spirit world.
>
> So use every piece of God's armor to resist the enemy whenever he attacks, and when it is all over, you will still be standing up (Ephesians 6:12–13; TLB).

If you find this hard to believe, you're not alone. But weigh the evidence. No one denies that people hear voices that tell them to harm themselves and kill others. It's *very* common:

> An Ohio man accused of killing 11 women . . . told police he suffered blackouts and heard voices in his head.[9]

> Serial Killer Herbert Mullin terrorized the San Diego, California, area at the same time the infamous Co-Ed Killer, Edmund Kemper, was active. Unlike Kemper, Mullin killed anyone. Young, old, men, women, children, and even a priest in a confession booth. He didn't adhere to a particular MO. The deadly voices told him to kill . . . and he killed.[10]

These voices begin as temptations to do evil. Jesus addressed this in "The Lord's Prayer" when He said, "Lead us not into temptation, but deliver us from evil" (Matthew 6:13; ESV). If we yield to the temptation to sin we give ourselves to evil, and that takes us into the demonic realm. When we serve sin, we give place to the devil (see Ephesians 4:27).

You can see this happen in the life of King Saul in the Old Testament. He was jealous of David, and the jealousy led to hatred, and that led to his attempted murder (see 1 Samuel 16:15–16, 23, 18:10, and 19:9). The Scriptures tell us that he *literally* had his demons, and like a number of those we have looked at who hear voices, the only way he could feel free from the tormenting depression was through music (see 1 Samuel 16:21–23). Saul eventually committed suicide (see 1 Samuel 31:4).

The Book of Timothy instructs the Christian on how to speak with contentious people:

> And a servant of the Lord must not quarrel but be gentle to all, able to teach, patient, in humility correcting those who are in opposition, if God perhaps will grant them repentance, so that they may know the truth, and that they may come to their senses *and escape* the snare of the devil, having been taken captive by him to *do* his will" (2 Timothy 2:24–26, italics added).

If you want to be free of the torment of demons, stay clear of evil. Sin is like quicksand. Step into it, it will take you down, and the more you struggle to get free, the deeper it will take you. You need a divine hand to *pull* you out before the quicksand of sin *takes* you out.

We tend to forget or even hide our secret sins. They are not pleasant thoughts in the light of a holy God. So we need His help. Have you been jealous of others? Are you given to lust? Has pride filled your heart? Have you honored your parents? Do you hate your father or mother, or hate other people? Are you holding on to some sort of bitterness? Sin is giving place to the devil. It is a cancer. So pray with the Psalmist:

> Search me, O God, and know my heart; try me, and know my anxieties; and see if there is any wicked way in me, and lead me in the way everlasting (Psalm 139:23–24).

You were successful, popular, and yet depressed and confused as to why you were continually depressed: "I can't think of the exact reasons." Like millions, you were like a tightrope walker with vertigo. Without the Savior, it was just a matter of time.

Bible Promise

"And the peace of God, which transcends all understanding, will guard your hearts and minds in Christ Jesus" (Philippians 4:7).

questions **?**

1. How did Kyla Dale describe depression?
2. Why did Newsweek think that Kurt Cobain "was at an increased risk to take his own life long before he found commercial success"?
3. What traumatic incident happened in his teens that may have exacerbated his fear of death?
4. Did you have any traumatic incidents happen to you in your childhood?
5. What "gives place" to the devil?

Endnotes

1. https://themighty.com/2015/08/what-depression-really-feels-like/.

2. "Kurt Cobain talks about depression, suicide and the what the future holds for NIRVANA"; https://www.youtube.com/watch?v=Da0w-Bpbm10.

3. https://consumer.healthday.com/encyclopedia/depression-12/depression-news-176/even-in-his-youth-644949.html.

4. http://www.rollingstone.com/music/news/kurt-cobains-downward-spiral-the-last-days-of-nirvanas-leader-19940602.

5. http://www.newsweek.com/five-kurt-cobain-myths-dispelled-montage-heck-328887.

6. https://www.quora.com/Why-did-Kurt-Cobain-kill-himself-1.

7. https://www.brainyquote.com/quotes/kurt_cobain_167119.

8. https://quizlet.com/180232189/music-presentation-set-2-flash-cards/.

9. http://www.smh.com.au/world/accused---serial-killer-heard-voices-20110715-1hhe9.html.

10. https://www.amazon.com/Deadly-Voices-Serial-Herbert-Homicide-ebook/dp/B019446HDG.

Chapter 29

Marilyn Monroe

"There are no windows within the dark house of depression through which to see others, only mirrors." — Miriam Toews, *Swing Low: A Life*[1]

Marilyn Monroe (born Norma Jeane Mortenson; June 1, 1926–August 5, 1962) was an American actress and model.

Marilyn Monroe was a close friend of actress Judy Garland, whose most famous role was as Dorothy in *The Wizard of Oz* (1939). Garland was wildly successful in film and in song, but she suffered from chronic depression. One of her husbands penned a memoir about her suicide attempts:

> In one incident in the early '50s, Luft claimed that Garland's depression was so debilitating that she slashed her throat in the bathroom of their Beverly Hills home. Luft, who rushed home to find her, writes:
>
> "Judy had cut her throat with a razor blade. . . . What demons inhabited her soul just when life seemed so rich and productive? It was a gigantic puzzlement that she would poison herself with pills, and that the toxic reaction to whatever she swallowed would create an impulse for self-mutilation."
>
> Afterwards, doctors rushed to the scene and saved Garland's life.
>
> He also revealed another suicide attempt in a D.C. hotel several years later.[2]

People Entertainment revealed a telling incident that happened just before the death of Marilyn Monroe:

> According to Luft, Monroe's death was "especially troubling to Judy since Marilyn had been one of Judy's telephone pals during her years of insomnia."
>
> The book also includes an excerpt from an article written by Garland about Monroe for *Ladies Home Journal* in 1967, in which she revealed a haunting conversation she'd once had with the star. In the article, Garland described a Hollywood party one evening in which Monroe followed her "from room to room."
>
> "I don't want to get too far away from you," she said. "I'm scared!"
>
> I told her, "We're all scared. I'm scared, too!"[3]

Once again, like millions of others, Marilyn Monroe was scared and chronically depressed but didn't know why:

> For those who believe that Marilyn's death was indeed a suicide, there are many indications of her emotional fragility and a description of a past suicide attempt. "Oh Paula," she wrote in an undated note to Paula Strasberg, "I wish I knew why I am so anguished. I think maybe I'm crazy like all the other members of my family were, when I was sick I was sure I was. I'm so glad you are with me here!"[4]

As usual, doctors told her that she was mentally ill:

> In February of 1961, Marilyn entered the Payne-Whitney Clinic in New York at the suggestion of her East Coast psychiatrist, Dr. Kris. From the start, Marilyn was not comfortable at Payne-Whitney. Surprised at the security precautions, which included barred windows and glass panes in the door so that nurses could glance inside, she rebelled at being treated "like a nut." She felt that the employees at the clinic were checking on her more often than on the other patients because she was a movie star.[5]

Banishing Her Demons

As seen in Lifetime's two-part miniseries "The Secret Life of Marilyn Monroe," she tried to redefine herself and banish her demons through her marriages to Joe DiMaggio (Jeffrey Dean Morgan) and playwright Arthur Miller (Stephen Bogaert), but they were not the answer to her problems. Doomed from her childhood by family mental illness, Monroe had a rough start — and all the fame and stardom couldn't ease her bottomless anxieties.[6]

Daily Reminders

Nothing acts as a reminder of our own mortality like losing someone we love. It cuts to the bone and escalates our fear:

Marilyn attempted to go into seclusion, but her efforts were thwarted by the announcement of Clark Gable's death on November 16. Gable had had a massive heart attack the day after The Misfits had wrapped, but many had believed he was improving.

His sudden death was a severe blow.

Marilyn took the news so badly that she was unable to make a coherent statement to the press, who kept calling for her comments.[7]

Her thoughts of death were made clear in one of her poems:

In one of the handful of sweet and affecting poems included in this archive, Marilyn, still in the first flush of her love for Miller and imagining what he might have been like as a young boy, wrote a poem about him:

my love sleeps beside me — in the faint light — I see his manly jaw give way — and the mouth of his boyhood returns with a softness softer its sensitiveness trembling in stillness his eyes must have look out wonderously from the cave of the little boy — when the things he did not understand — he forgot

The poem then turns dark, a premonition, perhaps, of how the marriage would end:

But will he look like this when he is dead oh unbearable fact inevitable yet sooner would I rather his love die than/or him? "Ah Peace I Need You — Even a Peaceful Monster"[8]

We All Have to Go Sometime

In an episode of the iconic *The Andy Griffith Show* called "The Medicine Man," the writers bravely went where few dare to go. The episode opened with Aunt Bea being depressed because a friend died. But her depression wasn't because the woman had died, but because the age at which she died was the same age as Aunt Bea. The death reminded her of her own appointment.

As she spoke of her fear of dying, Barney Fife, in typical thoughtless fashion, said, "We've all got to go sometime. . . ." It was a funny line, because he was so insensitive, but it's not funny when we say "We've all got to go sometime" but don't ask why. It's thoughtless. The Bible rightly says we are like sheep. They wait for their turn at the slaughterhouse.

I will never forget seeing an aged Burgess Meredith who played Rocky's trainer in the *Rocky* series of movies looking forlorn as he spoke about the beauty of life and why it had to end. Of course, this was just an elderly celebrity in a typical LA news candy clip talking about death, and we know that we all have to go some time.

It Couldn't Happen

There's a reason Super Bowl advertising is expensive:

> The average cost of a 30-second ad for the Super Bowl crept up to $5 million this year [2017], according to ad buyers, from an estimated $4.8 million last year.[9]

Advertising influences the human mind. Think of how often they use cool music and catchy lyrics to hit home their message. They do *that* because they know that if you tell enough people to do something, some will eventually do it. They will go out and buy what you are selling.

Imagine if someone wrote a song encouraging people to commit suicide . . . a song that talked about the hopelessness of life, that death was going to take us out anyway, and that it would be good to commit suicide. Of course, one would have to be insane to write such a song. And even if they did, no one would promote it in a society where there are so many people who are unstable and suicidal. To do so should be against the law:

> A teenage girl who sent her boyfriend text messages encouraging him to kill himself asked a judge Friday to keep statements she made to police out of her involuntary manslaughter trial. The request was among almost two dozen motions filed by lawyers for Michelle Carter, now 19, in Taunton Juvenile Court, *The Boston Globe* reported.
>
> The Plainville woman is charged with involuntary manslaughter in the 2014 death of 18-year-old Conrad Roy III, of Mattapoisett.
>
> "In sum, we conclude that there was probable cause to show that the coercive quality of the defendant's verbal conduct overwhelmed whatever willpower the eighteen year old victim had to cope with his depression, and that but for the defendant's admonishments, pressure, and instructions, the victim would not have gotten back into the truck and poisoned himself to death," Justice Robert Cordy wrote for the court in the unanimous ruling.[10]

So one would think that a song with lyrics encouraging people to commit suicide could never be promoted, let alone become a hit. But it did. There was one that was recorded by dozens of high-profile artists that encouraged suicide. Here are the lyrics:

> Through early morning fog I see
> Visions of the things to be
> The pains that are withheld for me
> I realize and I can see . . .
>
> That suicide is painless
> It brings on many changes
> And I can take or leave it if I please
>
> The game of life is hard to play
> I'm gonna lose it anyway

The losing card I'll someday lay
So this is all I have to say

The sword of time will pierce our skins
It doesn't hurt when it begins
But as it works its way on in
The pain grows stronger . . . watch it grin, but. . . .[11]

This world is insane.

questions **?**

1. What did Marilyn Monroe write to Paula Strasberg?
2. In February of 1961, Marilyn entered the Payne-Whitney Clinic in New York at the suggestion of her East Coast psychiatrist, Dr. Kris. How did she feel that she was being treated?
3. In "The Secret Life of Marilyn Monroe," what was it that "doomed" her from the beginning?
4. What was the average cost for a 2017 30-second Super Bowl advertisement?
5. What are your thoughts on the lyrics of the song "Suicide is Painless"?

Endnotes

1. http://www.azquotes.com/quote/663047.

2. http://people.com/books/judy-garland-drugs-suicide-husband-memoir/.

3. http://people.com/books/judy-garlands-shocking-revelation-about-marilyn-monroe-she-asked-me-for-help/.

4. http://www.vanityfair.com/culture/2010/11/marilyn-monroe-201011.

5. http://entertainment.howstuffworks.com/marilyn-monroe-final-years4.htm.

6. http://nypost.com/2015/05/30/new-miniseries-reveals-the-secret-life-of-marilyn-monroe/.

7. http://entertainment.howstuffworks.com/marilyn-monroe-final-years4.htm.

8. Ibid.

9. https://www.nytimes.com/2017/01/29/business/5-million-for-a-super-bowl-ad-another-million-or-more-to-market-the-ad.html.

10. http://www.dailymail.co.uk/news/article-3670166/Court-OKs-trial-girl-texted-boyfriend-urging-suicide.html.

11. "Suicide is Painless," written by Mike Altman, was the theme song for the *MASH* TV series, and recorded by numerous artists.

Chapter 30

Honesty in Anonymity

I was crossing at some traffic lights on my bike when I misjudged where the sidewalk curb began and when my front wheel hit it, I went over the handlebars. As I lay on the ground, my pain was secondary. I was more concerned that the many drivers who were waiting at the lights were staring at me. I was worried about looking foolish. If I had broken both legs, my arms, neck and ribs, I would have quickly gotten back onto the bike as though all was well.

I was once speaking in the open air when a woman in high heels walked between myself and the crowd and twisted her ankle. But she recovered immediately and walked on as though nothing happened. From my vantage point, I could see that she went another 20 or so paces until she thought she was out of sight, and then she buckled up in pain. We are proud creatures.

That is the reason so many are reticent to admit that they fear death. They don't want to look weak. However, I recently came across a gold mine of honesty. It was a website where a would-be filmmaker said,

> Hello Everyone. I personally don't have this fear — or at least not abnormally. I'm currently working as a Media Student and I'm about to start a new film. The plot is still being written and I was wondering if anyone could help me.
>
> My main character is called Evangeline — she's a young woman who suffers from the fear of her own death. As a child she suffered a near death experience by nearly drowning. Throughout her life Evangeline avoids anything which

could cause or be linked to her own death. She becomes very restricted and struggles to live a full life.

My film is going to be a thriller so it would be nice if anyone could message me some experiences or ideas. Anything to do with the fear of death. Thank you so much for your help![1]

People were able to respond anonymously, and the result was rare honesty-of-heart. No one was concerned about looking weak and vulnerable, and their responses are heartbreaking and hopelessly depressing. But they bolster my case that the Bible is right when it says that *every* human being is *all their lifetime* held a prisoner to the fear of death (Hebrews 2:15). Some have always been conscious of the fear, while some only realized it through a traumatic experience, and it became prevalent after that experience:

I Have a Severe Fear of Death. I Don't Know Why

Hey everyone, I had no clue that there was a group like this, but I am very glad that I found it. My story; I have feared death since I was 23 and I'm 48 now, it has not left my mind, not for one single day. I had an anxiety attack at the age of 23, and that's where it all began. Now for 25 years I have thought each day that it would be my last. I've been in therapy for this, and I'm back in it again. I can't understand why I just can't live a normal life, and just live? But I DO live each day in fear of death. It Will Not Leave My Mind. I wish it would, just for a day. I'm not sure if it's dying that I'm afraid of, or maybe just leaving the ones that I love. But it really seems that it's just death itself that I fear. I hate it and wish I could rid of my everyday fear; the fear of dying.

I Don't Know What Exactly

It's a combination of what will happen to me when I die, and what's dying actually like? It's so severe that anytime I hear anything to do with death I panic inside. I feel horrible ever since I can remember, it has scared me. It actually keeps me awake sometimes, or I start panicking at night time. I have a wonderful family and friends but this fear has had me feeling so alone at times. It's depressing because I feel like an idiot fearing the one thing we all face at some stage. Does anybody else feel the way I feel?

I Have a Severe Fear of Death

I have a severe fear of death. Unlike many people here I cannot tell you when this fear started. However my fear of aging is fairly new. I have had a lot of changes in my life from this past two years. My grandfather past away a couple months back, and then my aunt past away.

Random Attacks

I have random panic attacks about dying, even when I am not thinking about death.

Fear of Death Is Driving Me Crazy

Hello Everyone. I guess I will start off by saying my fear of death started as a child. Any time I think of it, of what happens after (do I just disappear? Everyone I love?). I have panic attacks. Just typing this is unsettling me. As a child I talked to my father and he settled my fears by promising to be there waiting for me in the after life. He passed away when I was 22 and in my heart I am still holding him to his promise! Now I am almost 39 and the youngest of my family, my mother will be turning 70, my brothers 49 and 42. Time seems to be flying by so fast and it seems that there is so few years left to us. I know this sounds illogical but I cant help it. Most of the time I am fine and then something clicks and I'm pacing back and forth across the floor just about to come out of my skin in fear.

I'm Going Crazy

I don't know who to talk to, because I really feel like I'm going crazy. My family is not very religious; I believe that there is more than this life, but I'm not sure and no one can prove it to me. This fear is starting to interfere with my life, lately I have been having a bit of chest pain. . . . I am having a hard time falling asleep this last week. The stupid thought that I'm going to die in my sleep keeps going through my head, and if I did what will happen to my mother and brothers? Who would find my body etc., etc. Even right now it is almost midnight and here I am. Does any one have any suggestions how I can cope with this fear? Please understand that saying trust in god is not going to help me.

Every one of us has an intuitive knowledge of God. We know He exists because the heavens declare His glory (see Psalm 19:1–2). The Scriptures tell us that the invisible things of Him from the creation of the world are clearly seen in the things that are made, so we are "without excuse" (see Romans 1:20). And we know that He requires morality because we have a conscience that is shaped by society but God-given.

It is because of his knowledge of right and wrong that this person, like a guilty criminal, cowers in the security of darkness. He wants to find God as much as a bank robber wants to find a police officer. The only way to bring him out of the darkness is to convince him that he is in big trouble with the Law, that he can't escape its wrath, and the convincing agent is his conscience under the light of the Ten Commandments. It is in that place of humility that he can find mercy — because of the Cross. When John Newton penned *Amazing Grace,* he said, "It was grace that taught my heart to fear, and grace my fears relieved." In other words, God first showed him his sins, but then that same amazing grace freely forgave him.

So this person doesn't need to be told to trust God at this point in time. Trust, to him, will be meaningless. He needs to be shown his sin *first* and the certainty of judgment, and once he has that knowledge, he needs to trust God in Christ for his salvation (deliverance). It's like me trying to convince you to trust a parachute when you don't see your need for one. It would be meaningless.

But if you were hung out of the plane by your ankles for a few seconds and told that you have to jump at any moment, you would say, *"Give me that parachute!"* And part of the parachute package is to have your fears relieved. You will be delivered from the fear of death.

On top of this, God will "seal" you with the Holy Spirit (2 Corinthians 1:22). That means that you will not only be made new on the inside, but you will have the knowledge that you have passed from death to life.

If I promised to give you $5 million tomorrow at midday, but gave you $2 million today as a token of good faith, it would be reasonable for you to believe that you have another $3 million coming tomorrow. When God seals us with His Holy Spirit, it is a token of good faith so that we can have complete confidence that He will keep his promise of everlasting life.

Fear

Hi, I'm not sure why I have never looked this up on the Internet before now. Basically ever since I can remember, I mean like my earliest memories when I was a child, I have had this overwhelming fear of death.

Fear of Death

Since I crashed my car, a month after passing my driving test, I haven't been the same. I hate going out just in case something happens and I don't come home. I don't sleep because I feel like I won't wake up the next day.

I Have a Paralyzing Fear of Being Dead

I don't really know how to explain it, but I have an extreme fear of being dead. I don't really have much of a story except that this fear has not allowed me to eat, sleep, I have nasty panic attacks, and I throw up a lot. I feel this feeling will never go away.

Fear of Death

My fear of death is related to not having anyone to relate my death with. There are two life events that matter; birth and death. The rest are just spaces we fill up in between.

The Afterlife or the Lack of It

For the last 8 months I have been consumed with my mortality. I know death is inevitable, but I fear it. It is not so much death, but what happens after death. Is there nothing; an empty void with no self-awareness, or is there truly some divine place of peace where I can reunite with the souls of my loved ones? I often struggle to sleep at night, so overwhelmed by thoughts of death. I wish I could go back to my normal self, and enjoy my wonderful life. I wish I was a spiritual person, but my rational mind will not allow me to believe in blind faith. Can anybody help?

Help

Ever since I was about 10 or 11 I've had a very frightening fear of death. When I was younger I used to obsess about being buried — not because I worried about being buried alive, but because I couldn't understand what happened and where I went, that thought still terrifies me.

I Do Fear Death!!

I can relate to all of your stories. I have had a fear of death since I was 15; mine though only comes every 4 yrs in the fall and winter months. I get so discouraged when I talk about it to family and friends and they tell me they have no fear!! Even talked to my doctor about it and he said, "We all die." A lot of help he was. I not so much worry about how I'm gonna die. I worry about what is after death, and the not knowing really scares me.

My Fear of Death

Is that once I'm gone, I'm just gone, like I never existed, and life goes on on this planet like it didn't even happen, and there's nothing left of me, no trace, no legacy, no statue, no building, not structures to remember me.

I Want This Thought to Leave!

The thought of dying is getting worse by the day, and I feel that I fear it more than anyone. . . . I know that many of us do have a severe fear, but my G-d! It Will Not Leave My Head!!! I've been online looking at caskets, headstones. Is this a sign that I am going to die?

Fear of Death

One day, like a slap across the face, it hit me. I acknowledged my own mortality. This was five years ago when two loved ones passed away. Before that, I saw SO MANY people die. I work in the medical field for goodness sake. People drop like flies!

So Scared

I was raised Methodist and I still identify as a believer in God. Regardless, I still feel terrified of the thought of death. What if I'm not a good person, and my afterlife is bad because of it? I'm so scared.

Terrified

Just within the last few weeks I started this death and dying "phobia." I think it stems from my loneliness and fear that I will die alone. I think about it as soon as I wake up and when I'm going to bed. I cannot imagine never seeing this earth and its people again.

Phobia

I have a severe fear of death and dying. And it's just not me, it's also fear that my mum, dad, and brother would die. I try to stay awake and avoid sleeping to make sure that I'm still breathing in the morning.

Not Religious

I'm not religious, even though I wish the after life is real, I believe it's not. So because of that I have a severe fear of death. I avoid thinking about it as much as possible because when I do, usually at night when I'm alone, I start shaking and crying. I have panic attacks thinking about it.

My Daily Torment

Ever since I was 11 years of age I started to think about death, but it didn't seem to affect me too much. However in the last few months the fear I have has become more severe, and now virtually every minute of the day is spent dwelling on it.

Every Day

I think about it daily. I really do get scared. Terrified.

This Fear Is All Consuming . . .

I have been having full-out panic attacks about this for years now. I can usually suppress it, but sometimes I just can't. I am absolutely terrified. I think about it at least 5 times a day. Today I became physically ill because of it.

This Feeling Will Never Go Away

I have had a severe fear of death for as long as I remember. It began as panic attacks about twice as a child. These thoughts have come back to me recently. As much as I push them away they return. I do not understand how everyone does not have this extreme fear.

As we have seen, everyone *does* have this extreme fear. The Bible not only tells us that, but it tells us of the beginnings of the human race, its supreme purpose on earth, and its ultimate and eternal destiny.

For our own good, the Bible warns of of the dangers of gluttony, lust, greed, and drunkenness, tells how to raise our kids, how to make nations prosper, and how to make our marriages blossom. It explains why there is evil, warns of the coming Day of Judgment, offers sinful man God's mercy, and it displays His great love. It tells us why there is suffering, aging, death, how to overcome the fear of death, and how to find everlasting life without being religious.

questions?

1. Have you ever fallen over in public and felt foolish? Why did you feel foolish?
2. Put Hebrews 2:15 in your own words.
3. How would you give evidence for the existence of God?
4. What were your emotions as you read these anonymous cries for help?
5. If you're a Christian, are you fearful to share the gospel? Why?

Endnotes

1. http://www.experienceproject.com/groups/Have-A-Severe-Fear-Of-Death/226030..

Chapter 31

Doctors Bury Their Mistakes

I admire doctors. When I visit one and see a sea of sick humanity waiting to see him (or her) about a problem, I wonder how he makes it through each day. That's why I usually ask mine how he's doing and try to make him laugh. I feel the same about dentists, and thank God that He has made us different. I would go crazy peering down human drains. Then there are amazing surgeons. How could anybody slice living, bloody human skin with a blade and have a slither of job satisfaction? But they do.

Gifted though they may be, doctors are human, and in being mere mortals, they are capable of making mistakes. They also get depressed. They are just like the rest of us, yet they are portrayed in drug advertising as miracle-workers. "If you have a problem or a question, see your doctor." It's as if they can fix anything. But they can't.

Take a Guess

If you had to make an estimate as to how many Americans die each year through medical mistakes, how many would you say? If there were as many as a *thousand* fathers or mothers or precious children dying because of human error, I would think that there would be an outcry. But there are *more* than a thousand:

> Based on an analysis of prior research, the Johns Hopkins study estimates that more than 250,000 Americans die each year from medical errors. On the CDC's official list, that would rank just behind heart disease and cancer, which each took about 600,000 lives in 2014, and in front of respiratory disease, which caused about 150,000 deaths.

Medical mistakes that can lead to death range from sur-
gical complications that go unrecognized to mix-ups with
the doses or types of medications patients receive.[1]

These sobering statistics tell us that we are justified in questioning
the medical community when they say that depression is a disease,
and that its sufferers are mentally ill.

Wind-chasing

The favorite football team is trailing by ten points with 20 minutes
to go. *They could still win the game.* Hope is present. Time passes. It's
now two minutes to go with ten points needed. Less than a minute.
Winning is now *impossible.* All hope is gone. Even the faithful begin
leaving before the game is over.

When someone has a fear of death and no end to their nightmare, they lose all hope of winning. They begin to consider leaving
the game early. Suicide becomes their only way of escape. Without
hope, life is futile. It is as Solomon said — chasing the wind. The
1960 hit song by Peggy Lee about the futility of life hit the mark:

> Is that all there is, is that all there is
> If that's all there is my friends, then let's keep dancing
> Let's break out the booze and have a ball
> If that's all there is. . . .[2]

But what do you do if even the "ball" loses its bounce? What do you
do when dancing and booze no longer cut the mustard — when
you have had your little song and dance in the line of mortality?
Chronic depression rains a monsoon of fear on your parade, and
you don't even have an umbrella.

The shadow of death falls on you in your hopeless futility.

The Apostle Paul quoted the Book of Isaiah when he spoke of
what to do if we find ourselves without hope. He said, "Let us eat
and drink, for tomorrow we die" (see Isaiah 22:13 and 1 Corinthians 15:32). It's the common philosophy of the hopeless. Death is
coming, so squeeze whatever happiness you can get out of this life
before that happens. Party. And do it today, because tomorrow may
not come.

The context of Paul's lament was that if the gospel wasn't true, then we have *reason* to be chronically depressed. If Jesus Christ was just another religious teacher and God didn't raise Him from the dead as Jesus said He would, then we have no hope: "If in this life only we have hope in Christ, we are of all men most miserable"(1 Corinthians 15:19; KJV). We are like this hopeless world.

The experts would have us believe that every person in the previous chapter was suffering from mental illness — because they thought about death incessantly. But any *sane* person does . . . just as a condemned-to-death criminal thinks of his appointment. It looms over him as it nears.

Each of us wait to be executed because we have broken God's Law. But the moment Jesus cried, "It is finished!" (John 19:30) the debt to the moral Law was paid, and the Judge could then *legally* commute our death sentence. He could dismiss our case. The prisoner could be set free:

> I am he that liveth, and was dead; and, behold, I am alive for evermore, Amen; and have the keys of hell and of death (Revelation 1:18; KJV).

Notice how the word "hope" is referred to as a *living* hope:

> Blessed be the God and Father of our Lord Jesus Christ, who according to His abundant mercy has begotten us again to a living hope through the resurrection of Jesus Christ from the dead, to an inheritance incorruptible and undefiled and that does not fade away, reserved in heaven for you, who are kept by the power of God through faith for salvation ready to be revealed in the last time (1 Peter 1:3–5).

questions ?

1. How many Americans die each year through medical mistakes?
2. What did the 1960 hit song by Peggy Lee say about the futility of life?
3. Put Revelation 1:18 in your own words.

4. According to 1 Peter 1:3–5, what is the inheritance of the Christian?

5. Why do you think so few share the gospel with this tragic and lost world?

Endnotes

1. http://www.npr.org/sections/health-shots/2016/05/03/476636183/death-certificates-undercount-toll-of-medical-errors.

2. "Is That All There Is?" by Jerry Leiber and Mike Stoller.

Chapter 32

He Gave England Hope

Sir Winston Leonard Spencer-Churchill (born November 30, 1874–died January 24, 1965) was a British statesman who was the Prime Minister of the United Kingdom from 1940 to 1945 and again from 1951 to 1955.

Winston Churchill was a lighthouse in perhaps the darkest of storms in human history. Hitler was showering England with bombs in the early years of the Second World War, and the prognosis was chronically depressing. The United States was isolated from what was called the "European" war, and it seemed that it would just be a matter of time until Great Britain was conquered.

But Churchill would have none of it.

He gave rousing speeches that gave England living hope. People hung onto every syllable as life-giving water in a parched desert. Here are some of his wonderfully inspiring words:

> I would say to the House, as I said to those who have joined this government: "I have nothing to offer but blood, toil, tears and sweat."
>
> We have before us an ordeal of the most grievous kind. We have before us many, many long months of struggle and of suffering. You ask, what is our policy? I can say: It is to wage war, by sea, land and air, with all our might and with all the strength that God can give us; to wage war against a monstrous tyranny, never surpassed in the dark, lamentable catalogue of human crime. That is our policy. You ask, what is our aim?

I can answer in one word: It is victory, victory at all costs, victory in spite of all terror, victory, however long and hard the road may be; for without victory, there is no survival. Let that be realized; no survival for the British Empire, no survival for all that the British Empire has stood for, no survival for the urge and impulse of the ages, that mankind will move forward towards its goal. But I take up my task with buoyancy and hope.[1]

Arguably, the climax of all Churchill said in those dark days was in this marvelous exhortation:

We shall go on to the end, we shall fight in France, we shall fight on the seas and oceans, we shall fight with growing confidence and growing strength in the air, we shall defend our Island, whatever the cost may be, we shall fight on the beaches, we shall fight on the landing grounds, we shall fight in the fields and in the streets, we shall fight in the hills; we shall *never* surrender, and even if, which I do not for a moment believe, this Island or a large part of it were subjugated and starving, then our Empire beyond the seas, armed and guarded by the British Fleet, would carry on the struggle, until, in God's good time, the New World, with all its power and might, steps forth to the rescue and the liberation of the old.[2]

The Irony

There is an irony when it came to this powerfully positive and courageous man. *He suffered from chronic depression.* According to modern medicine, he was mentally ill. Yet there are clues that this isn't true — that he merely understood the precious nature of his life:

Little did they know how shaky those hands were. For decades, Churchill had avoided standing too close to balconies and train platforms:

I don't like standing near the edge of a platform when an express train is passing through. I like to stand back and, if possible, get a pillar between me and the train. I don't like to stand by the side of a ship and look down into the water. A second's action would end everything. A few drops of desperation.[3]

Such respect for life shouldn't be construed as an abnormality, but rather a sober appreciation that death could be but a moment away. These are the musings of a sane and thoughtful mind. "The fear of death" is an expression for *self-preservation* and the *love* of life. Those who lack a fear of death, and would without any concern stand on the edge of balconies and close to a passing train, are the ones who could be more rightly labeled mentally ill.

His battle started young:

Churchill knew it and named [depression] his "black dog," following Samuel Johnson (who, like many great men, suffered from the great disease of manic-depression). Churchill was so paralyzed by despair that he spent time in bed, had little energy, few interests, lost his appetite, couldn't concentrate. He was minimally functional – and this didn't just happen once or twice in the 1930s, but also in the 1920s and 1910s and earlier. These darker periods would last a few months, and then he'd come out of it and be his normal self.[4]

Like the very sane and likable Carrie Fisher and Stephen Fry, Churchill had great wit. He once said: "I am very fond of pigs. Dogs look up to us, cats look down on us, but pigs treat us as equals." But in the light of his chronic depression, the BBC said,

Winston Churchill led Britain to victory over the Nazis against all the odds. He courageously conquered Hitler and his own personal demons. But how would we view Churchill today? Would his bouts of depression be a stumbling block in the public mind? Not to mention his flamboyant behavior, his gambling, his love of fine food and alcohol at a time of austerity.

A man like Churchill would send the spin doctors into a spin, but perhaps we would like our politicians to have more character and to be more open about their failings. In her darkest hour Britain needed a prophet, a heroic vision- ary, a man who could dream of victory when all seemed lost. Winston Churchill was that man, but would we want him back?[5]

How dare they even ask. Yes! We want those like Carrie Fisher, Bruce Springsteen, Stephen Fry, Robin Williams, and Winston Churchill. Don't tell them they are insane and medicate them out of their sane thinking. Medication is nothing but a bandaid on terminal cancer — the contemporary straight-jacket to stop the patient from doing himself harm. Instead, they should be told that they can be delivered from the fear that they will have to fight all their lifetime, unless they come to Christ. That fear has only two cures: faith in Jesus or death.

The Bible says of Jesus that it was "not possible" that death could hold Him, and when you and I yield our lives to Him, death cannot hold us either. We whisper, "O death, where is your sting?" (1 Corinthians 15:55). This is the soul-stirring, life-giving, hope-filled message those who are hopelessly lost in darkness need to hear. When someone calls upon God, like Lazarus, they are roused by the voice of Jesus of Nazareth. They find light in their darkness, and hope bursts into the soul like the early morning sun bursts through an open door. Without that living hope, you will be left alone to sing a somber, *Is that all there is?* Churchill's last words were, "I'm so bored with it all."[6]

questions **?**

1. Who was Sir Winston Churchill?
2. What did he offer the United Kingdom in the face of war?
3. What was the irony when it came to this powerfully positive and courageous man?
4. What did Churchill call his depression?
5. What were Winston Churchill's last words?

Endnotes

1. https://www.presentationmagazine.com/winston-churchill-speech-blood-toil-tears-and-sweat-7878.htm.

2. https://www.presentationmagazine.com/winston-churchill-speech-we-shall-fight-them-on-the-beaches-8003.htm.

3. http://theconversation.com/winston-churchill-and-his-black-dog-of-greatness-36570.

4. Ibid.

5. http://www.bbc.co.uk/guides/zqjpsbk#z8wpsbk.

6. https://en.m.wikiquote.org/wiki/Last_words.

Chapter 33

Veteran Suicide — Frightening Conclusions

There is an epidemic of suicides among our veteran soldiers. A recent VA study found that 20 veterans commit suicide *each day*. And no one can put their finger on why this is happening:

> Roughly 20 veterans a day commit suicide nationwide, according to new data from the Department of Veterans Affairs — a figure that dispels the often quoted, but problematic, "22 a day" estimate yet solidifies the disturbing mental health crisis the number implied.
>
> In 2014, the latest year available, more than 7,400 veterans took their own lives, accounting for 18 percent of all suicides in America. Veterans make up less than 9 percent of the U.S. population.
>
> About 70 percent of veterans who took their own lives were not regular users of VA services.
>
> The new data, being released publicly today, is the most comprehensive suicide study ever conducted by the department.[1]

And as usual the response has been to say that those who committed suicide suffered from mental disease. The alternative is to say that they were normal, stable, sane human beings, and in the face of their suicide, that makes no sense. Sane people don't kill themselves.

The National Alliance on Mental Illness in their Depression and Veterans FACT SHEET said,

There is no single cause of major depression. Psychological, biological and environmental factors may all contribute to its development. . . . Scientists have also found evidence of a genetic predisposition to major depression. There is an increased risk for developing depression when there is a family history of the illness.[2]

But that leaves them with some frightening conclusions:

In addition, mental health rates have risen 65% in the military since 2000, with 936,000 troops diagnosed with at least one mental health issue in that time, according to the new data.[3]

They end up with results that show that 936,000 American soldiers are running around with guns, and they have mental problems.

Many of these efforts were catalyzed by VA's February 2016 Preventing Veteran Suicide — A Call to Action summit, which focused on improving mental health care access for Veterans across the nation and increasing resources for the VA Suicide Prevention Program.[4]

A study reported by CNN showed:

What's causing soldiers to kill themselves at a record rate . . . suicides last year among active and non-active military personnel — are the same mental health problems that can be found in the general population, according to the study authors: depression, manic depression and alcohol abuse.[5]

The conclusion is that veterans are killing themselves for the same reason non-military people kill themselves: depression. The problem is that they don't know what causes depression, nor do they know why the rate is so much higher in the military.

In February of 2013 CNN reported,

Military experts have long said one of the enduring challenges is that there doesn't appear to be a direct link

between suicides and the stress of being in the combat zone.
. . . Nobody knows No. 1, why all the suicides.[6]

The National Center for Veterans Studies at the University of Utah
published a study that also found that the reason veterans take their
lives is the same reason non-military people kill themselves:

> When researchers asked 72 soldiers at Fort Carson,
> Colo., why they tried to kill themselves, out of the 33 rea-
> sons they had to choose from, all of the soldiers included one
> in particular — a desire to end intense emotional distress.
>
> "This really is the first study that provides scientific data
> saying that the top reason . . . these guys are trying to kill
> themselves [is] because they have this intense psychologi-
> cal suffering and pain," said Craig Bryan, co-author of the
> study by the National Center for Veterans Studies at the
> University of Utah that will be published in the coming
> months.
>
> But military scientists say that finally, after years of con-
> gressional funding and the launch of randomized studies of
> a subject rarely researched, a few validated results are begin-
> ning to surface.[7]

In April of 2015, PBS featured a story on "What We Still Don't
Understand about Military Suicides," which used information from
a recent study by *JAMA Psychiatry*:

> The JAMA study found two subsets of military service
> members who seem to be especially at risk. It examined the
> records of 3.9 million service members who served in the
> military from October 7, 2001, when the Afghanistan war
> began, through Dec. 31, 2007.
>
> Researchers found a higher risk of suicide among those
> who either left the military before their four years of service
> were up, or who received a less-than-honorable discharge.
>
> The new data leaves another unanswered question: If
> deployment alone is not a factor, and military members are
> affected by the same everyday stresses as the rest of the pop-
> ulation, why has the suicide rate risen now?

"That is exactly the question everyone is working so hard to understand," said Mark Reger, the JAMA study's main author and deputy director of the DOD's National Center for Telehealth and Technology. "The answers that we have are not satisfying at this point."[8]

There is an answer to this question, and we can get clues by reading what the soldiers themselves write on the subject in answer to the question, *How does a soldier overcome the fear of death in combat?*

One problem with the fear of death is that after a while it becomes so ingrained that even when the real danger is long over the soldier still can't shake it off. The fear is eating your soul. And even long after the war when you might have forgotten all about it, a sound or a smell, the mentioning of a name or the look at a picture might bring back this fear. Then you are screwed. Fear of death is the strongest emotion. You can't overcome it and in the end it might get you.[9]

Another soldier addresses the same question:

Mostly though, fear is overcome by one's extreme concentration on executing the mission. No other thoughts seem to filter into your overloaded mind at the time. One's training takes over and you act accordingly. Training and the desire to accomplish one's mission and protect all who are in harm's way with you takes over most all one's brain cells and synapses. Thus the already overcrowded brain does not allow fear to sneak in. Fear is overcome by action, based upon extensive training.[10]

Notice that the question "How does a soldier overcome the fear of death in combat?" uses the words "the fear of death" in the question. This helps the soldiers to *unashamedly* shape their answer.

Here's the problem. During service, the soldier in training knows that it's normal to fear death. He therefore rationalizes it. It makes sense, and as a soldier he trains himself to fight it. He could die at any moment. That's what being a soldier is about. Live with your justified fear. The fear of death makes sense. It's nothing to be depressed about.

But when he leaves the military, *he still has the fear.* But he is not in training. He therefore thinks that his uncontrollable fear is irrational. It makes no sense. He's home with family. There's no danger, but there's dread. And so, thanks to modern psychiatry, he begins to believe that he's mentally unbalanced.

But we know better. Dear soldier, you are not insane. You love life. You love your precious family, your liberty, and you love God and country. You need not surrender to depression, alcohol, legal and illegal drugs, or to suicide. Instead, take courage. Drop to your knees as a guilty sinner and make peace with your Creator. The solution is simple.

questions ?

1. How many U.S. veterans commit suicide each day?
2. What's the alternative to saying that these people are mentally ill?
3. How many of our soldiers do experts say are mentally ill?
4. What was the number one reason (in the Fort Carson, Colorado, study) why veterans tried to kill themselves?
5. Explain how a soldier rationalizes his fear of death while in training.

Endnotes

1. http://www.militarytimes.com/story/veterans/2016/07/07/va-suicide-20-daily-research/86788332/.

2. https://www.voaww.org/pdf_files/signs-depression.

3. http://usatoday30.usatoday.com/news/military/story/2012-07-10/army-study-soldiers-suicides/56136192/1.

4. http://www.va.gov/opa/pressrel/pressrelease.cfm?id=2801.

5. Jen Christensen, "Study: Mental Illness, Not Combat, Causes Soldier Suicides," CNN, August 6, 2013; http://www.cnn.com/2013/08/06/health/soldier-suicides-cause-study/.

6. Tom Watkins and Maggie Schneider, "325 Army Suicides in 2012 a Record," CNN, February 2, 2013; https://www.cnn.com/2013/02/02/us/army-suicides.

7. Gregg Zoroya, "Study Reveals Top Reason Behind Solders' Suicides," USA Today; http://usatoday30.usatoday.com/news/military/story/2012-07-10/army-study-soldiers-suicides/56136192/1.

8. Sarah Childress, "What We Still Don't Understand about Military Suicides," Frontline, PBS, April 3, 2015; http://www.pbs.org/wgbh/frontline/article/what-we-still-dont-understand-about-military-suicides/.

9. https://www.quora.com/How-does-a-soldier-overcome-the-fear-of-death-in-combat.

   Publisher's note: There are online resources available for those at risk for suicide in the military including: https://dod.defense.gov/News/Special-Reports/0916_suicideprevention/ and https://dod.defense.gov/News/Special-Reports/0915_suicideprevention/.

10. Ibid.

Chapter 34

Tough Talk

Steve Jobs famously said,

> Remembering that I'll be dead soon is the most important tool I've ever encountered to help me make the big choices in life. Almost everything — all external expectations, all pride, all fear of embarrassment or failure — these things just fall away in the face of death, leaving only what is truly important. Remembering that you are going to die is the best way I know to avoid the trap of thinking you have something to lose. You are already naked. There is no reason not to follow your heart. No one wants to die. Even people who want to go to heaven don't want to die to get there. And yet, death is the destination we all share. No one has ever escaped it, and that is how it should be, because death is very likely the single best invention of life. It's life's change agent. It clears out the old to make way for the new.[1]

Tough talk is easier when the enemy is at a distance. But when he was nearing the final weeks of his cancer battle, he began to have sober and personal thoughts of God and the afterlife. He said, "I saw my life as an arc. And that it would end and compared to that nothing mattered. You're born alone, you're gonna die alone. And does anything else really matter? I mean what is it exactly is it that you have to lose Steve? You know? There's nothing."[2]

Jobs' biographer said,

> I remember sitting in his backyard in his garden one day and he started talking about God. He said, "Sometimes I

believe in God, sometimes I don't. I think it's 50-50 maybe. But ever since I've had cancer, I've been thinking about it more. And I find myself believing a bit more. I kind of — maybe it's 'cause I want to believe in an afterlife. That when you die, it doesn't just all disappear."[3]

We don't know what happened between Steve Jobs and his Creator in his final days. However, we do know his final words:

> Steve Jobs's sister Mona Simpson has a moving tribute in the *New York Times* detailing some of his final moments and his last words. According to the article, titled "A Sister's Eulogy for Steve Jobs," Jobs's last words were "OH WOW. OH WOW. OH WOW." (The words were rendered in all capital letters in the essay.)[4]

Early in 2017, I received the following email from a young man in Ireland:

> I have always suffered from anxiety, but since September 2016 that anxiety has increased and turned into crippling depression. I would wake up constantly during nights, I would cry uncontrollably and I would beg God to take this pain away from me.
>
> I would have suicidal thoughts, and in November I had a plan to do exactly that. It was 4am and I was in my dad's garage with a bottle of diesel, and the only thing that stopped me was the thought of my parents and how they will be destroyed.
>
> I have been going to a suicide prevention clinic and have been given a small dose of medication to balance my hormones. I desperately need advice and help because I'm losing hope in the Lord. I never thought I would say that, but I am.

I shared much of the following with him.

I'm sure you know the famous Bible verse speaking of faith, hope, and love. Here it is in context:

When I was a child, I spoke as a child, I understood as a child, I thought as a child; but when I became a man, I put away childish things. For now we see in a mirror, dimly, but then face to face. Now I know in part, but then I shall know just as I also am known. And now abide faith, hope, love, these three; but the greatest of these is love (1 Corinthians 13:11–13).

Faith, hope, and love are linked together for a reason. If you lose hope, it's because you've lost faith, and if you lose faith it's because you have lost sight of love.

On Saturday, December 30, 2016, at Buena Park, California, a ride at Knott's Berry Farm became stuck at 148 feet in the air. The theme park is just ten minutes down the freeway, and Sue and I had been on that particular ride. It wasn't a death-defying upside down, insane, roller coaster. It was just one of those slow moving, very safe, non-stressful, high-rise, sight-seeing rides for families. But it got stuck high in the air with 21 people on board, including 7 children.

Firefighters tried to reach the stranded passengers by using a massive ladder, but it was too short. Everything else they attempted was unsuccessful. Fire crews had no choice. They would have to lower each passenger from 148 feet in the air, harnessed to a single rope. Orange County Fire Authority Capt. Larry Kurtz told Eye-witness News,

> We have firefighters in the cab with the occupants. No one is in any medical distress. So we're going to affix a harness onto each one of them and one at a time we're going to lower them down to the ground.

A father of three children who were on the ride at the time said he wasn't worried about the situation:

> This is America. We (are one of the safest) countries in the world. It sounds scary, but these guys, they train for this all the time. We have very, very strong ropes that have 9,000 pounds of breaking strength on them.

All of 20 passengers and the ride operator were lowered safely to the ground just before 10 p.m. that night.[5]

Think of those 20 people who were stuck high in the air. A stranger was going to put a rope around each one of them and accompany them to the safety of the ground. Each person had to go alone with the firefighter, swung out 148 feet over the earth knowing that certain death awaited if something went wrong.

The captain had good reason to say, "It sounds scary, but these guys, they train for this all the time. We have very, very strong ropes that have 9,000 pounds of breaking strength on them." He was building the *faith* of those who were trapped. He was giving them information *that if believed* would dissipate their fears. All he could do was give them the knowledge, but it was up to each person to believe what he said and place their trust in the firefighter.

Let's zero in on one of the youngsters, and say his name was Luke. He's seven years old — old enough to feel terror as he looks over the edge to the ground 148 feet below.

His dad places Luke into the hands of the firefighter. The firefighter looks Luke in his eyes, and with a steadying voice says, "Trust me, Luke. I won't let you go. Your life is *very* precious to me, and I will have you down before you know it."

Luke listens to him speak. He thinks about what he heard about the "very, very strong rope." He believes the firefighter's reassuring words and trusts him completely. Besides, he has no choice. This is his only hope of getting to safety. If he doesn't have faith, then he doesn't believe that the firefighter cares for him. He would then lose his only hope of reaching the ground. Faith, hope, and love are bound together.

Giant Despair

You may have heard of the famous allegory *Pilgrim's Progress*. It was written by John Bunyan in the 17th century, after he was put in prison for 13 years for preaching the gospel without a license from the Anglican Church. While in prison he wrote his amazing book:

The Pilgrim's Progress is the ultimate English classic, a book that has been continuously in print, from its first publication to the present day, in an extraordinary number of editions. There's no book in English, apart from the Bible, to equal Bunyan's masterpiece for the range of its readership, or its influence on writers as diverse as William Thackeray, Charlotte Bronte, Mark Twain, CS Lewis, John Steinbeck and even Enid Blyton.[6]

It begins with a man reading a book that convinces him that the entire sinful world will come under the wrath of God, so he begins a journey to find eternal life. After finding everlasting life through faith in Jesus, Christian meets a man named *Hopeful*. They are sidetracked from the straight and narrow path and are confronted by a giant named *Despair*. He says that they are trespassing and locks them in a deep, dark dungeon in Doubting Castle, where they lie for days without food or drink. After some time, *Giant Despair* appears, beats them almost senseless, and advises them to commit suicide so that he won't have to return and kill them.

When all seems hopeless, Christian suddenly says, "What a fool am I, thus to lie in a stinking dungeon when I may as well walk at liberty. I have a key in my bosom called Promise which will (I am persuaded) open any lock in Doubting Castle."

He does that and escapes the clutches of *Giant Despair,* getting back on the straight and narrow path where they should be.

If you doubt God's promises, you will find yourself in Doubting Castle being tormented by *Giant Despair*. Don't ever doubt God — ever — *unless you enjoy the feeling of despair and thoughts of suicide.*

So do what Christian did. He reached into his own breast and found the Key of Promise. I can't do that for you. Nobody can "trust" for you. You have to do that yourself. God has given you the key to your own release. Just like that seven-year-old boy whose father couldn't do the trusting for him. If Luke totally trusts the firefighter he will even enjoy the ride down. He will have no fear at all. That's why Jesus said that we must become as little children to enter the kingdom of God (Matthew 18:3). Little children don't have a problem with doubt. They simply trust.

Say to yourself: What a fool am I, thus to lie in a stinking dungeon of depression with despairing thoughts of suicide! I have a key to get out of this prison, and I am going to use it right now. I trust God. I will never doubt Him again — ever. And if temptation to doubt comes to my mind, I will dismiss it as I would a disgustingly filthy thought.

Cling to the Firefighter. There's nothing to fear when you are in His trustworthy hands. He is faithful who promised.

Bible Promise

> Why are you cast down, O my soul? And why are you disquieted within me? Hope in God; for I shall yet praise Him, the help of my countenance and my God (Psalm 43:5).

questions ?

1. What was Steve Jobs' most important tool that helped him make the big choices in life?
2. What odds did he give for the existence of God?
3. How would you witness to someone who gave those odds?
4. What were the last words of Steve Jobs?
5. According to the famous allegory *Pilgrim's Progress*, who appears the moment we doubt God's promises?

Endnotes

1. https://www.goodreads.com/quotes/427317-remembering-that-i-ll-be-dead-soon-is-the-most-important.

2. https://www.christianpost.com/news/steve-jobs-biography-religious-views-changed-due-to-cancer-59153/.

3. http://oregonfaithreport.com/2011/10/steve-jobs-on-god-afterlife-were-challenged-at-the-end/.

4. Christopher John Farley, " 'Oh Wow': What Do Steve Jobs's Last Words Really Mean?" *The Wall Street Journal*, October 31, 2011; http://blogs.wsj.com/speakeasy/2011/10/31/oh-wow-what-do-steve-jobss-last-words-really-mean/.

5. ABC Eyewitness News; http://abc7.com/news/21-rescued-after-knotts-berry-farm-ride-stops-midway/1679992/.

6. Robert McCrum, *The Guardian*; https://www.theguardian.com/books/2013/sep/23/100-best-novels-pilgrims-progress.

Chapter 35

When it's Okay to Be Depressed

We all have our ups and downs, and at times if we do get depressed, we're not alone. The Apostle Paul said:

> For we do not want you to be ignorant, brethren, of our trouble which came to us in Asia: that we were burdened beyond measure, above strength, so that we despaired even of life (2 Corinthians 1:8).

Life is filled with troubles that can make us depressed, but as we face our lion's dens we have the promise that God is working all things together for our good (see Romans 8:28). And we know that even if the lions don't have their mouths stopped and the unthinkable happens, God allowed it in His perfect wisdom. Therefore, we trust Him. And as evidence of that trust, we rejoice in tribulation, as the Bible tells us to.

Are you going through trials? Look at Paul's list:

> From the Jews five times I received forty stripes minus one. Three times I was beaten with rods; once I was stoned; three times I was shipwrecked; a night and a day I have been in the deep; in journeys often, in perils of waters, in perils of robbers, in perils of my own countrymen, in perils of the Gentiles, in perils in the city, in perils in the wilderness, in perils in the sea, in perils among false brethren; in weariness and toil, in sleeplessness often, in hunger and thirst, in fastings often, in cold and nakedness (2 Corinthians 11:24–27).

But he contrasted his depressing suffering with what was in store, and brought it all into perspective. He called our sufferings a "light" affliction:

> For our light affliction, which is but for a moment, is working for us a far more exceeding and eternal weight of glory, while we do not look at the things which are seen, but at the things which are not seen. For the things which are seen are temporary, but the things which are not seen are eternal (2 Corinthians 4:17–18).

There are a number of other cases in the Bible of people feeling down in the mouth because of depression. One was Jonah. King David also battled depression. That's perhaps why millions find his psalms so comforting. King Saul suffered from terrible depression. He was the first king of Israel and as we have seen, he "had his demons."

Depression in Paradise

Tragically, there is an epidemic of depression and suicide among the surfing world. In an article titled "Mental Waves: Battling Depression in Paradise," surfer Sean Nee wrote about the sudden death of Andy Irons, three-time world surf champion. He said,

> Depressed, anxious, scared, and numb. There I was, living at an amazing surf camp in the Mentawais. I surfed every day at epic spots with cool people from around the world and I was feeling depressed, anxious, scared, and numb . . . more surfers are killed each year from suicide than are killed surfing heavy waves.
>
> Well, I am a surfer with a mental illness. I have thoughts of self harm and suicide more often than I would like.
>
> I never met him personally, but I do feel a connection with the late, great Andy Irons. . . . Andy had been diagnosed with bipolar depression at a young age and had been struggling with it throughout his career. I found this out when a family statement was released after his death. Andy was in an industry where it wasn't ok to be open about his mental health issues.[1]

Depression and Suicide Among Doctors and Nurses

There is a huge problem with chronic depression and suicide within the medical profession:

> According to the Robert Wood Johnson Foundation Interdisciplinary Nursing Quality Research Initiative (INQRI), nurses experience clinical depression at twice the rate of the general public. Depression affects 9% of everyday citizens, but 18% of nurses experience symptoms of depression.[2]

In September of 2016, the Australian Broadcasting Corporation said,

> Female doctors and nurses [are] at least three times more likely to commit suicide. This was the first time Australian researchers have conducted a nationwide review of suicides in the medical profession, and they say what they found was alarming. The research revealed that female doctors take their own lives at nearly three times the rate of the general population.
>
> Female nurses had a suicide risk almost four times greater than women in other jobs.[3]

Nursing journals reported:

> Younger nurses consistently reported stronger fear of death and more negative attitudes towards end-of-life patient care. Nurses need to be aware of their own beliefs.[4] The rate of depressive disorders among health-care workers compared with the general population is alarming and is an issue that spans the medical profession.[5]

Police Officers, Entrepreneurs, and Suicide

Law enforcement suicide is real and yet the police culture continues to ignore the facts. The #1 one killer of police officers is law enforcement suicide.[6]

There is also a problem with chronic depression and suicide among entrepreneurs:

> 1 in 3 entrepreneurs lives with depression. . . . You don't
> have to look far to see that many bright and promising
> young entrepreneurs have tragically taken their lives.[7]

There is no doubt an epidemic of depression among those who aren't entrepreneurial and who are not police officers or medical professions, as well at those who are into skiing, cycling, swimming, climbing, walking, racing, yachting, football, baseball, jumping, eating, drinking, and breathing. Depression is everywhere.

Or could it just be that as the nations become more secular, shaking off the faith of their fathers, it comes with a hefty price? As faith has receded and depression and suicide have rushed in to fill the vacuum, even established explanations for depression have had to be reconsidered. The longstanding biological explanation of depression — that people with the disorder have low levels of the neurotransmitter serotonin — is now considered overly simplistic.[8] Sociologists in general believe that when society robs people of self-control, individual dignity, or a connection to something larger than themselves, suicide rates rise.[9] That's a nebulous reference to, dare I say it, fearing God. In the United States back in the 1950s, the Ten Commandments were upheld, doors were left unlocked, rape and murder were not as prevalent, police were respected, self-abuse through drugs was relatively rare, obesity was uncommon, and almost everyone went to church and believed in God and country. A lack of self-control not only leads to over-eating but alcohol and drug abuse, anger, wife-beating, road rage, jealousy, bitterness, and a host of other self-destroying sins.

Back in the 1950s the average American had a measure of faith, and their personal faith kept fear in its place. They had a connection to something larger than themselves. That has now gone, depression takes its place, and so suicide rates explode.

As the world continues to diagnose hundreds of millions as being depressed, and therefore having a mental disease, it has paved a highway for moral relativism. There is no right nor wrong, because there are no moral absolutes. Anyone who becomes depressed, hears voices, and kills people isn't a criminal but a victim of mental disease. The murderer is therefore not a criminal, and he shouldn't be punished, but instead treated for his disease and rehabilitated so that he can reenter society. Such is the insanity of secular humanism.

questions ?

1. According to 2 Corinthians 4:17–18, what did Paul call the trials of this life?
2. How does this help us as Christians?
3. What did surfer Sean Nee say about his state when he wrote about the sudden death of Andy Irons (three-time world surf champion)?
4. What are the statistics regarding depression in nurses?
5. Why do you think that female doctors and nurses are at least three times more likely to commit suicide?

Endnotes

1. https://www.theinertia.com/surf/mental-waves-battling-depression-in-paradise/.

2. Lynda Lampert, "Minority Nurse," March 1, 2016; http://minoritynurse.com/depression-in-nurses-the-unspoken-epidemic/.

3. Bridget Brennan, ABC News, September 18, 2016; http://www.abc.net.au/news/2016-09-19/female-health-professionals-at-higher-risk-of-suicide/7856968.

4. *The Open Nursing Journal*; https://www.ncbi.nlm.nih.gov/pmc/articles/PMC3565229/.

5. "Suicide Among Health-care Workers: Time to Act," The Lancet, January 2017; http://www.thelancet.com/journals/lancet/article/PIIS0140-6736(17)30005-3/fulltext?rss=yes.

6. Pamela Kulbarsh, "2015 Police Suicide Statistics," Officer.com; http://www.officer.com/article/12156622/2015-police-suicide-statistics.

7. Breena Kerr, "Depression Among Entrepreneurs Is an Epidemic Nobody Is Talking About," The Hustle, October 26, 2015; http://thehustle.co/depression-among-entrepreneurs-is-an-epidemic-nobody-is-talking-about.

8. https://www.scientificamerican.com/article/robin-williams-depression-alone-rarely-causes-suicide/.

9. http://www.newsweek.com/2013/05/22/why-suicide-has-become-epidemic-and-what-we-can-do-help-237434.html.

Chapter 36

John Wayne and Mary Tyler Moore

Think about some of our heroes of the past. We would like to think that John Wayne just rode off into the sunset. He starred in over 150 movies, and in 9 of them he died. But that didn't prepare him for the real thing.[1]

During a visit to London in January 1974 to appear on *The Glen Campbell Goodtime Hour* (1969) and *Parkinson* (1971), Wayne caught pneumonia. For a 66-year-old man with one lung this was very serious, and eventually he was coughing so hard that he damaged a valve in his heart. This problem went undetected until March 1978, when he underwent emergency open heart surgery in Boston.

On Friday, January 12, 1979, Wayne entered hospital for gall bladder surgery, which turned into a nine and a half hour operation when doctors discovered cancer in his stomach. His entire stomach was removed. On May 2, Wayne returned to the hospital, where the cancer was found to have spread to his intestines. He was taken to the 9th floor of the UCLA Medical Center, where President Jimmy Carter visited him, and Queen Elizabeth II sent him a get well card. He went into a coma on Sunday, June 10, 1979, and died at 5:35 P.M., in the late afternoon the next day, Monday, June 11, 1979.[2]

Or think of America's sweetheart, Mary Tyler Moore, tossing her hat in the air and living a happy, carefree life after she faded from the public eye. Not so:

TV icon Mary Tyler Moore was living in pain before passing away . . . at age 80. Her "The Dick Van Dyke Show" co-star and close friend Rose Marie, 93, told RadarOnline, "Oh, my God she suffered so much these last few years. She had a tumor and she had diabetes. She was going blind and she couldn't hear very well, either." Along with those ailments, Radar reports that Moore also battled Alzheimer's and heart and kidney problems.[3]

As we get older, our immune system breaks down. We may slow it down, but our genes are instructing our body to shut down. We call this in scientific terms "entropy" (dict. "lack of order or predictability; gradual decline into disorder"). The Bible calls it "corruption":

Now this I say, brethren, that flesh and blood cannot inherit the kingdom of God; nor does corruption inherit incorruption. Behold, I tell you a mystery: We shall not all sleep, but we shall all be changed — in a moment, in the twinkling of an eye, at the last trumpet. For the trumpet will sound, and the dead will be raised incorruptible, and we shall be changed. For this corruptible must put on incorruption, and this mortal must put on immortality. So when this corruptible has put on incorruption, and this mortal has put on immortality, then shall be brought to pass the saying that is written: "Death is swallowed up in victory."

"O Death, where is your sting?" (1 Corinthians 15:50–55).

Life is tough. Everywhere we look, we see sickness and suffering, disease and death. And it is all the result of the sin of Adam each of us have inherited. It's in our rebellious nature.

Sin is like a carbon monoxide leak at a dance party. The gas is poisonous, invisible, and odorless, and as guests mysteriously begin to fall to the floor and die, some try desperately to revive them. But they too succumb to the poisoning. Others say that trying to do anything is futile, so they keep dancing, bring out the booze, and have a ball. Others have a list of some of the different foods on the menu that they want to try before they die. But those who think know that something is wrong and that they need to find a way out.

Hollywood's Values

Despite these past heroes dying almost daily, an inordinate amount of them are bankrupt when it comes to faith in God. There's a reason for this. The movie industry attracts people who are proud and who, by their own admission, are driven by their egos. They want applause, recognition, praise, money, and the power that comes with it. They are most often good-looking, confident, and talented, and they know it. They aren't the sort who gravitate to the humility of Christianity. They are pro-choice, pro-homosexuality, and pro-almost-everything the Bible speaks of as being morally wrong. And so we have a powerful industry of people who are godless in their philosophy. Any celebrity who publicly has faith in the God of the Bible is blacklisted as a troublemaker on set. No sex scenes, no gay scenes, no blasphemy, no mockery of Christian values. That means problems in production and loss of money. Christians are weeded out and becomes as rare in Hollywood as a hen's dentist.

It is with this godless philosophy that Hollywood has influenced the world; and its influence has been massive. It has been responsible for the wholesale export of fornication, violence, the occult, homosexuality, blasphemy, and mockery of Christianity. The result has been generations of millions who reflect Hollywood's values, and that has left them without faith, floating in a sea of hopelessness. Frank Sinatra so eloquently summed up what has happened. In his famous song "My Way," he said, "I did it my way . . . not the words of one who kneels,"[4] and if we hold onto that rebellion by refusing to bow the knee to mercy, we will bow the knee to judgment.

The War with God

You eat wisely, watch your weight and stay fit. Some don't seem to care about their health. But not you.

One day you wake up with pain which gets progressively worse during the day and keeps you awake at night, and so you decide to see your doctor. He seems a little concerned and sends you to a specialist. The specialist says that he would like to take x-rays and do a biopsy.

The results are not good. You are devastated to find you have cancer. It's your worst fear. But you are determined to fight it tooth and nail. But even if you win the battle, without the Savior you are going to lose the war. Death will eventually be the victor. Cancer is just a horrible reminder that you are terminal.

By failing to adhere to the words of Jesus, you are like the man who built his house on sand. Life has many storms and like everyone else, one of them will cause you to come crashing down. And Jesus said, "Great was the fall of it." Yet, in a moment of time, through faith in the words of Jesus, you can build on rock. Please do that now. Stop reading this book for a moment, and call the name of the Lord. Stop running. Make peace with Him.

questions?

1. How many movies did John Wayne make and how many times was he killed in those films?
2. How did he die in real life?
3. Do you find life depressing? If so, how do you deal with it?
4. Why is Hollywood so bankrupt when it comes to genuine faith in God?
5. What did Frank Sinatra reveal in the song "My Way."

Endnotes

1. http://www.angelfire.com/zine/timetraveler/FAQ.html.

2. IMDb; http://www.imdb.com/name/nm0000078/bio.

3. "Inside Mary Tyler Moore's Heartbreaking Final Days," Celebrity News, January 26, 2017; http://extratv.com/2017/01/26/inside-mary-tyler-moores-heartbreaking-final-days/.

4. "My Way," lyrics by Paul Anka.

Chapter 37

How to Fight Suicidal Thoughts

In a video on the subject of suicide, Kevin Hines tells of his survival after jumping off the Golden Gate Bridge in San Francisco. He said,

> The last thought before I went over was "Jump now!" I have had auditory hallucinations and they were just screaming. They were just screaming in my head, "You must die, you must die now! Jump now!" and I did. I was compelled to die. In four seconds I fell, 75 miles an hour, 25 stories, and I hit the water.

The Coast Guard said that he was the only one they found to be alive, out of the 57 bodies they had picked up.[1]

If you're fighting depression and having suicidal thoughts, never forget that your battle is against demonic forces that came to " steal, and to kill, and to destroy" (see John 10:10). The Bible tells us to "Submit to God. Resist the devil, and he will flee from you" (see James 4:7). So submit your life to God and do what Jesus did when Satan tempted Him to commit suicide. He resisted the devil by quoting the Word of God:

> Then the devil took Him up into the holy city, set Him on the pinnacle of the temple, and said to Him, "If You are the Son of God, throw Yourself down. For it is written: 'He shall give His angels charge over you,' and, 'In their hands they shall bear you up, lest you dash your foot against a stone.'" Jesus said to him, "It is written again, 'You shall not tempt the Lord your God' " (Matthew 4:5–7).

So when fear and suicidal thoughts attack your mind, pray something like this:

> It is written, "Submit to God, resist the devil and he will flee from you" (James 4:7). I have done that. I have been delivered from the kingdom of darkness and now belong to the Kingdom of Light. I stand in the righteousness of Christ and resist every work of darkness in the name of Jesus. I pray for great wisdom, a love for righteousness, a hunger for the Word of God, and a deep concern for the lost. It is written in Psalm 56:3–4: "Whenever I am afraid, I will trust in You. In God I have put my trust; I will not fear." In God I have put my trust; I will not be afraid. For You have delivered my soul from death. Have You not kept my feet from falling, that I may walk before God in the light of the living? In Jesus' Name I pray. Amen.

Be consistent with this prayer. Don't give up. *Every* time a negative thought comes, pray this positive prayer, believing what you pray. Any time you are attacked, it will become a reminder to pray. You will turn every negative fear and suicidal thought into a positive and powerful prayer.

Cultivate a Special Fear

As we've seen, there are fears that are intuitive and beneficial. I am grateful for a fear of heights. Years ago my buddies would jump off a 50-foot cliff into the ocean — for something to do when there was no surf. They had to time the jump for when there was an incoming wave. The first one to try it did so to see if the water was deep enough to jump. He came up with a bleeding nose. When they tried to goad me into jumping, I refused. I was newly married and was beginning to see the precious nature of life. I feared losing it and wasn't going to put it at risk for some cheap thrill. Many a thrill-seeker has ignored that common-sense fear and has lost his life. Fear tells you to put on a parachute before you jump. It clicks the buckle of your seat belt in a car. It doesn't shoot heroin, take LSD, or drink and drive. That fear is married to self-preservation. And that's good.

When I see someone who lacks that sort of fear, I pity them. They are the thrill-seekers — the adrenaline junkies that the world admires and portrays as heroes. I have friends whose thrill-seeking son fell to his death at the prime of life, leaving his parents shattered. His thoughtless thrill-seeking brought them unspeakable grief. They don't go for a moment in any day without the pain of his loss.

The special fear we should seek is one that is despised by this world. It is shunned, frowned upon, vilified, and discouraged, and those who promote it are categorized as being hateful. Yet the Bible is filled with exhortations to obtain it, because is it more precious than silver and gold. It is called "the beginning of wisdom" (see Proverbs 9:10) and "the fountain of life" (see Proverbs 14:27). It will cause us to depart from evil and will lead us to everlasting life (see Proverbs 16:6, 19:23).

Psalm 34:4 says, "I sought the LORD, and He heard me, and delivered me from all my fears." This is the testimony of King David and of every other person who has sought the Lord. He delivers us from all of our fears, including the tormenting King of Terrors. Then, just a few verses later there are a number of seeming contradictions about fear:

> The angel of the LORD encamps all around those who fear Him, and delivers them (verse 7).

> Oh, fear the LORD, you His saints! There is no want to those who fear Him (verse 9).

> "Come, you children, listen to me; I will teach you the fear of the LORD (verse 12).

Proverbs 2:5 says that the fear of God comes through "understanding," and that leads us to the knowledge of God. Never despise the fear of God. It is to be coveted, if you want to live. This world doesn't fear a God. It uses His Name to cuss, and it does so because of idolatry. It has an erroneous image of God. Don't be like them. Instead, fill your mind with understanding by studying Scripture and its revelation of the character and nature of God.

Steve Jobs wasn't the only one who in his youth was courageous about death. Mark Twain boldly said, "I do not fear death. I had been dead for billions and billions of years before I was born, and had not suffered the slightest inconvenience from it."[2] But time took its toll and left him overcome him with depression:

> He was believed to have suffered depression when his friend Henry, who inspired him to learn steamboat piloting died. Twain felt responsible for his death arguing that he foresaw the accident in a dream days before it occurred. He was also reported to have suffered depression after the tragic death of his wife and three children.[3]

Those who reject a parachute have good reason to be swallowed by depression and fear. But you are not like them. You are going to cultivate the fear of God, and trust in Him as you prepare yourself for the big jump. Charles Spurgeon had this advice about overcoming the fear of death:

> I would say, first, let us die every day. "I die daily," said the Apostle Paul. The man who practices dying every day, the man who has, as it were, a daily rehearsal of it, will not be afraid of the reality when it comes! We are wise to talk of our last hours, to be familiar with the thought of our departure from this world. Every night, when we go to our bed, we ought to have a rehearsal of death. We lay aside our clothes for the night just as we shall have to lay aside our bodies in death. I like that idea best on Saturday night, for then we take off our workday clothes and they are put away, and we fall asleep. And then, in the morning, there are our Sabbath Day garments laid ready for us and oh, what wonderful Sabbath Day clothes we shall have when we awake in the morning in heaven and are "arrayed in fine linen: clean and white," which is "the righteousness of saints."
>
> So, die daily, brothers and sisters, in this fashion! Get into the habit of so doing. I remember an old Christian woman who used to say that she had dipped her feet in the river of death every morning before she left her bedroom, so she did not mind when she was called to go through it, she was so accustomed to "die daily."

The next piece of advice I have to give you is this — hold very loosely everything on earth. Have you a great many possessions and friends? Mind that you do not cling too closely to them, for there is danger about them all. As one once observed to a rich man who took him over his parks and gardens, "Ah, sir, these are the things that make it hard to die!" The poor have little enough to leave and when they go, they have not the regrets which the covetous and greedy rich man oftentimes has, or the man who has added field to field and farm to farm, till he owns all the land in the region where he lives. "Must I leave you? Must I leave you?" has often been the miser's cry, as he has tried to clutch his money-bags with his dying fingers! O beloved, hold everything loosely! You are in a dying world and everything about you is like yourself, shadowy and fleeting. Do not build your nest here as if you were to abide here forever.[4]

A 2014 study of prison inmates concluded that solitary confinement "can cause a specific psychiatric syndrome, characterized by hallucinations; panic attacks; overt paranoia; diminished impulse control; hypersensitivity to external stimuli; and difficulties with thinking, concentration and memory." In other words, normal human beings don't like being left alone.[5]

We have been created to be social creatures. God Himself said of the first solitary man "It is not good that man should be alone; I will make him a helper comparable to him" (Genesis 2:18).

But when we die, we will die alone. We may surround our deathbed with 100 relatives who comfort us while we are still alive, but when that moment comes, we die alone. "Alone" that is, if we die without the Savior. If we are trusting in Jesus when death comes, we can't lose. If we are not trusting Him, we can't win.

I came into this world with nothing. But I when I leave, I leave with my hand in the hand of Jesus and with my soul in the hands of God. There is no safer place in the universe. It is the peaceful eye of the storm. The King of Terrors has been dethroned.

"I'm walking to the bridge," begins a Golden Gate Bridge suicide note. "If one person smiles at me on the way, I will not jump." The writer jumped.[6]

We are surrounded by a world that lives in a secret despair. They are looking for light. Do more than smile. Love them. Reach out to them with the gospel. Let your light shine.

Over 2,000 people have committed suicide by jumping off one bridge in China. Mothers and fathers, sons and daughters, brothers and sisters have so despaired of life that they killed themselves. However, one wonderfully compassionate man named Chen Si faithfully patrolled the Nanjing Yangtze bridge every Saturday and Sunday for 13 years. He would physically grab those who were about to jump, hold them, and then take them to an apartment, away from that awful scene. He saved 321 lives.[7]

May this book be like that man. Please pass it on to others.

For further books and videos by Ray Comfort, see www.livingwaters.com.

questions ?

1. Do you believe in demonic entities? Why?
2. What two things are we to do, according to James 4:7?
3. What did Jesus do when the devil suggested He throw Himself off the temple?
4. What does the Bible say about the fear of the Lord?
5. Have you made peace with God? Are you trusting in Jesus?

Endnotes

1. https://youtu.be/LytKNC405oI.

2. https://www.goodreads.com/quotes/25647-i-do-not-fear-death-i-had-been-dead-for.

3. http://www.famousbipolarpeople.com/mark-twain.html.

4. http://www.spurgeongems.org/vols55-57/chs3125.pdf.

5. http://www.pbs.org/wgbh/frontline/article/what-does-solitary-confinement-do-to-your-mind/.

6. http://www.newsweek.com/2013/05/22/why-suicide-has-become-epidemic-and-what-we-can-do-help-237434.html.

7. http://www.dailymail.co.uk/news/article-3968696/Meet-man-dedicates-life-preventing-suicides-China-s-notorious-jumping-spot-saved-321-people-13-years.html.

Answers to Chapter Questions

Chapter 1

1. 100 people every minute, 6000 people every hour, and 54 million every year.
2. Having riches and being famous does not overcome the haunting fear of death and the sense of futility that comes with that.
3. Answers will vary.
4. Only one in five respond well to antidepressants.
5. It may only add to their depression, to be told that they're not in their right mind, especially people who are in the public eye.

Chapter 2

1. The answer is subjective.
2. Daily news is depressing. It majors on death. If it bleeds it leads: cancer, and who has it, who has been killed in car accidents, terrorism, kids who have cancer, war, plane crashes, fires, murders, tornados, suicides, and of course, highly publicized celebrity deaths.
3. No matter how sweet the moment, that dreaded storm is coming.
4. For normal thinking people, the fact of impending death justifies being depressed.
5. Like faith in a parachute, we have the ability to control our fear of death by faith in God.

Chapter 3

1. Faith in Jesus and His finished work on the Cross gives us a living hope in our death. We see the "end" as the beginning. Plus, we also have the wonderful promise of Romans 8:28.

2. Trusting in Jesus as Lord and Savior is the only prep we need. He will take care of the rest.
3. A building is evidence of a builder and a painting is evidence of a painter. Creation is absolute proof of the Creator. See Romans 1:20.
4. It is outside of the realm of possibility for nature to be eternal — because of the second law of thermodynamics. That says that everything is subject to corruption. It runs down. In 100 million years, everything we can see will have turned to dust. If the universe was eternally preexistent, it would have turned to dust 500 trillion plus years ago.
5. Faith in God for the future provides immediate peace and joy in this life.

Chapter 4

1. It would seem that he had built his house on sand, evidenced by his godless lifestyle.
2. We have to have faith in the pilots, planes, banks, elevators, taxi drivers, doctors, surgeons, and a multitude of other things, from history books to restaurants that prepare our food, and sodas prepared by companies for us to guzzle down without a second thought. We build our human relationships on faith. If you don't trust someone, you have no basis for a relationship. Faith isn't weak as some would suggest: it is a building block of life.
3. An implicit trust.
4. With God, nothing is impossible. Nothing can stop Him from keeping His Word to us. He is trustworthy.
5. Idolatry. We tend to create a god in our own image, one with whom we feel comfortable.

Chapter 5

1. "Depression is a side effect of dying."
2. People who are depressed are more vulnerable to abusing alcohol than those who don't experience depressive episodes.
3. "Everything. It's just a general all-round arggghhh. It's fearfulness and anxiety."

4. God is often offered as a means of help in life, as a kind of heavenly Buddy.
5. "So why am I depressed? That's the million-dollar question, baby, the Tootsie Roll question; not even the owl knows the answer to that one. I don't know either."

Chapter 6

1. "The bravest thing I ever did was continuing my life when I wanted to die."
2. "Don't do it, Mom! Don't do it!" Wynonna pleaded with her mother. "People will think you're crazy and I know you're not!"
3. "Those thoughts of suicide don't come anymore. But I'm vulnerable. I know I can backslide."
4. Many in the country music industry have an intellectual knowledge of God that falls short of conversion.
5. When we obey the gospel, God gives us the gift of faith. The Holy Spirit helps us in our weakness.

Chapter 7

1. "Sadness is more or less like a head cold — with patience, it passes. Depression is like cancer."
2. He said that in terms of choosing between "the closet" and coming out, the stigma of mental illness is most closely analogous to LGBT status.
3. An estimated 350 million people in the world suffer from depression, according to the World Health Organization.
4. In the gospel, God offers him everlasting life, freedom from the fear of death and the hopelessness that comes with it.
5. ". . . we will not fear."

Chapter 8

1. Electroshock therapy at the Menninger Clinic.
2. 61.
3. "A legacy of addiction, mental illness and suicide across generations."
4. It is more truthful to say that all thinking men who reject the gospel live in a constant state of depression.
5. Child-like faith.

Chapter 9

1. The battle for happiness. That is the mistake of the ungodly. They think the chief end of man is our personal happiness. But there is something far more important than our happiness. It is righteousness. We should never ask, "Does this make me happy?" without asking, "Is this right in God's eyes?"
2. Attention Deficit Disorder, tartrazine food coloring, dairy produce, and air pollution.
3. An indignant atheist is like a man who walks into a lighted room, turns out the light, and then complains about the darkness. The Bible gives light for us to see why there is suffering. But atheists turn that light out.
4. One that is easily dismantled by the person making the argument, making themselves look intelligent.
5. The moral Law was given universally — to leave the "whole world guilty before God" (see Romans 3:19–20).

Chapter 10

1. Here are the "Common Side Effects of Librium": confusion; depressed mood, thoughts of suicide or hurting yourself.
2. She literally drank herself to death.
3. She said, "In 10 years' time I'm gonna be looking after my husband and our seven kids. I'd really like to get everyone in one place and sit down and eat a meal together. I would like to uphold certain things, but not the religious side of things, just the nice family things to do. At the end of the day, I'm a Jewish girl."
4. Guilty sinners don't like the thought of being morally responsible to God.
5. Her last words were, "I don't want to die," spoken to her doctor over the phone two hours prior to her death.

Chapter 11

1. Hope.
2. She said, "Death is my biggest phobia ... I used to have panic attacks when I was little, saying, 'Mum, I don't want to die.' I've been to therapy and still try to go every week."

3. "Jesus Christ... has abolished death and brought life and immortality to light through the gospel" (2 Timothy 1:10).

4. The difference is called "works of righteousness." Traditional religion says that you must do something to get to heaven. You have to work at it to obtain righteousness; and that is your ticket into heaven. Christianity maintains that there is nothing you can do to save yourself from death and hell. It says that we can only be saved by "grace."

5. God saves us because He's good and kind. We don't deserve eternal life, but it is freely given to us because of His favor — His amazing grace.

Chapter 12

1. "I have so little time left!" Jane Fonda, 76, reveals she can't stop crying as she comes to terms with her own mortality.

2. With all of its problems and pain, life is wonderful ... with its friends and family, its love and laughter, sunrises and sunsets, playful puppies and cute kittens, with its beautiful birds and colorful flutter-by butterflies. Life is more than good. And so the more it is loved and its blessings are appreciated, the greater the wrenching will be as death rips this precious possession from our unwilling hands.

3. He said, "The fear of death never left me; I couldn't get used to the thought; I would still sometimes shake and weep with terror. By contrast, the fact of existence here and now sometimes took on a glorious splendor."

4. We should never think of the pleasures of sin without thinking of the pain of death. The two are bedfellows.

5. Nothing.

Chapter 13

1. "I fear death!"
2. It took courage and humility.
3. Grope.
4. Blindness.
5. We are spiritually blind until God opens our eyes.

Chapter 14

1. He said, "I was writing jokes when I was 15 — not out of happiness, but to escape."
2. Fearing the stigma of mental illness and convinced change was impossible, Dangerfield suffered in silence for years.
3. Researchers from the University of Queensland concluded that depression and anxiety exist in every society in the world today.
4. You humorously put yourself down.
5. If there is one hallmark of Jewish humor, says Rabbi Telushkin, it is the absurd ability to keep us "laughing in order not to cry."

Chapter 15

1. Through medication and yoga — and by hanging upside down for up to 30 minutes each day.
2. The Columbine High School massacre was what pushed her over the edge.
3. Patrick Swayze said, "The longer your life goes on, the more death you face."
4. This life is called "the shadow of death," and the Scriptures tell us that all humanity "sits" in the shadow.
5. 150,000 human beings, people who are just like us — with a love of life and a fear of death, will die. If there was ever a justified cause for chronic depression, that is it. We need to, we must, reach out to them with the gospel.

Chapter 16

1. Sleep was her only refuge from the nightmare of real life.
2. Our hearts should break — to think that so many are tormented by depression and fear. If we don't reach out to the unsaved, our love is a mere self-deceiving lip service.
3. He described himself as "incapacitated for about eight years with clinical depression."
4. "Pain must never be a source of shame. It's a part of life, it's part of humanity."
5. That means that 65 million Americans suffer from mental disease.

Chapter 17

1. He said, "I think the trauma was that I realized ... this ends! It comes to a point where one day you vanish. You totally vanish for ever. You're gone. Period."
2. "I'm not afraid of death; I just don't want to be there when it happens."
3. In one interview he used the word "grim" three times to describe it.
4. It is without the realm of possibility for such a complex instructional language to create itself.
5. "Blessed is the man who fears the Lord."

Chapter 18

1. He hoped to drop dead of a heart attack on stage.
2. He said, "The immediacy of life, and how fragile life is, stayed with me."
3. He said, "He couldn't get his breath, he was drowning in his own fluids. What a difficult way of passing. His death affected me a great deal. ... no matter how famous you are, it's dust, it's over in the blink of an eye so nobody remembers your name."
4. "Humble yourselves in the sight of the Lord, and He will lift you up" (James 4:8–10).
5. Scripture promises: "Draw near to God and He will draw near to you." (James 4:8–10)

Chapter 19

1. Her full quote is, "I wish I was in a full body cast, with every bone in my body broken. ... Then, maybe, people would stop minimizing my illness because they can actually see what's wrong with me."
2. "I hated every minute of it and I lost every ounce of energy and enthusiasm for the deal. There were several times when I was really going to throw in the towel and give it up."
3. After overcoming his addictions, Bowie came to terms with the depression that he had been hiding from for many years.
4. He said, "Searching for music is like searching for God."

5. He said, "It's because I'm not quite an atheist and it worries me. There's that little bit that holds on: Well, I'm almost an atheist. Give me a couple of months."

Chapter 20

1. "I've suffered through depression and anxiety my entire life, I still suffer with it every single day."
2. She said, "I suppose you could say I'm quite a religious woman but very confused about religion."
3. He said, "When they stop believing in God, they believe in anything."
4. They should cry out to God, read the New Testament with an open heart and a humble attitude of "Please, show me the truth."
5. The Bible says, "For God has not given us a spirit of fear, but of power and of love and of a sound mind." (2 Timothy 1:7)

Chapter 21

1. She said, "I have studiously tried to avoid ever using the word 'madness' to describe my condition. Now and again, the word slips out, but I hate it. . . ."
2. "I got a fear of death that creeps on every night. I know I won't die soon, but then again I might."
3. God has provided us with a living hope through the gospel.
4. "People fear death even more than pain. It's strange that they fear death. Life hurts a lot more than death. At the point of death, the pain is over. Yeah, I guess it is a friend."
5. "The Lord is on my side; I will not fear. What can man do to me?" (Psalm 118:6).

Chapter 22

1. Suzanne Collins.
2. To say a depressed person is mentally ill is to add a diagnosis of insanity to their depression. Her statement issues from a misdiagnosis.
3. She said, "There is such an extreme stigma about mental health issues, and I can't make heads or tails of why it exists."

4. As of 2016, 44.7 million America adults were included in the category of being mentally ill.

5. Research has revealed that this self-injury is practiced by as many as 4% of the adult population the United States.

Chapter 23

1. He said, "Who wants mortality? Everybody wants immortality."

2. He said, "I think growing old is the ugliest, the most, the ugliest thing. When the body breaks down and you start to wrinkle, I think it's so bad. I don't ... that's something I don't understand."

3. Rabbi: So do you want to die before that happens?
   Michael Jackson: Um ... I don't want to grow old.
   Rabbi: Are you afraid of death?
   Michael Jackson: Yes.
   Rabbi: We all are.

4. Everything fell when Adam fell. In time, the most vibrant and cutest of little puppies becomes a deaf, blind, slow-moving, and smelly old dog. Leaves fall and die, roses lose their petals, trees bend and crack, elephants wrinkle, horses sag, and frogs croak. Everything grows old, dies, and turns to dust.

5. We go vegan, work out, juice, Botox, use moisturizers, and try and slow down the process by using so-called anti-aging products.

Chapter 24

1. Realists.

2. The death of his son and his parents.

3. He said, "I've always wondered if that answer hides a denial so deeply seated it cannot be faced by most."

4. He said, "I've unearthed a fear so overwhelming my mind has been turned aside as if my imagination and the idea of my own end were two magnets of identical polarity, unwilling to meet no matter how hard I tried to make them."

5. God and God alone.

Chapter 25

1. He said, "It's odd, sad, and slightly contradictory that Ms. McCready recently checked out of a psychiatric hospital before

completing treatment because, according to Dr. Drew, she feared the stigma."

2. The person committed suicide, therefore that is the evidence that they had mental problems.

3. In commenting about her death, a leading doctor said, "But let me be clear. Mindy's tragic situation is about mental illness. Chronic mental illness."

4. In Christ they would find:

    A. God is the lover of their soul

    B. Purpose for their existence

    C. Freedom from the fear of death

    D. A hope that the Bible says "is both sure and steadfast, an anchor for the soul."

5. "I sought the Lord, and He heard me, and delivered me from all my fears" (Psalm 34:4).

Chapter 26

1. Telling her, "I'm so down, I'm so depressed, I'm so scared, I'm so worried."

2. Her dog. She said, "But when my dog came in and sat in my lap, I thought, 'Who's going to take care of Spike?'"

3. The answer is subjective.

4. The answer is subjective.

5. "Do not fear therefore; you are of more value than many sparrows."

Chapter 27

1. The answer is subjective.

2. God. Ultimate truth, which is alone in Jesus.

3. "I'm not sure, it may have helped me out of a jam a little bit."

4. "A low level of despair."

5. That he knows little of biblical Christianity.

Chapter 28

1. "It feels like you've swallowed a bag of stones. A heavy feeling somewhere between your heart and stomach."

2. "He had a serious family history of suicide and depression."

3. "In addition, the biography recounts an incident, from when he was in eighth grade, of Kurt Cobain discovering the swinging corpse of a classmate who committed suicide by hanging."
4. The answer is subjective.
5. Sin.

Chapter 29

1. She wrote: "I wish I knew why I am so anguished."
2. "Like a nut."
3. They said she was "Doomed from her childhood by family mental illness. . . ."
4. $5 million.
5. The answer is subjective.

Chapter 30

1. The answer is subjective.
2. The answer is subjective.
3. Romans 1:20 tells us that creation is absolute evidence of the Creator.
4. The answer is subjective.
5. If you are fearful to share the gospel, don't pray for less fear, pray for more love. Because that is the problem.

Chapter 31

1. A Johns Hopkins study estimates that more than 250,000 Americans die each year from medical errors.
2. "Is that all there is, is that all there is? If that's all there is my friends, then let's keep dancing. Let's break out the booze and have a ball. If that's all there is."
3. The answer is subjective.
4. It's "an inheritance incorruptible and undefiled and that does not fade away, reserved in heaven for you, who are kept by the power of God through faith for salvation ready to be revealed in the last time."
5. The answer is subjective.

Chapter 32

1. The Prime Minister of the United Kingdom from 1940 to 1945 and again from 1951 to 1955.
2. "I have nothing to offer but blood, toil, tears, and sweat."
3. He suffered from chronic depression.
4. His "black dog."
5. Churchill's last words were, "I'm so bored with it all."

Chapter 33

1. Approximately 20 per day.
2. The alternative is to say that they were normal, stable, sane human beings, and in the face of their suicide, that makes no sense. Sane people don't kill themselves. So they say.
3. "Mental health rates have risen 65% in the military since 2000, with 936,000 troops diagnosed with at least one mental health issue in that time, according to the new data."
4. All of the soldiers included one in particular — a desire to end intense emotional distress.
5. During service, the soldier in training knows that it's normal to fear death. He therefore rationalizes it. It makes sense, and as a soldier he trains himself to fight it. He could die at any moment. That's what being a soldier is about. Live with your justified fear. The fear of death makes sense. It's nothing to be depressed about.

Chapter 34

1. Steve Jobs famously said, "Remembering that I'll be dead soon is the most important tool I've ever encountered to help me make the big choices in life."
2. He said, "Sometimes I believe in God, sometimes I don't. I think it's 50-50 maybe."
3. It's like a man sitting in his house and thinking that the chances that there was a builder are 50/50. Perhaps the building made itself.
4. Jobs's last words were "OH WOW. OH WOW. OH WOW."
5. Giant Despair.

Chapter 35

1. He called them "our light affliction, which is but for a moment."
2. It gives us a living hope. There is brilliant light at the end of the tunnel.
3. He said, "There I was, living at an amazing surf camp in the Mentawais. I surfed every day at epic spots with cool people from around the world and I was feeling depressed, anxious, scared, and numb ... more surfers are killed each year from suicide than are killed surfing heavy waves. "
4. Depression affects 9% of everyday citizens, but 18% of nurses experience symptoms of depression.
5. They are continually dealing with death, reminding themselves of their own inevitable appointment with the Grim Reaper.

Chapter 36

1. He starred in over 150 movies, and in nine of them he died.
2. He died of cancer.
3. The answer is subjective.
4. The movie industry attracts people who are proud, and who, by their own admission, are driven by their egos. They want applause, recognition, praise, money, and the power that comes with it. They are most often good-looking, confident, and talented, and they know it. They aren't the sort who gravitate to the humility of Christianity. They are pro-choice, pro-homosexuality, and pro-almost-everything the Bible speaks of as being morally wrong.
5. "I did it my way ... not the words of one who kneels...."

Chapter 37

1. If you're fighting depression and having suicidal thoughts, never forget that your battle is against demonic forces that came to "steal, and to kill, and to destroy" (see John 10:10).
2. The Bible tells us to "Submit to God. Resist the devil, and he will flee from you."
3. "Then the devil took Him up into the holy city, set Him on the pinnacle of the temple, and said to Him, 'If You are the Son of God, throw Yourself down. For it is written: "He shall give His

angels charge over you," and, "In their hands they shall bear you up, lest you dash your foot against a stone." ' Jesus said to him, 'It is written again, "You shall not tempt the Lord your God" ' " (Matthew 4:5–7).

4. Proverbs 2:5 says that the fear of God comes through "understanding," and that leads us to the knowledge of God. Never despise the fear of God. It is to be coveted if you want to live. This world doesn't fear God. It uses His Name to cuss, and it does so because of idolatry. It has an erroneous image of God. Don't be like them. Instead, fill your mind with understanding by studying Scripture and its revelation of the character and nature of God.

5. The answer is subjective.

First printing: October 2018

New Leaf Press is a division of the New Leaf Publishing Group, Inc.

ISBN: 978-0-89221-761-8
Library of Congress Number: 2018955417

Cover by Diana Bogardus

Please consider requesting that a copy of this volume be purchased by your local library system.

Printed in the United States of America

Please visit our website for other great titles:
www.newleafpress.com

For information regarding author interviews,
please contact the publicity department at (870) 438-5288.

New Leaf Press
A Division of New Leaf Publishing Group
www.newleafpress.com

THE FINAL CURTAIN:

RAY COMFORT